POWER TOOLS

for
Ableton Live 9

POWER TOOLS

for
Ableton Live 9

Master Ableton's Music Production and Live Performance Application

INCLUDES DVD-ROM!

Jake Perrine

HAL LEONARD BOOKS
An Imprint of Hal Leonard Corporation

Published in 2013 by Hal Leonard Books
An Imprint of Hal Leonard Corporation
7777 West Bluemound Road
Milwaukee, WI 53213

Trade Book Division Editorial Offices
33 Plymouth St., Montclair, NJ 07042

Printed in the United States of America

Book design by Kristina Rolander

Library of Congress Cataloging-in-Publication Data
Perrine, Jake.
 Power tools for Ableton Live 9 : master Ableton's music production and live performance application / Jake Perrine.
    pages cm. -- (Power tools)
1. Ableton Live. 2. Digital audio editors. I. Title.
ML74.4.A23P46 2013
781.3'4536--dc23
                                        2013021720

ISBN 978-1-4584-0038-3

Contents

CHAPTER 4
ARRANGEMENT VIEW

CHAPTER 6
RECORDING AUDIO WITH LIVE   123

CHAPTER 7
MIDI AND CONTROLLERS IN LIVE   133

CHAPTER 8
MIXING AND AUTOMATION IN LIVE 187

CHAPTER 9
USING LIVE...LIVE! 203

CHAPTER 10
BEST PRACTICES

Introduction

MISSION

I know the feeling. Symphonies of sound flow through you. If only you had a way to express the rivers of vibration that only you can hear in your head! The size, the impact, the dynamic range, the subtlety, the grandeur, the raw emotion, and the unique blend of timbres that makes you, you!

It can be frustrating, harboring a wellspring of inspiration with no means to share your unique voice. So, like millions before you, you decide to undertake a lifelong journey, seeking out a point on the horizon that will take you to your goal. Like a painter picking up a paintbrush, you search for the tools that will enable your expression. And that is what has led you to this book. Well done. As Obi-Wan Kenobi once wisely said to Luke, "You have just taken your first step into a larger world."

And while this decision to learn a craft is an important step—perhaps the most important step—it is by no means the first step: You have known music and sound all your life, and you've spent countless hours formulating imaginary melodies, beats, lyrics, soundscapes, rises and falls, builds and breakdowns, at times to the exclusion of any other thought or activity. This wealth of experience is infinitely valuable. It is the palette of colors that you will draw your inspiration from. Hold onto that. Feed it. Nurture it. Treat it with the utmost respect. Your song is unique in all the universe.

And if you are just starting, there is good news! There has never been a better time to get into electronic-music creation. Never before in the short history of electronic music making have the tools been so powerful, available, inexpensive, and easy to use. Gone are the days when there was no way around splicing tape and rooms full of gear. With a laptop and some headphones, you can make world-class, major label-caliber music wherever and whenever inspiration strikes.

There are many different music applications available to choose from. You've made an excellent choice in selecting Ableton Live! I am not shy about my passion for this program—you'll find it on every page of this book—and I hope to inspire the same passion in you. In my humble opinion, Ableton Live represents the best know-how of more than a century of electronic-music makers. It does some very powerful things simply and gracefully in a streamlined interface that is easy to learn, easy to use, and enjoyable to work with.

On the surface, there are many similarities between Live and other multitrack recording and editing packages. Live will definitely do a majority of what those programs can. But in addition to all that standard functionality, Live really shines in its additional ability to work with audio in a non-linear fashion on-the-fly, or "live." As its name implies, it was built with live performance in mind, and in this regard, no other program even comes close.

Another aspect of Live that impresses me is its versatility. Often there are many ways to accomplish similar results within Live: Instead of being locked into one way of doing things, Live's simple yet flexible design allows people to create in their own way. And because there are so many ways to combine Live's features, people are continually discovering new things to do with it! I've used it for composing, arranging, scoring, jamming with other musicians, remixing, DJ'ing, live looping, art installations, teaching music theory, and sound design for theater, dance, film and videogames. I'm sure there are many more uses I've not yet tried.

Add to that an avid community of users who love to exchange ideas, tips, and techniques! In all my years of music making, I've never seen a group of users so fanatic about a product or as open about sharing what they know with other users. It really is a true community endeavor. Have a question? Jump on the Ableton forum. Wonder how somebody made that sound? Look it up on YouTube. Looking for a new way to DJ your tunes to a crowd? Download another user's templates and controller mappings they've created. You could spend all your waking hours exploring the wealth of materials available online—believe me, I've tried—and you would have hardly scratched the surface.

So let's get started!

HOW TO USE THIS BOOK

The goal of this book is not to explain to you every single feature of the program. You already have Ableton's excellent reference manual for that. The goal is to get you making music quickly as possible using the key features that you will use every day, and learning specific techniques that will help you reach your goals.

If you are just getting started, I recommend moving through this book in a linear fashion. The lessons are sequential, building a song from the ground up, as you learn about Live's features in a hands-on fashion. Each new lesson builds upon the techniques discussed in previous chapters, referencing the previous terms and techniques discussed there. However, if you already have some experience with the program, you can jump in where it feels appropriate, as each exercise has its own corresponding Live Set to get you started at that point.

Appendices

One feature of this book I am excited to bring to you is that of the appendices. These topics are isolated from the rest of the book because they cover subjects that will be referenced throughout the lessons, and I did not want to impede the focus of the exercises with a bunch of digressions. If you are unclear about one of the appendix topics referenced in a lesson, take the time to study it.

However, I've included these appendix topics for another important reason. For more than a decade I have taught audio production concepts, including MIDI, sound design, and Ableton Live to budding new audio engineers. Professional audio engineers make it their job to understand a wide array of concepts, because their careers depend upon it. But in the past decade, I have seen a massive influx of what I like to refer to as "The Laptop Producer." This is someone, perhaps like yourself, who does not aim to sit in a studio behind a console recording and mixing bands, but rather wants to use a laptop and perhaps a few controllers to make music. Laptop Producers do not need to know how to calibrate a 2-inch analog tape machine, but there are a few key audio-related concepts that do affect them that they often have no knowledge about. I get asked questions about these topics—such as frequency and amplitude, or sample rate and bit depth—all the time, and while there is a lot of information online about such topics, there is even more misinformation about them. So, the appendices are a subset of topics that are not necessarily Ableton Live specific, but will greatly aid you in working with the program and making computer music in general. I have intentionally tried to give you enough depth in these topics so that you can work with them confidently and yet not get bogged down in a lot of technical detail that won't serve your needs.

Supplemental Content

Included with this book is a collection of materials that we will be using as a basis for many of the exercises herein. They are available on the accompanying DVD-ROM in the printed version and downloadable online for the ebook version. Follow the included instructions in Appendix G for downloading and installing this content to your hard drive before starting the exercises.

The content folder contains several subfolders:

- **Book Exercises Project**—This folder contains a series of Live Sets that are the starting point for each exercise in the book, so you can jump in wherever you like. Our friends over at SoundsToSample. com have provided a great collection of raw audio materials to get you started. If you like what you hear, head over to the company's website and check out its comprehensive supply of loops and samples for sale. I have yet to find another site that has as much to choose from with such a user-friendly interface. Highly recommended!

- **Install**—This folder contains some of my favorite third-party plug-ins. Some of the plug-ins are freeware that you can use for free indefinitely, and some of them are demo versions. The instructions for installing these tools are included in each Device's subfolder, as well as a link to each company's website should you decide to purchase some of your favorites.

- **Warp Academy Videos**—I am also the Lead Trainer at a new online Ableton Live training academy called Warp Academy, and we produce classes and training videos on using Ableton Live. I have included some videos detailing nine new features of Live 9 by some of our trainers, plus some excerpts from my Mixing and Mastering class, one of many online classes we offer.

ASSUMPTIONS

This book makes a few basic assumptions that are worth mentioning beforehand so that we are all on the same page. They include the following:

Basic Computer Experience

Making music with computers is not rocket science, but neither is it as easy as surfing the web or writing a letter in a word-processing program. That you are interested in pushing your computer and your creativity to higher levels leads me to believe that you feel some basic level of comfort with things like hooking up your computer, installing applications, saving files to a hard drive, navigating through folders, and so on. It's even better if you have a bit of experience troubleshooting your computer, because periodically things inevitably don't function the way you expect them to, especially when you are pushing your computer to its limits making music. If these kinds of tasks seem overly challenging or beyond your level of computer experience, you may want to spend some time obtaining some basic computing skills before moving on to digital audio wrangling. There are a plethora of schools, books, and online tutorials for just this sort of thing.

Understanding Basic Music Terminology

While I don't expect that you have necessarily had lots of music theory training, I do expect that you will understand basic musical terminology such as bars, beats, octaves, tempo, time signature, quarter notes, sixteenth notes, and the like. If this kind of language seems foreign to you, you can still make it through this book, but knowing the basics of music will help you to not only understand this material but also communicate with other musicians. I encourage you to seek out this understanding either through books, school, private tutoring, or the Internet.

Versions of Live

For the purposes of this book, I will assume that you are using the full version of Ableton Live 9—the current latest version of the program—but that is not a requirement. You can happily enjoy a vast majority of this instruction using a previous version of the program, because many of the core concepts remain the same.

The same can be said of Ableton Live 9 Intro, the highly affordable feature-limited version of Live. You may run into some limitations of Intro while using this book, but the majority of the concepts are very much applicable.

As well, while I may make an occasional reference to Ableton Live Suite 9—the fullest version of the program that additionally includes a sizeable library of Instrument Devices and Presets—the Suite is not required in order to use this book.

Optional Useful Audio Gear

You need no other gear besides a computer and a copy of Live to make music or complete most of the book's exercises. However, appendix E, "The Makings of a Producer's Studio," will give you some ideas for future expansion. Here is a short list of optional gear that would be useful to have when working with Live, and this book, in order of importance:

- **A pair of good-quality, closed-ear headphones**—Closed-ear headphones surround the ear, giving better sound isolation and a far better sound than earbuds and the like. If you can't hear the sounds that you are making in detail, you have no way of knowing if what you are doing sounds good. Sony MDR7506 headphones cost about $100 and are my personal favorites over other headphones costing many times more.
- **A USB MIDI keyboard controller**—This is an external USB controller with keys and/or drum pads for playing in notes, with sliders and knobs for adjusting parameters. Even if you don't have a lot of proficiency at playing an instrument, having a tactile hardware device to input MIDI notes and gestures is just a lot more fun than using your mouse! Novation and Akai make some great controllers for under $300, and now Ableton has created a ground-breaking new hardware controller built specifically for Live called Push, which should be available by the time you read this. More on this in chapter 9.
- **A USB or FireWire audio interface with MIDI I/O, and two powered near-field studio monitors**—Headphones are fine for getting started, but if you are serious about learning how to mix audio proficiently, you will need a way to get quality audio out of your computer and moving through the air via studio monitors. A wide range of these monitors are available today, and generally you get what you pay for, so try not to skimp on these when you decide to buy. An entry-level audio interface will cost from $150 to $500, and a basic pair of studio monitors will run from about $200 to $1,000.

Caution: If making computer music is your passion, you will find that once you get on the gear-purchasing escalator it is very hard to get off, so be prepared for addiction!

CONVENTIONS

What follows is a list of the shorthand conventions used in this book. Keeping these conventions streamlined and consistent will allow you to move smoothly and quickly through the exercises.

Keyboard Shortcuts

I am a keyboard shortcut fanatic! In Live, there are typically multiple ways of doing most tasks. I will list them all, but you will note that I always put the keyboard shortcut first. I heartily encourage you to try to memorize the keyboard shortcuts as quickly as possible.

Write them down if that helps you, or keep Ableton's own keyboard shortcut list open in another window so that you can refer to it as needed. I like to try to commit to learning one new shortcut each time I sit down in front of a program. If it is a program you work with regularly, you will learn them quickly and steadily. You might ask, "Why learn shortcuts?" One very simple answer: speed. The more keyboard shortcuts you know, the faster you can work. The faster you can work, the faster you can translate the idea in your head to something you—and everyone else—can hear.

I will always write out the keyboard shortcuts in the following format:

[(Macintosh modifier key)-(key)/(Windows modifier key)-(key)]

And I will be abbreviating the modifier keys like so:

- ctrl = Control (Macintosh and Windows)
- opt = Option (Macintosh)
- alt = Alternate (Windows)
- cmd = Command (Macintosh)
- shift = Shift (Macintosh and Windows)

So, when I write the following command:

"To save your session use [cmd-s/ctrl-s]."

This means "Use [Command and "s"] on the Macintosh, or [Control and "s"] on Windows."

If the keyboard shortcut is the same on both platforms, I will use only one command. For example:

"Press [spacebar] to begin playback."

This means that the spacebar will begin playback on both Mac and PC.

Menu Items

I also have a shorthand for executing menu commands, and it looks like this:

- Go File > Save.

This simply means, "Click on the File menu, and in that menu click on the Save function." If there is a further submenu, it might look like this:

- Go Edit > Record Quantization > Sixteenth-Note Quantization.

This simply indicates, "Click on the Edit menu, scroll down to the Record Quantization submenu item, and then select Sixteenth-Note Quantization." Easy!

Control-Click/Right-Click

Often PC mice will have a right-click button in addition to the standard left-click button. Some Mac mice do as well, but a lot of them do not. In Live (and in a lot of other apps) on Mac, the equivalent to a right-click is a Control-click (holding down the Control button while clicking on something). To indicate this gesture I will use a convention similar to keyboard shortcuts:

- [Ctrl-click/right-click]

This means "On a Mac, hold down Control and click, or on a PC, click the right mouse button."

DO IT! When you see this heading, there is a task or series of tasks that I am asking you to try out. Not every one of these is essential to complete before moving on to the next task, but the majority are, so as the sign says, do it!

IMPORTANT! This heading indicates a key concept that you should pay special attention to before moving on.

COOL! These asides are little tidbits of geekery that are typically for fun and impressing friends with your trivia knowledge! I've thrown these in to add a little color and context to what you are learning.

NEW FEATURE! Where indicated, the feature that follows is new in Live 9, and will not be the same—or perhaps even exist at all—in previous versions of Live.

The Ableton Live Interface

I know you are eager to make some sound. But before jumping into making some music, we should have a look around at the various parts of the Live interface and get familiar with them.

COOL! The graphic interface of Live was designed from the start to be easy to look at for long hours and easy for your computer to display quickly, which becomes increasingly important when you are working on a complex song or mixing a Set live, pushing your computer to its limits. The simpler the interface graphics, the less time and processor power your computer spends rendering the interface, and the more power it has left over to create high-quality audio. And if you don't like the classic default black-on-gray color scheme, you can simply jump into Live's Preferences to radically change it.

TWO VIEWS: SESSION AND ARRANGEMENT

The first feature I'd like to introduce you to in Live is not only its most important feature but also the one that sets it apart from all other audio programs: its two different views. If you just opened Live, you are currently looking at what is called Session View. Before we learn about Session View, let's visit the other view, Arrangement View, and learn our first keyboard shortcut.

DO IT! Here are three ways to switch between Session View and Arrangement View:

- Press the [tab] key on your keyboard.
- Click on one of the View selection buttons.
- Go View > Arrangement or View > Session.

Pic. 1.01: The two View selection buttons.

Repeat one of the methods outlined above to switch back and forth as needed.

The relationship between these two views is the heart and soul of Ableton Live's power, and we will explore it in detail. Essentially, the two views offer two ways of interacting with your music. For now, just note the parts of the interface that change (the center area) and the parts that stay the same (the rest) when switching between the views.

COOL!   Did you notice that Ableton's company logo is made out of the Session View and Arrangement View Selector buttons? That should give you an idea of how central these two views are to using Live!

SESSION VIEW INTERFACE

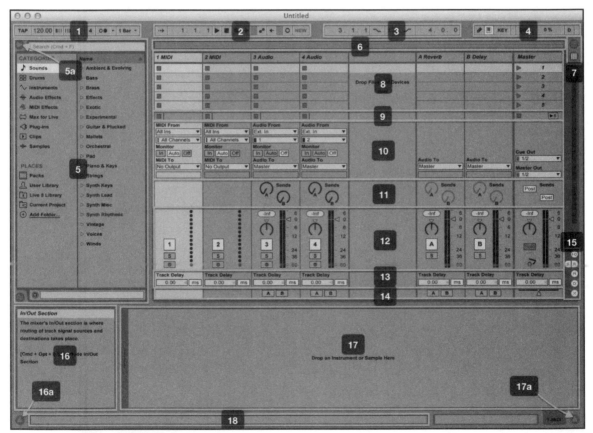

Pic. 1.02: Session View areas.

When you first launch the program, you are looking at a blank Session View. Session View is made up of the following areas:

1. Tempo, Time Signature and Global Quantize controls
2. Transport and Automation / Session Record controls
3. Arrangement Loop controls
4. Draw Mode, Keyboard/MIDI mapping controls, and the CPU/Disk Activity Meters
5. Browser and (5a) the Browser Show/Hide button
6. Overview
7. View Selector
8. Session View Clip Slot Grid and Scene Slots
9. Track Status Display, Stop All Clips button, and Back to Arrangement button
10. In/Out section
11. Sends section
12. Mixer
13. Track Delay section
14. Crossfader section
15. Session View Show/Hide buttons
16. Info View area and (16a) the Info View Show/Hide button
17. Detail View area and (17a) the Detail View Show/Hide button
18. Status Bar

COOL! Many of the dividers between areas can be moved, thereby resizing their bordering areas. For example, click-and-drag the black vertical divider between the Browser area and the main Session View Clips grid to the left and right. Try the same thing, but vertically this time, on the divider between the Mixer and the Detail View area. You can make an area larger or smaller as your focus changes. Nice!

We'll go through each of these areas and a few more as they come up. For now just note their names and locations. Note as well that many of these areas can be hidden from view to make more room for the parts of the interface that you are currently using.

DO IT! Here are three ways to show or hide many of these areas:

- Use a keyboard shortcut (all of which are shown in the View menu).
- Click on the appropriate Show/Hide button on the interface (item 15 in Pic. 1.02 above).
- Go View > (the area you wish to Show/Hide).

COOL! One area you might want to keep open all the time while you are learning the program is the Info View located in the lower left corner. This area will give you a brief description of any item you roll your cursor over, and will often tell you the keyboard shortcut for that item as well. The keyboard shortcut for Show/Hide Info View is, not surprisingly, the question mark [?], also known as [shift-/]. Turn it on, and leave it on!

AN INTRODUCTION TO LIVE PROJECTS AND LIVE SETS

Pop quiz: What is the most important keyboard shortcut of all?

Answer: [Cmd-s/ctrl-s], which saves your work!

Let's take a moment to understand how Live handles the important task of saving and organizing your work using two important concepts: Live Projects and Live Sets.

- A Live Set contains the work you do in Live, much the way a text file is a collection of the typing you do in a text editor. A Live Set's name is typically appended with the .als extension.
- A Live Project is a folder that contains one or more Live Set files and a series of folders and files referenced by those Sets. This includes the Samples folder, which contains any recordings made in that Project.

Think of it this way: When you make a song, you may want to make multiple versions of that song: different arrangements, different tempos, or even multiple remixes. Each of those versions could be a different Live Set. Live also assumes that you would likely want all the different versions of that song together in a single place, as they probably would share some of the same recordings: perhaps the vocal takes are the same for all versions of the song, even if different combinations of them are used in each version. The Live Project is a folder containing all of the versions of your song and some of the audio elements common to all the Sets.

A typical Live Project folder may contain the following:

- **Ableton Project Info** (folder)—Live uses files in this folder to keep track of settings for the Project. You should not delete, move or rename this folder for any reason. Leave it as it is.
- **The Live Set** (file with the extension .als)—One or more Live Sets you have created in this Project.
- **Samples folder**—This folder is where Live keeps the various media that you create while working on your Set. We'll get into details about this folder and its usage later.

IMPORTANT! Although the Live Set plays back audio, the Live Set file (.als) does not contain any audio itself! If you look at the size of the Live Set file, you will see that it has a relatively small file size compared to most audio files. The Live Set references other audio files on your hard drive, some of which may be in the Project folder's Samples folder.

When Live first opens, it creates a new, blank Set. This Set is not yet saved, and as such exists only in a temporary folder until you save it. I find it a very good practice to immediately save the Set before you even get started working, so you can consciously choose where you want the saved files to live on your computer.

| DO IT! | Let's get your Set and Project folders set up right:

1. Press [cmd-s/ctrl-s] or go File > Save Live Set.

When you hit the Save command for the first time in a new Set, you are presented with a standard Save File dialog box where you can name your file, choose a location, and click on the Save button.

2. Navigate to a sensible folder on your hard drive.
3. Name the Set "My Exercise" and be sure to note what folder you are saving to.
4. Click on Save.
5. Now, switch out of Live into your computer's standard file navigator (that is, Finder/Windows Explorer) and navigate to the location you just saved your Set to.

It should look something like this:

Name	Kind
▼ 🗂 My Exercise Project	Folder
▶ 🗂 Ableton Project Info	Folder
📄 My Exercise.als	Ableton Live Set

Pic. 1.03: The Live Project folder and its contents (Mac).

Even though you issued a command to save the Live Set, note that what Live really saved was an entire Live Project folder that contains the Live Set as you named it. Live takes the liberty of naming your Project folder with the name of your Live Set, and adding the word "Project" on the end. So, the first time you save a Set, you actually save a Project that contains that Set. Note that there is not yet a Samples folder, because you have not yet added any audio to this Project.

6. Return to Live and go File > Save As... or press [cmd-shift-s/ctrl-shift-s].

Notice that you are now back inside the Project folder, where you see the current Live Set you saved previously.

7. Choose a new, similar name, such as My Exercise 1.als, and save it in the Project folder.

This time, Live does not save an entire new Project folder, rather just a second Live Set with a new name within the same Live Project folder. Perfect.

- If you wanted to save your current Set as an entirely new Project, go File > Save As... and select a new location outside of the Project folder. Live will create a new Project based on the name you choose.

- If you wanted to start an entirely new Project, you would go File > New Live Set [cmd-n/ctrl-n], and then save it as described above.

LIVE LIBRARY

Historically, music recording has consisted of a group of musicians playing in a recording studio, and these performances being blended into a finished recording. Since the advent of computers and sampling in the 1980's, some styles of music making have evolved into more of a collage-like process, using multiple pre-recorded sounds blended together to create new works. Today, there are companies that create and sell vast, royalty-free sound libraries specifically for this purpose, and it would not be unusual to never make a single new audio recording during the creation of a song. Knowing this, Ableton Live ships with, and installs a sizeable collection of "raw materials" known as the Live Library. You can access this content—as well as any other files on your hard drive—through the Live Browser, and since this content is royalty-free, you can use it in just about any way you like to help you make music.

LIVE 9 BROWSER

While working with Live, you will find you regularly want to add a particular audio file, a plug-in, preset, or some other file to your Set. The Browser is where you access these resources. Think of the Browser like a painter's palette, and the Live Set as your canvas to paint on.

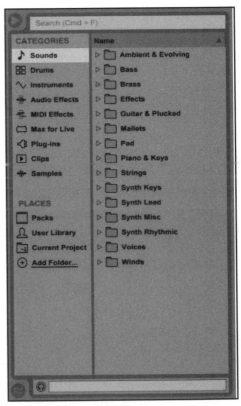

NEW FEATURE! Live 9 has a brand new, greatly enhanced Browser that offers many new features to speed up your work flow.

Likely the Browser is already visible if you are looking at a new Set. Regardless, here are three ways to Show/Hide the Live Browser:

- Press [cmd-opt-b/ctrl-alt-b].
- Click on the Show/Hide Browser Arrow button.
- Go View > Browser > Show.

Live 9's new two-pane Browser window sorts your resources into two groups: Categories and Places. Categories contain handy ways to find files, Devices, and Presets from Live's built-in

Pic. 1.04: The Live 9 Browser.

Library, and Places helps you locate files that are elsewhere on your computer. Click on an item in the left-hand column and see what that item contains in the right-hand column. Let's go through them one at a time:

Categories

- **Sounds**—This is a listing of Presets for Live's installed virtual Instrument Devices sorted by the type of sound made, rather than by the specific device that makes it. For example, in the Bass Category, you might have bass patches generated by a Simpler, Operator, Analog, or even an Instrument Rack with several Devices in it. (Instrument Devices, Instrument Racks, and MIDI Effects will be discussed in chapter 7: "MIDI and Controllers.")
- **Drums**—This is a listing of Live's Drum Rack Presets, as well as a listing of individual drum hits sorted by type.
- **Instruments**—When you want to browse your Instrument Devices, this is the place to go. Click on the triangle next to an Instrument Device to see a list of its Presets.
- **MIDI Effects**—This is a listing of Live's MIDI Effect Devices, and their Presets.
- **Plug-ins**—If you have installed any third-party (non-Ableton) effects or instruments (VST or AU for Mac, VST for PC), such as any of the demo-ware included with this book, they will be listed here. (Third-party plug-ins will be discussed in chapters 5 and 7.)
- **Clips**—Clips are a container for audio or MIDI files that allow you to save certain Live-specific playback settings with the file. Live's included Clips are browseable here, and you can make and save your own. (Audio Clips will be covered in detail in chapter 2 and MIDI Clips in chapter 7.)
- **Samples**—This is a comprehensive listing of all of the audio files that ship with Live. Unlike Clips or Device Presets that may use these files, this category give you just the "raw", unmodified audio files for you to use in any way you like.
- **Max for Live**—This category is only available if you have Live 9 Suite installed. Max for Live is an incredibly vast and deep tool for creating your own Devices for Live, and due to its complexity, is beyond the scope of this book. Read more about Max for Live at Ableton.com.
- **All Results**—If you have searched for a term in the Search field at the top of the Browser, the results appear in a category called All Results which shows you the results of your search across all categories.

Places

- **Packs**—Additional content, such as Device Presets, Live Sets, and sound collections, can be added into Live's Library, and this typically is done by way of a proprietary Ableton file type known as a Live Pack (.alp). Packs that have been installed can be browsed here.
- **User Library**—This allows you to browse other parts of the Live Library not included in the categories above, such as the Defaults folder, where you can add or amend various default settings in Live.
- **Current Project**—This is a very convenient way to quickly browse your current Live Project folder, where you may have additional Live Sets, sounds, or other files you might need access to.
- **Add Folder**—This very handy feature allows you to add any folder from your computer to the Places list for easy access. You might add your sample library folder, music library folder, synth presets folder, or any other place you need access to regularly to speed up your work flow.

Other Browser Features

- **The Search field**—Use the Search field to enter a word to search your file system for files, Devices, or Presets that contain this word. You can filter your search results by choosing a Category or Place to restrict the results.
- **The Groove Pool Show/Hide button**—This area is for choosing and working with Live's Groove templates. This will be discussed in chapter 3, "Warping, Quantization and Grooves".
- **The Preview Tab**—When previewing an audio file in the Browser, a small waveform overview will display in this box. Enable the headphones switch to play a selected audio file through the Cue Out. This is covered more thoroughly in the next chapter.

As you move through the exercises in the book, you will experience the Browser in greater detail. For now, click on each of the Categories and Places and scroll through what you find there to familiarize yourself with its functionality.

SUMMARY

- There are two main Views in Live—Session View and Arrangement View—and you can use [tab] to switch between them.
- Most of the various areas of the Live interface can be shown, hidden, and resized as needed.
- The question mark key [?] shows Info View, which will give contextual help for any part of the program you place your mouse over.
- Live saves your work into a Project folder, which contains (among other things) your Live Sets.
- Live Sets contain the edits you make, but Sets do not contain any audio unto themselves. Instead, a Live Set merely references the audio files you choose.
- Live comes with an extensive Library of raw materials to jump-start your music making.
- The Live Browser is your interface to access audio and MIDI files, Instruments, and Effect Devices.

Audio Clips and Session View

Okay, you've gotten the lay of the land. Let's make some music!

The primary building block of any Live Set is the Clip. Clips come in two flavors: Audio Clips and MIDI Clips. This chapter will deal with Audio Clips, and constructing a Set in Session View.

When you use a digital audio file in your Set, Live creates what is called a Clip out of it. A Clip is simply a wrapper for the audio content it contains that allows for a wide assortment of playback parameter assignments such as pitch, volume, looping parameters, Warp Markers, Launch Modes, and Clip Envelopes. These are some of the primary functions that make Live the powerful sound-sculpting tool that it is.

There are five kinds of Tracks in Live: Audio Tracks, MIDI Tracks, Group Tracks, Return Tracks, and the Master Track. We will explore each of these eventually, but let's begin with Audio Tracks. Audio Tracks can record and play back Audio Clips. An Audio Track in Live is a lot like a channel on a hardware audio mixer: an Audio Track takes in an audio signal; allows you to change the signal's volume, panning, EQ, and effects settings; and then hands that signal on to the Master Track, where is it combined with other signals for output so you can hear these combined signals through your speakers or headphones.

When you first open Live 9, the program starts you off with four Tracks: two MIDI Track called 1 MIDI and 2 MIDI, and two Audio Tracks called 3 Audio and 4 Audio. In Session View, the vertical columns under these names are called Tracks. The gray boxes on these Tracks are called Clip Slots. This is where we will put (and later record) our Audio and MIDI Clip data.

Here are a few things you should know about Audio Clips and Audio Tracks:

- An Audio Clip plays on an Audio Track.
- An Audio Track can play back only one Audio Clip at a time.
- An Audio Clip can be either mono (one channel) or stereo (two channels).

- All Tracks in Live are always stereo, regardless of their content.
- An Audio Track can have both mono and/or stereo Audio Clips on it at the same time.

Let's see Audio Clips in action!

EXERCISE 2.1—AUDIO TRACKS AND CLIPS IN SESSION VIEW

For this exercise—and most of the exercises—you will need the supplemental content that came with your book, either from DVD or via a download.

2.1.1—Importing and Launching Your First Clip

DO IT! Here are several ways to set up your Exercise 2.1 Project:

- You can continue from right where you left off at the end of Exercise 1 and use File > Save As… to save the Set as My Exercise 2.1.als inside the same Project folder, or…
- Open the supplied Exercise 2.1.als from the Book Content > Book Exercises Project folder. Incidentally, this Set is exactly the same as a new Set. Save it as My Exercise 2.1. Or…
- Go File > New Live Set, and save this new Set as My Exercise 2.1.

Ready?

1. It should be already, but if it is not, make the Browser is visible in one of the following three ways:

- Click on the Show/Hide Browser triangle in the upper-left corner of the screen.
- Press [cmd-opt-b/ctrl-alt-b] until it is visible.
- Go View > Show Browser.

2. In the Browser under Places, find and click Current Project. Live displays the contents of the Book Exercises Project folder.
3. In the Book Exercises Project folder—among many other things—you will find a folder named Samples. Double-click this folder to take the Browser view inside Samples. In here you should see a folder named Sounds to Sample.

NEW FEATURE! Making Places—The Sounds to Sample folder is one that we will be using over and over again during these tutorials, so saving it to our Places list just makes good sense. You can do that in one of two ways: Since we are already looking at it in the Browser, the easiest way is to simply drag the Sounds to Sample folder from the right pane to somewhere in the list of Places in the left pane. Easy! Alternately, you could click the Add Folder option under Places, which brings up a dialogue box for finding and selecting the folder you wish to add. From here on, I will simply reference the Sounds to Sample folder directly, and you can now get to it easily in your Places.

4. Now navigate to Sounds to Sample > Drum Loops, and find the file called MT_Beats_125_07.wav. Click on it just once to highlight it.

A small waveform appears at the bottom of the Browser in the Preview Tab showing you a visual representation of the audio. To the left of the waveform is a button with a pair of headphones on it; this is known as the Preview switch. Turn on the Preview switch to listen to the file. Alternately, you can use [shift-return] or [right arrow] to preview a highlighted file in the Browser.

Pic. 2.01: The Sounds to Sample folder added to Places in the Browser

Pic. 2.02: The Preview Tab and Preview switch in the Browser.

5. Click-and-drag the MT_Beats_125_07.wav Clip onto the top Clip Slot on the track named 3 Audio.

Your Clip grid should now look something like this:

You now have an Audio Clip on an Audio Track! Live assigns a random color to the new Audio Clip in the Session View Clip grid. Note the new Clip View box that comes up at the bottom of your screen when you add a new Clip. For now, leave this alone. We'll get into that shortly.

6. On the left-hand side of the MT_Beats_125_07 Clip in the Clip grid, you will see a triangle pointing to the right. This is the Clip Launch button. Click on it. You should hear your Clip play.

Notice that the Clip loops automatically. In the Track Status Display just below the Clip grid, you'll see a number, a small and animated pie chart, and another number while the Clip plays.

- The first number shows the number of times the Loop has played.
- The small pie chart is a visual representation of the percentage of the loop that has played so far this time around.
- The final number is the number of quarter-note beats in the current Clip.

Pic. 2.03: The Audio Clip MT_Beats_125_07.wav on the Audio Track 3 Audio.

You may be wondering, "How do I stop the Clip?" There are several different ways to stop a Clip that is playing, each of which does something slightly different. Try them all:

- Click on any of the Clip Stop buttons (the squares) in any of the empty Clip Slots of the same track.

Pic. 2.04: The Track Status Display area just below the Clip grid.

- Click on the Clip Stop button in the Track Status Display. This does the same thing as clicking on an empty Clip Slot's Stop button, but sometimes all the Clip Slots are full of Clips, so this provides a Clip Stop button that is always visible.

Pic. 2.05:
The Stop All
Clips button
and the Back
To Arrangement
button on the
Master Track.

- Click on the Stop All Clips button on the Master Track all the way to the right. This will stop all Clips on all Tracks, but leaves global playback of the Set still running. You'll discover why this is useful later.
- Click on the square Stop button in the Control Bar at the top-middle of the interface, or press [spacebar]. This stops playback of the entire Set.

Pic. 2.06: The Stop button

2.1.2—Adding a Second Clip

Before moving on, let's get rid of the two MIDI Tracks. We won't be using these for this exercise.

7. Click on the 2 MIDI track name to highlight it, and the press the [delete] key on your keyboard, or go Edit > Delete. Do the same for the 1 MIDI track.

Better. Now let's add our second Clip while the first one is playing!

8. Click on the Launch button on the MT_Beats Clip you added previously to the recently renamed track 1 Audio so that it plays.
9. With that Clip still playing, return to the same Drums folder as before in the Browser. Click on another loop in the same folder.

If the Preview button is still lit blue at the bottom of the Browser, you should now hear the new file you selected playing in sync with the MT_Beats Clip. Very cool! This is made possible by Live's Warping engine and it is part of the magic of Live! Scroll through the list, single-clicking on each file one at a time or using the Up/Down Arrow keys, previewing each of these loops with your first loop. Some will sound good together, while others not so much.

 How a file plays back when previewed in the Browser depends on whether Live is currently playing:

- If Live is currently stopped (the Play button is black in the Control Bar area) and you click on a file in the Browser, Live will play back that Clip at its original tempo.
- If Live is already playing (the Play button is green in the Control Bar) and you click on a file in the Browser, Live will attempt to play back the file at the Set's master tempo, in sync with your other Clips.

- If Live is already playing and you want to preview a Clip at its original tempo and not in sync with the Set's master tempo, click on the Raw button to the right of the preview waveform at the bottom of the Browser window. This may be useful for Clips without a lot of rhythmic content, such as atmospheric backgrounds, sound effects, or spoken-word Clips to name a few.

Okay, let's continue:

10. Preview the file s2s_tt_lightribal_125_lawn3.wav. These two sound pretty good together.
11. Drag s2s_tt_lightribal_125_lawn3.wav into the first Clip Slot of 2 Audio, which is the box directly to the right of the MT_Beats_125_07 Clip.
12. The new Clip on the 2 Audio Track is currently not playing. Launch s2s_tt_lightribal_125_lawn3 with its Launch button. The Launch button may flash for a moment or two, and then when the beat comes around again, the Clip launches in sync with the first Clip.

IMPORTANT! You may notice that the level meter on the Master Track turns red intermittently. This means that the combined volume of all your Tracks has exceeded the total available dynamic range, and has gone into "clipping," which is harsh, digital distortion. You can always correct this in one of three ways:

- Lower the Master Volume slider until the Master level meter turns green again.
- Lower the Track Volume slider on your individual Tracks until the Master level meter turns green again.
- Lower the Clip Gain of individual Clips. We'll talk more about this control shortly.

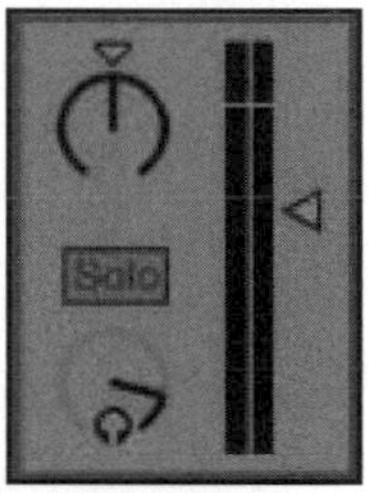

Pic. 2.07: The Master Volume slider lowered by 10.3 decibels.

Each of these accomplishes the task, but each will impact future volume-related decisions as well. For now,

13. Lower the Master Volume slider to –10.3 dB. You can see the exact level as you move the slider in the Status Bar at the bottom of Live's interface.

You may want to increase your speaker's volume slightly to compensate for the drop in volume.

2.1.3—Set Tempo and the Global Quantize Value

IMPORTANT! The synchronization of these two Clips is made possible by two very important controls at the top left of your screen:

- The first control is the Tempo box where you see the number 125, which stands for 125 beats per minute (bpm). The Tempo value sets the tempo for the entire Set, and when new Clips are added to the Set, Live will attempt to play the Clips back at this tempo, in sync with all of the Set's other Clips.
- The second control is in the middle at the top, where it says 1 Bar. This is the Global Quantize value. When you attempt to launch a new Clip during playback, Live will wait until the next Global Quantize value to start playback of the Clip. At the current setting of 1 Bar, Live will wait until the

next new bar after you click on the Launch button to actually play the Clip. Depending on when you click on the Launch button, this could be almost instantaneously, or several beats later.

Pic. 2.08: The Global Tempo and Global Quantize value in the Control Bar.

 Let's explore these two concepts in practice:

14. With either or both of the Clips playing, click-and-drag in the Tempo box and hear the tempo change. Try going to the far extremes (20, then 999) to hear your Clips do some crazy things. When done, set the tempo to 120 bpm.
15. Launch one Clip, either will do.
16. Change the Global Quantize value to 4 Bars.
17. Now click on the Launch button of the second Clip.

The Launch button flashes until the next bar number divisible by four comes around, such as 4, 8, 12, or 100.

18. Stop the second Clip.
19. Change the Global Quantize value to 1/4.
20. Play the second Clip.

It will start at the next quarter note now, which is much more often, and can make for some very interesting syncopated rhythms!

21. When you are done experimenting with this, set the Global Quantize value back to 1 Bar.
22. Stop playback. The [spacebar] is your friend.

We will return again and again to these two concepts. They are foundational to what makes Live such a unique program.

2.1.4—A Third Clip and Launching Scenes

 This groove needs some bass! Let's add our third Clip and then explore the concept of Scenes:

23. In the Browser, head over to Sounds to Sample > Bass. Audition some bass lines. MT_Bass_125_A_04.wav sounds pretty good with the two Clips we've chosen. Rather than drag the file over to a Clip Slot, this time do one of the following:

- Double-click on the file name.
- Highlight the file and press [return].

Either of these actions will create a new track and put the selected file into the top Clip Slot on the new track, here called 3 Audio.

24. Click on the Stop All Clips button in the lower-right corner of the grid.

This will stop any previously playing Clips.

Notice that if you press [spacebar] to start playback after clicking on Stop Clips, nothing plays. Even though the global bars and beats indicator is incrementing in the Control Bar, none of the Clips have been launched since you pressed Stop Clips.

Look all the way to the right in the Clips grid to the track called Master. Notice that instead of empty Clip Slots, this track has numbers and Launch buttons already. These are known as Scenes.

25. Click on the Launch button in the top Scene named 1.

All three Clips on all three Tracks begin to play! You have just launched your first Scene.

A Scene is simply an elegant way to launch an entire horizontal row of Clips across all the Tracks at once. As you are about to see, Scenes also give you an easy way to experiment with groupings of Clips and to create some arrangement possibilities.

26. Select your very first Clip, MT_Beats, by clicking once on the Clip's name (not the Launch button). The Clip is highlighted with a blue background.

Now duplicate it by doing one of the following:

- Press [cmd-d/ctrl-d].
- Go Edit > Duplicate.
- [Ctrl-click/right-click] on the Clip to bring up a contextual menu and choose Duplicate.

You can do this on multiple Clips at once as well:

27. Make a multi-selection of all three Clips in the first Scene across all three Tracks by doing one of the following:

- Click-and-drag a box around the three Clips in Scene 1.
- [Cmd-click/ctrl-click] on the three Clips in Scene 1 one at a time.
- Click once on the MT_Beats Clip, hold down Shift, and [shift-click] on the MT_Bass_125_A_04 Clip.

28. Press [cmd-d/ctrl-d] twice to duplicate the selected row of Clips twice. You should now have three rows of all three Clips.

Pic. 2.09: Scene Launch buttons in numbered Scenes on the Master Track

Pic. 2.10: Three Scenes of three Clips on three Tracks.

This action can be performed on Scenes as well, but for now, do not duplicate any Scenes.

How is this useful, you ask? Time to chisel at the marble and reveal the statue within! You can get rid of Clips as easily as you duplicate them:

29. Select the first Clip on 2 Audio and do one of the following:

- Press the [delete] key.
- Go Edit > Delete.
- [Ctrl-click/right-click] on the Clip and choose Delete from the contextual menu.

30. Also delete the first and second Clips on the 3 Audio Track. Your Clip grid should now look like this:

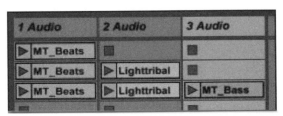

Pic. 2.11: Three different Scene variations of three Clips.

Here is an another useful way that you can launch Scenes:

31. Click on the name of the first Scene (not the Launch button) on the Master Track to highlight the Scene. The Scene Slot turns yellow, and the rest of the Scene is highlighted white.
32. Press the [enter] key. The first Scene launches, and the second Scene is now highlighted.
33. After the Scene has played for a few bars, hit [enter] again. The second Scene is launched, and now the third Scene is highlighted.
34. Launch the third Scene in the same way when you are ready.

Want to play a previous Scene? No problem:

35. Use the [up/down arrow] keys to highlight the desired Scene, and then press [enter] to launch it.

COOL! With minimal keystrokes you can step through your Scenes at any pace you like. No need for precision mouse clicking! Sometimes aiming and timing a mouse-click on those small Launch buttons can be tricky. Using [up/down arrows] and [enter] offers a much easier and more reliable method. You can also configure a MIDI controller to do the same thing, and then you won't need the keyboard or the mouse!

As you step through these three Scenes, notice the blend of these three simple Clip combinations. As you can hear and see, we have the beginnings of a simple arrangement emerging.

Note that you can play the Scenes in any order you like, remixing your basic arrangement on the fly. Since each of these Scenes currently loops indefinitely, we have not yet had to commit to determining how long each of these Scenes will ultimately play. Instead we have simply identified that these Clip combinations work well together and might be used in these groupings in our final arrangement. You could make Scenes for different verses, a chorus, a bridge, an intro, and a finale. Ultimately, I will show you how to turn your Session View Clips and Scenes into an arrangement in Arrangement View. For now, let's explore Audio Clips a bit more.

2.1.5—Renaming Scenes, Tracks, and Clips

It is a great idea to get in the habit of renaming things as you go along so that you can quickly identify the elements of your Set. In Live, this is very simple: highlight the object you would like to rename and do one of the following:

- Press [cmd-r/ctrl-r].
- Go Edit > Rename.
- [Ctrl-click/right-click] on the item and choose Rename from the contextual menu.

DO IT! Let's rename your three Tracks:

36. Click on the track name 1 Audio. Use one of the three previous methods to rename it to "Beats."
37. Instead of pressing [return] to commit your renaming, instead press [tab], which jumps you to the next track and highlights the name of 2 Audio for renaming. Much easier! Rename 2 Audio as "Perc."
38. Press [tab] again, and rename 3 Audio as "Bass."
39. Click in the first Scene on the Master Track currently named 1, and rename it as "Intro." Press [tab]. Rename the second Scene as "Add Perc." Press [tab] again and rename the third Scene as "Add Bass."
40. Rename the Beats track's Clips as "MT_Beats," the Perc track's Clips as "Lightribal," and the Bass track's Clip as "MT_Bass."

> **IMPORTANT!**   Renaming a Clip does not rename the file on your hard drive.

Don't forget!:

41. Save your Set by pressing [cmd-s/ctrl-s].

EXERCISE 2.2—CLIP VIEW PROPERTIES

When you click on a Clip's colored box (not the Launch button), Live displays the Clip's Clip View properties and Sample Editor in the Detail View at the bottom of the interface. The Clip View boxes contain many variables and concepts worth exploring.

At the bottom left of the Clip View area, you will notice three little yellow buttons: one is the letter L, one is a small image of a waveform, and one is the letter E. Each of these buttons shows and hides a box of the Clip View:

- The Clip box is always shown and cannot be hidden.
- The L button shows and hides the Launch box.
- The waveform squiggle button shows and hides the Sample box.
- The E button shows and hides the Envelopes box.

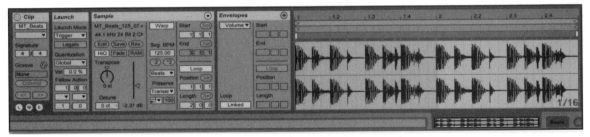

Pic. 2.12: The Clip View properties boxes, their Show/Hide buttons, and the Sample Editor.

Go ahead and turn all three buttons on if any of them are off. We will go through each of them.

To the right of these four boxes is the Sample Display. Here you can view a Clip's progress as it plays back and make other adjustments depending on whether the Sample or Envelopes box is currently active. You can toggle between which box is active by clicking on either the Sample or the Envelopes box's title bar.

Here is what each of these Clip View boxes does in a general sense:

- **Clip**—The Clip box is for activating/deactivating, renaming, changing the color, changing the time signature, or changing the applied Groove of the current Clip.
- **Launch**—The Launch box controls how the Clip responds to Launch commands, and what it does after it has been launched.
- **Sample**—The Sample box controls Clip Gain, Tuning, Warping and Warp Mode, and Clip Start, End, and Looping values.

- **Envelope**—The Envelopes box is where you apply Clip Envelopes, allowing you to automate (vary over time) just about any parameter associated with the Clip.

The following exercises will walk you through several of the Clip View's key features.

2.2.1—Clip Gain (Volume)

DO IT!   Get ready to learn about Clip View. There are two ways to get started:

- You can continue from right where you left off at the end of Exercise 2.1 and use File > Save As… to save the Set as My Exercise 2.2.als, or
- You can open Exercise 2.2.als from the supplied Sets in Book Content > Book Exercises Project, and then perform a Save As… and save your Set as My Exercise 2.2.als.

The relative volume level of the Lightribal Clip on the Perc track seems a little high to my ears. While you could lower the Track Volume in the mixer, that would also lower the volume of future Clips that you may want to put on this track. Instead, lower the Clip's gain, which you can think of as another word for "volume."

1. Click on the first instance of the Lightribal percussion Clip in Clip Slot 2 on the Perc Track. The Clip's properties come up in the Detail View at the bottom of your screen.
2. Make sure that the Sample box is visible (which it should be already) by enabling the squiggly waveform radio button at the bottom-left corner of the Detail View.

Pic. 2.13: The Clip Gain slider.

In the Sample box, note the vertical slider with 0.00 dB appearing below it. This is your Clip Gain slider.

3. Lower this Clip's gain (volume) to −8.09 dB by doing one of the following:

- Click on the triangle and pull it downward.
- Click anywhere on the Clip Gain slider and use your computer keyboard's [up/down arrow] keys to adjust it.
- Click on the 0.00 dB value at the bottom: a box appears around it, and you can now type in any value you like.

Doing this means that every time this Clip is played back, it will play back at a little more than eight decibels less than it was recorded at.

4. Now click on the duplicate of Lightribal just below this Clip in Clip Slot 3 of the Clip grid. Notice that the volume of this Clip still reads as 0.00 dB.

IMPORTANT!   Clip Gain and all other Clip parameters are specific to that Clip only! Adjusting one Clip will not adjust the parameters of its duplicates. Every Clip in the grid can have radically different Clip View properties, even though they all reference the same original audio file. This is an awesomely powerful feature of Live, as you will see!

If you want the Gains of both of these Clips to be the same, you can accomplish this in one of several ways:

- Manually lower each of the individual Clip Gains one at a time.
- Change the Gain of the first Clip and duplicate that Clip again, overwriting your previous Clip.
- Multiselect all of the Clips whose Gain you wish to change and change them simultaneously.

At different times, each of these techniques will be the way to go depending on what needs doing. Let's try each of these:

5. Since you have already changed the first of the two Lightribal Clips' Gain, let's just duplicate it over the second Clip: Highlight the first Clip (whose Clip Gain you already changed to read –8.09 dB) and hit [cmd-d/ctrl-d] to duplicate the Clip down to the next Slot. Although it does not look as though anything has happened, since there was already a Clip in the third Slot, the third Clip Slot is now an exact copy of the second Clip Slot, including the Gain change you made. Confirm this by clicking on the Clip in the third Slot: its Clip Gain should now also read –8.09 dB.
6. Click on the first MT_Beats Clip in Clip Slot 1 on the Beats track. Hold down [shift] and click on the third (and last) Clip in Slot 3 to multiselect all three duplicate Clips. When you do so, the Clip View changes to something like this:

Pic. 2.14: Multiselected Clips.

The "candy cane" diagonal stripes are there to indicate that you have selected multiple Clips and are potentially about to adjust the parameters for multiple Clips simultaneously.

7. With all three MT_Beats Clips still multiselected, bring the Clip Gain slider down to –2.31 dB. All three Clips' Gain values have been adjusted.
8. Select MT_Bass Clip on the Bass track so you can see its properties in the Detail View area. Click on the Gain value of 0.00 dB, type in "–3", and press [return]. The volumes are a bit more balanced now.

2.2.2—Clip Transposition

DO IT! Let's change a new parameter: Clip Transpose. Tuning elements—even drums—so that they work together is essential for making a harmonious mix:

Pic. 2.15: The Transpose dial and Detune box.

9. Launch your third Scene, Add Bass, so that all three Clips are playing.
10. Select your MT_Bass Clip on the Bass track by clicking on its name, which will bring up Clip View for that Clip.

11. Click-and-drag the Transpose dial and listen to the pitch of your bass line change in semitone (st) steps. As you go beyond a few semitones in either direction, you will hear the tone of the sound change more and more dramatically.

12. While you are at it, go ahead and click-and-drag in the Detune box as well. This is a subtler pitch adjustment using cents (ct). There are 100 cents in a semitone, so the Detune adjustment could be used for fine-tuning a performance that might be less than a semitone out of pitch with your Set. Note that you can adjust this value indefinitely in either direction, and the value will "wrap around," working in tandem with the Transpose value. Once you go upward in pitch past 50 cents (ct) (the value, not the rapper!) in the Detune box, you will notice that the Transpose value increments by 1 and the Detune value becomes –49 ct. The same is true when rolling the Detune value downward.

> **COOL!** Just about every adjustable parameter in Live can be reset to its default state by clicking on the parameter to select it, and then pressing the [delete] key on your keyboard. A few controls, such as Transpose and Detune controls, also have a small triangle that accomplishes the same thing when clicked.

13. Click on the Transpose and Detune's triangle's to reset them both to 0, their default value.

The Transpose and Detune values work closely with the Warp Mode settings (described in chapter 3, "Warping, Quantization, and Grooves") and with the Transpose Envelope described later in this chapter.

2.2.3—Looping and Non-Looping Clips

Thus far we have worked exclusively with Clips that repeat, or loop, as well as with Clips that are Warped to fit the tempo of our Set. Let's explore what these controls are for, and find a few instances in which these controls are not necessarily desirable.

14. In the Browser, head on over to Sounds to Sample > Atmospheric and preview a file called TEMFX01-Atmospheric11.wav. Spooky and delicious! Drag this file into the big open gray area in the Clip grid that is labeled Drop Files and Devices Here, and do what it tells you to do: drop it there! Live creates a new Audio Track and puts this Clip in the first Clip Slot, parallel with your first instance of MT_Beats, in the Scene you labeled as Intro.

15. Rename this new track—currently named 4 Audio—as "One Shots," and rename the new Clip as "Atmospheric."

16. This Clip, being as long as it is, is not a Clip that you would necessarily want to hear over and over; hearing it once through as an introductory atmospheric mood setter should be enough. So, in the Clip View, on the Sample box, turn off looping by deselecting the Loop button. Play the Intro Scene now, and listen to this Clip playing along with MT_Beats until the Atmospheric Clip completes. It will not loop—it just ends, while MT_Beats continues. I call these non-looping types of Clips (you guessed it) "one-shots."

At the same time, those two Clips by themselves get a little boring. Let's do something to add a little variation.

Loop

Pic. 2.16: The Loop button.

If you are playing the Intro Scene and you click on the Launch button for Scene 2, Add Perc, the Atmospheric Clip will stop playing because there is a Stop button in the second Clip Slot on your new One Shots track. If you were to duplicate the Atmospheric Clip in Clip Slot 1 to this second Clip Slot, you would hear the Atmospheric Clip restart when you triggered the Add Perc Scene, and that is not very interesting, either. Instead, do this:

17. Click in the second (empty) Clip Slot on One Shots, below the Atmospheric Clip, and do one of the following:

   • Press [cmd-e/ctrl-e].
   • Go Edit > Remove Stop Button.
   • [Ctrl-click/right-click] on the empty Clip Slot and choose Remove Stop Button from the contextual menu that appears.

This removes the Stop command from being triggered when this Scene is launched. If a Clip on this track is already playing when you launch this Scene it will continue to play, since there is no longer a Clip Stop button to stop it.

18. Now, launch Scene 1, Intro, and let it play for a few measures. Once it has established itself, launch Scene 2, Add Perc.

The Atmospheric Clip continues to play while the Lightribal Clip on the Perc track is added. Nice! It adds a bit of interest while the Atmospheric Clip continues to evolve.

Now do something similar with a short Clip of a crash cymbal to punctuate the entrance of your Bass Clip in Scene 3.

19. Navigate to Sounds to Sample > Crashes and drag the file The 80s.wav onto Clip Slot 3 of One Shots next to your MT_Bass Clip. Take the Clip Gain slider down to –8 dB. Turn looping off for this Clip as well, so that it plays only once. (A looping crash cymbal is a terrible thing! It sounds like a marching band, doesn't it? Ouch!)

20. Play through your first three Scenes, advancing when it feels right to do so. You needn't wait for the end of the Atmospheric Clip. When the time feels right, click on the Add Bass Scene and get your groove on with the bass line. It's starting to feel like a song now, right?

These are two examples of non-looping Clips that can add variation to your Session View arrangement. Here is what your Clip grid should look like by now:

Beats	Perc	Bass	One Shots
▶ MT_Beats	■	■	▶ Atmospheric
▶ MT_Beats	▶ Lighttribal	■	
▶ MT_Beats	▶ Lighttribal	▶ MT_Bass	▶ The 80s

Pic. 2.17: The Clip grid in progress.

2.2.4—Sample Editor Navigation Controls

Let's learn how to navigate the Sample Editor.

21. Click on the Stop All Clips button on the Master Track.
22. In the Clip grid, click on the Atmospheric Clip's name in the first Clip Slot on the One Shots track
     to bring up its Clip View properties.

> **COOL!**   If you want to make the Sample Editor larger so you can see more detail of
> the waveform, remember that you can click on and vertically drag the
> black divider between the Mixer and the Detail View area.

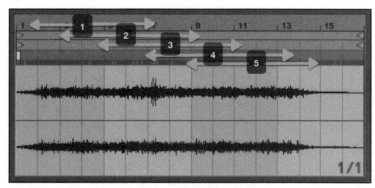

Pic. 2.18: The Atmospheric Clip's Sample Editor.

Depending on whether a Clip's Warp button is enabled, the number and type of available controls in the Sample Editor will logically change. The more complex of these two states, and the one you may find yourself using most often, is when Warp is set to On (the way it presently is in this Clip), so let's look at these controls. The navigation controls in the Sample Editor with Warp set to Off represent a simplified version of these controls, as you will see.

Let's define some of the areas of the Sample Editor window when Warp is set to On:

- **1. Sample Display Timeline**—The timeline shows the bar and beat divisions for the Clip. It is also used for navigation: As you mouse over the timeline, your cursor changes to a magnifying glass icon. Clicking-and-dragging up or down on the timeline will zoom the display, while click-dragging left and right will scroll your view of the Clip's waveform horizontally.
- **2. The Loop Brace**—The Loop Brace is a visual representation of the Clip's Loop Start and End points. Clicking-and-dragging either end of the Loop Brace will adjust the Loop Start or End, respectively, and clicking-and-dragging in the middle of the Loop Brace will relocate the entire loop, both Start and End simultaneously (provided that the loop length has been shortened, creating room to move the Loop Brace either forward or backward in time).

- **3. Clip Start/End/Playback**—The third area down from the top has triangle markers representing the Clip's Start and End values. These can be set independently from the Loop Start/End Brace above it. Mousing over the area between the Clip Start and End markers turns your cursor into a speaker icon, and clicking there will launch the Clip from that point on the timeline. Note that the actual playback point and timing is governed by the current Global Quantize value, so that launching the Clip in this manner will still keep it in sync with your other Clips. Also note that mousing over the lower half of the waveform display will turn your cursor into a speaker icon and clicking there will also launch the Clip from that point in a similar fashion.
- **4. The Warp Marker zone**—The next area down concerns Warp Markers. Note the single yellow Warp Marker at the start of this Clip. Warp Markers are for manipulating a Clip's relationship to tempo, and are covered in chapter 3, "Warping, Quantization, and Grooves." For now, do not click in this area.
- **5. Transient zone**—This area just above the waveform works together with the Warp Marker zone above it. In essence, this thin strip indicates sudden jumps in the waveform's amplitude (volume) with little white marks, suggesting logical places to add a Warp Marker. Transients are also explored in chapter 3, "Warping, Quantization, and Grooves."

Let's see some of these controls in action:

23. Launch the Atmospheric Clip by itself (not the whole Intro Scene). As the Clip plays, a vertical line shows the position of playback within the Clip, moving slowly across the waveform.
24. Roll your cursor anywhere over the timeline at the top of the Sample Editor: it changes to a magnifying glass icon. Click with the magnifying glass and drag it downward a ways: The waveform magnifies, or "zooms in." (You can also use the [+] and [-] keys to zoom horizontally.)
25. Before releasing the mouse button, drag left and right: The waveform scrolls left and right. (You can also use [left arrow] and [right arrow] to scroll the view horizontally.)
26. Would you like the Sample Editor view to follow the playback position? Easy: Click on the Follow button in the Control Bar or press [cmd-shift-f/ctrl-shift-f].

Pic. 2.19: The Follow button in the Control Bar.

If you zoom or scroll the view at all, Follow is turned off and you must re-enable it. That is why knowing the keyboard shortcut for this feature is essential. Also, you can toggle between page-by-page or continuous scrolling in Live's Preferences on the Look/Feel page.

IMPORTANT! In the lower-right corner of your screen, you will see a small duplicate waveform down below the main one. This is known as the Clip Overview. Its purpose is to provide you with an overview of your Clip's waveform when you are zoomed in on a portion of it. The black box that currently frames a portion of the waveform, which is known as the Zooming Hot Spot, indicates the segment that you are currently viewing in the Sample Editor. And here's a bonus: The same navigational gestures you just learned for working with the timeline in the Sample Editor also work on the Clip Overview. You can jump the Zooming Hot Spot to any point in the timeline with a single click on the Clip Overview, and you can click-and-drag on the Zooming Hot Spot to zoom and scroll the view here as well. Try it!

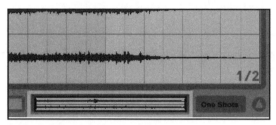

Pic. 2.20: The Clip Overview area.

27. Use the magnifier on the timeline to continue to resize and scroll the Sample Editor View. Notice how the Zooming Hot Spot interacts with the Clip Overview.

28. Click on the Clip Overview to jump the Zooming Hot Spot to that location. Click-and-drag on the Zooming Hot Spot to zoom and scroll the Sample Editor window.

2.2.5—Alternate Loops

As mentioned before, one audio file can be played back in an infinite number of ways using different Clip View settings for each duplicate. That is one of my favorite features of Live, for sure. Let's make some new variations of your primary three Clips to create a little buildup to the next section.

29. Multiselect the three left-most Clips in Scene 3: MT_Beats, Lightribal, and MT_Bass. Press [cmd-d/ctrl-d] to duplicate these three Clips onto the fourth Scene.

Click on the new MT_Beats Clip you just made in the fourth Clip Slot. In the Clip View Sample box, find the Position and Length value boxes under the Loop toggle button. These control the start position and length of your loop within the Clip. Currently, they are set to 1.1.1 and 2.0.0, respectively, which means "Start the Loop at (Position) bar 1, beat 1, sixteenth 1 (also known as the beginning of the Clip) and restart the Clip after playing for (Length) 2 bars, 0 beats, 0 sixteenth notes" (which happens to be the length of the entire Clip: 2 bars). In short, the entire Audio Clip is looping every two bars. Let's change that.

Pic. 2.21: The Loop Position and Length values in the Sample box.

30. Click in the middle Length box (currently 0), and then press the [down arrow] key until the Length reads 0.1.0, or one beat. Notice what happens in the Sample Editor to the right: The gray bar above the waveform (known as the Loop Brace) shortens to one beat and the rest of the sample is grayed out. If you launch this Clip right now, it will loop only the first beat of this Clip.

31. Now change the Position values to 2.4.1, so that the last beat of the second bar of the Clip Loops. Notice what the Loop Brace is doing: it has moved over to the end of bar 2 and still covers only one beat. Launch it!

Let's move on to the newest Lightribal Clip, to the right of the one you were just working on. This time let's use the Loop Brace to change the Length and Position values.

32. Put your cursor over the right end of the Loop Brace where the left-pointing triangle is. This is the Loop End indicator. Click-and-drag it to the left to 2.4.
33. Mouse over the left-most end of the Loop Brace: this is the Loop Start indicator. Drag it to 2.3. Notice that the Position value in the Sample box now reads 2.3.1 and the Length value reads 0.1.0. Play the Clip.
34. For a bit of variation, click-and-drag the Clip Start triangle (not the Loop Start triangle—the one just beneath that) all the way to the left to 1.1.1. Launch the Clip (or the Scene) and see the result of this.

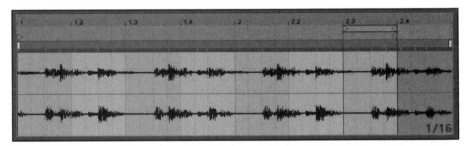

Pic. 2.22: The Loop Brace, Loop Start/End, and Clip Start/End indicators in the Sample Editor.

COOL! By moving the Clip Start away from the Loop Start you can have a Clip that starts playback from one point in the Clip and then loops at a different place in the Clip. One common use of this is to have a series of Clips in a Scene that starts with a fill (perhaps a drum roll) and then moves into a repeating loop without the fill. By putting it at the beginning of a series of Clips, you can choose when you want to transition into the Scene with the fill, but then loop the rest of the Scene normally. There are lots of other useful applications for this.

Finally, let's have a go with the MT_Bass Clip…

35. In the MT_Bass Clip in Scene 4, drag the Loop End indicator to 1.3 on the Sample Editor timeline, making the Clip Loop length two beats long, and starting at 1.1.1.
36. Launch the entire Scene 3, Add Bass, and then after a few bars launch into the Scene 4 you just made. A nice little buildup!
37. Let's rename this Scene and call it "Buildup."

Although we have been making changes to some Clip View controls, up until this point we had not drastically altered any of these Clips, and they still retain a vast majority of the original file's feel and sound. But now that we have versions where we are looping a small segment, this seems like a reason to start renaming a few Clips. Let's rename the three Clips in the Buildup Scene.

38. Rename MT_Beats in the fourth Slot as "MT_Beats Buildup 1."
39. Rename Lightribal in the fourth Slot as "Lightribal Buildup 1."
40. Rename MT_Bass in the fourth Slot as "MT_Bass Buildup 1."

Another thing I like to do to Clips that are different is to change their color so I remember that they are unlike the other Clips on the track with the same name.

41. [Ctrl-click/right-click] on one of the Clips in the fourth Scene that you have just modified. See all the colorful boxes at the bottom of the contextual window? Pick one of these that is not the current color. Do this for all three Clips in the Buildup Scene.

I like to choose a color that is similar to the one it was before, so I can still associate it with the Clip it came from. If it was blue before, make this new version light blue. You will likely come up with your own ways of using Clip color to make sense of your Sets.

> **COOL!** You can recolorize Tracks and Scenes in exactly the same way. [Ctrl-click/right-click] on any track or Scene name and choose a new color for it.

You may not be able to read the full titles of all your Clips at this point, as the track is not wide enough. Let's expand the width of the Tracks so you can:

42. Put your cursor over the gray vertical divider between the track names Beats and Perc. Your cursor changes to a bracket icon ( ]):
43. Click-and-drag this divider to the right to expand the width of the Beats track. Repeat this for all the Tracks until you can read all the Clip names.

You can resize the Master Track and Return Tracks as well.

So you see, with a couple of simple variations of the Clip View properties, we have a very different-sounding Scene using the same three Clips.

2.2.6—Follow Actions

This is another unique feature of Live that I just adore. Follow Actions allow you to control (or randomize) how a series of sequential Clips on a track relate to each other. You can create wonderful variations of Clips and then set their Follow Actions to determine what order to play them in. The following exercise will walk you through one of many possibilities.

Let's make Scene 5 return to the original Groove, and then add some new layers to explore Follow Actions.

44. Click on the Add Bass Scene name (not the Launch button) so the third cell down on the Master Track is highlighted. Then do one of the following:

- Press [cmd-c/ctrl-c] for Copy.
- Go Edit > Copy.
- [Ctrl-click/right-click] and select Copy from the contextual menu.

You've now copied the Add Bass Scene to the Clipboard.

45. Click in the fifth Scene down (currently called 5) to highlight it, and do one of the following:

- Press [cmd-v/ctrl-v] for Paste.
- Go Edit > Paste.
- [Ctrl-click/right-click] and select Paste from the contextual menu.

46. You now have a fifth Scene. Rename it as "Main Groove."

All set. Now for three new Clips to use with Follow Actions:

47. Head over to Sounds to Sample > Synth Loops, then select the file s2s_dt_synth_128_postwarvar1_Am.wav. Now hold down [cmd/ctrl] and click on , s2s_dt_synth_128_postwarvar3_Am.wav and s2s_dt_synth_128_postwarvar4_Am.wav to multi-select all three files in the Browser. Drag all three files simultaneously onto a new track in the fifth Scene Clip Slot next to your other new Clips in Main Groove.
48. Rename this new track as "Synth 1." Rename the three new Clips as "Postwarvar1," "Postwarvar3," and "Postwarvar4," respectively.
49. Select all three of these new Clips and lower their Clip Gain to –6dB.

Your Clip grid should now look something like this:

Beats	Perc	Bass	One Shots	Synth 1
▷ MT_Beats	■	■	▷ Atmospheric	■
▷ MT_Beats	▷ Lighttribal	■		■
▷ MT_Beats	▷ Lighttribal	▷ MT_Bass	▷ The 80s	■
▷ MT_Beats Build	▷ Lighttribal Build	▷ MT_Bass Build	■	■
▷ MT_Beats	▷ Lighttribal	▷ MT_Bass	▷ The 80s	▷ Postwarvar1
■	■	■	■	▷ Postwarvar3
■	■	■	■	▷ Postwarvar4

Pic. 2.23: The Clip grid in progress. Sample Editor.

When you launch Scene 5, Main Groove, you will hear the first of the three new Clips play. Let's use Follow Actions so that all three will play in order and then loop back to the start:

50. Click on Postwarvar1, the top-most Clip of the three. In the Clip View, on the Clip box, you will see the Follow Actions section:

The three settings here are the following:

- **Follow Action Time**—This is the interval after which a Follow Action may occur.
- **Follow Action A and B**—Each of these two pull-downs represents a Follow Action that may occur at the Follow Action Time interval.
- **Follow Action Chance A and B**—These values express what the likelihood is that either Follow Action A or B will occur. If A is set to 5 and B is set to 1, there is a five to one likelihood that A will occur, and a one in five likelihood that B will occur. If either of these is set to 0 (the default), that action will never occur.

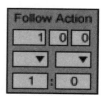

Pic. 2.24: The Follow Actions controls.

Yes, these controls are a little daunting at first glance, but stay with me! We will use them in a very straightforward way to get you started:

51. Set the Follow Action Time for this Clip to 4.0.0. Set the Follow Action A to Next. Set the Follow Action Chance A to 1.

This means that "after four bars, there is a one in one chance (or 100%) that the next Clip below will start playing." Easy enough? Try it! Play the Main Groove Scene and watch what happens: After all the Clips are triggered, the Clip below this one's (Postwarvar3) Launch button begins flashing right away, as if to say "I'm going to play next!" After four bars, it does just that. Let's keep going:

52. Click on the second Clip, Postwarvar3, and set the same settings for this Clip as the previous Clip: Follow Action Time to 4.0.0., Follow Action A to Next, Follow Action Chance A to 1.
53. Click on the final Clip, Postwarvar4. Notice that this Clip is only two bars long. Set the Follow Action Time for this Clip to 2.0.0. Set the Follow Action A to First. Set the Follow Action Chance A to 1. Play the Main Groove Scene to see what is happening.

Each of the three Clips plays in turn, and when the third one is done, it goes back to the first one and starts over. We've just created a 10-bar repeating phrase.

54. Just for fun, go back to the Clip called The 80s in the fifth slot on the One Shots track, and set this Clip to loop every ten bars: Turn Warp on, Loop on, and set the Loop Length to 10.0.0. This way, every time your Postwarvar Clip phrase repeats, the crash cymbal will also sound.

Wow, we've done a lot so far. Congrats! Take a deep breath. Stretch. Grab a cup of tea, and come back: we've still got two more Audio Clip exercises to go, and I've saved the best two for last! Speaking of saving:

55. Save your Set: [cmd-s/ctrl-s].

EXERCISE 2.3—CLIP ENVELOPES

The next feature, Clip Envelopes, offers a simple way to vary Clip parameters over time, which opens up all kinds of new sonic possibilities.

Clip Envelopes come in two flavors: modulation and automation. When you automate a parameter—such as Track Pan—the parameter moves, just as if you were moving it yourself, according to the Envelope's value. Modulation, on the other hand, is often expressed as a percentage value that operates *in addition to* whatever the parameter's current value is. You can even use modulation and automation at the same time.

Although we will explore only three basic Clip Envelopes to begin with, they can be used to add variety to virtually any parameter you can think of. Moreover, you can make an infinite number of Clip variations from a single piece of audio or MIDI, allowing for incredible variety and flexibility. The specific settings that you select in each Clip are saved and stored in your Set and can be saved to the Live Library for future use in other Sets as well.

2.3.1—The Volume Clip Envelope, Draw Modes, and Grid Values

DO IT! Let's get ready to work with Clip Envelopes. Here are two ways to get started:

- You can continue from right where we left off at the end of Exercise 2.2 and use File > Save As… to save the Set as My Exercise 2.3.als, or
- You can open Exercise 2.3.als from the supplied Sets in Book Content > Book Exercises Project, and then perform a Save As… and save your Set as My Exercise 2.3.als.

Now that you know how to navigate in the Sample Editor, let's grab a new Clip to work with:

1. Head over to the Sounds to Sample > FX folder and double-click on the first file, CST 1.wav, to put it on its own new track.
2. Move the Clip down to the fifth Clip Slot, which is on the Main Groove Scene.
3. Rename this track as "Synth 2." (No need to rename the Clip. It is already pretty simple and memorable.)
4. Play the Main Groove Scene to hear it in context.
5. If it is not already visible, click on the CST 1 Clip name in the Clip grid to ensure that the Clip's Clip View properties are visible in the Detail View at the bottom of your screen.

This CST 1 Clip is a little loud, and there is a raspy low note at the end of this phrase that doesn't sound great and conflicts with several other Clips' tonalities. You could use Clip Gain or Track Volume to fix the overall volume, but what about turning off that last note of the phrase? For that, you can use the Volume Clip Envelope.

IMPORTANT! The Sample Editor has two modes: Sample Editor and the Envelope Editor. Thus far we have been working in Sample Display mode as we worked with the controls on that box. Notice the right-pointing arrows to the right of the Sample and Envelopes box names. The highlighted arrow indicates which Sample Editor mode you are currently in. Clicking on these arrows, or any control in either box, will switch you to the mode associated with that box. Easy.

6. In the Clip View area of the CST 1 Clip, click anywhere in the Envelope box to switch to the Envelope Editor mode.

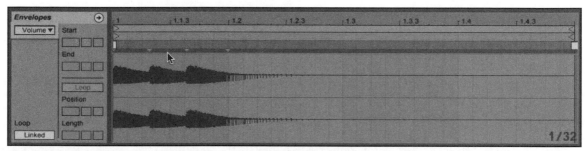

Pic. 2.25: The Envelope box Device Chooser and the Volume Clip Envelope.

In the upper left corner of the Envelopes box, you will see a pull-down menu: This is known as the Device Chooser, and it allows you to choose which part of the interface you'd like to see an Envelope for. When you choose an item from this list, a second pull-down menu appears, which is called the Clip Envelope Control chooser. This menu allows you to select the specific parameter you want to automate or modulate. The default Device is Clip and the default Control is Clip Gain, which is what we want for the following exercise. As it happens, you can *only* modulate—not automate—controls in the Clip Device list. More about this shortly.

The CST 1 waveform is overlaid with a dotted Volume Clip Envelope, which signifies that this parameter is currently unmodulated. Place your mouse over this dotted line, and the entire region turns pink. Think of this pink area as a graph representing the Clip's relative volume level as it plays back, with 0% of the current volume at the bottom of the waveform and 100% of the current volume at the top. The Envelope is currently at 100% all the way across, so the Clip plays back at its current volume set in the Clip Gain. Let's change that.

In Envelope Editor mode, there are two Draw modes for modifying envelopes:

- **Draw mode On**—In this mode, your cursor becomes a Pencil icon and you may draw in your envelopes by hand.
- **Draw mode Off**—This mode is called Breakpoint Editing, and it is more like pinning down a rubber band to create smooth, gradual shifts from one breakpoint to another.

To toggle the Draw mode on and off, do one of the following:

- Press the [B] key on your keyboard.
- Go Options > Draw mode.
- Click on the Draw mode switch, the Pencil icon in the upper right of your screen.

Pic. 2.26: The Draw mode switch enabled.

For now, turn Draw mode on: make sure that the Pencil icon at the top of your screen is lit yellow, and your cursor turns into a pencil when it is over the Envelope Editor area.

7. Click in the Envelope Editor and draw the Volume Envelope any way you like. Go crazy with it. Paint a landscape if you like. Hills and valleys. Play it back and hear the result.

Pic. 2.27: The current Sample Display grid value.

Sounds pretty choppy. Look down in the lower right corner of the Sample Display/Envelope Editor. There's a fraction there, and yours likely says 1/16. (No, I'm not a mind reader—that is the default.) That is your Snap to Grid value. The envelopes you draw are currently snapping to a grid that is currently divided into sixteenth notes, hence the choppiness.

You can change the grid value in one of three ways:

- Pressing [cmd-1/ctrl-1] makes the grid value smaller, and pressing [cmd-2/ctrl-2] makes the grid value larger.
- Go Options > Narrow Grid or Options > Widen Grid.
- [Ctrl-click/right-click] and choose a grid value from the contextual menu.

Since the three notes are each eight note triplets, let's set the grid to 1/8T:

8. Press [cmd-2/ctrl-2] once to get to the 1/8-note grid value.
9. Press [cmd-3/ctrl-3] once to turn triplets on. (The other two methods described above have equivalents here as well: Options > Triplet Grid, or [ctrl-click/right-click] and choose Triplet Grid.) The grid value now reads 1/8T.
10. Using the Pencil icon, click anywhere on the waveform: the Volume Clip Envelope jumps to meet your Pencil. Click-and-drag the envelope to about 80% for the first three 1/8T divisions, which are the notes that we want to be slightly quieter.
11. Now draw all the remaining quarter-note divisions after the first three down to 0% so that they will not sound at all. This gets rid of the buzzy low note altogether.

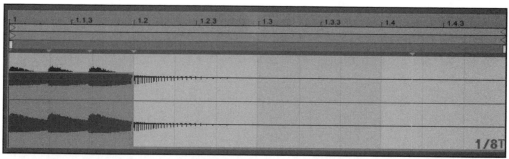

Pic. 2.28: The final Volume Clip Envelope for CST 1.

One question you might be asking yourself at this point is, "Why do the units for measuring the volume envelope use a percentage as the scale? Wouldn't decibels be a better unit of measurement here?" I'm glad you asked!:

IMPORTANT! Many modulated Clip Envelope graphs are expressed as a percentage of the Clip's current value. In the case of Clip Volume, the red line at the top represents "100% of the current Clip Gain," and dragging the red line below 100% yields smaller percentages of the current Clip Gain value, down to 0%. This way you can still change the Clip Gain slider, and whatever pattern you have drawn here will still be a relative amount (and therefore a percentage) of the Clip Gain value. In fact, if you watch the Clip Gain setting for CST 1 while it plays, you will see a little orange dot indicating the Envelope's current modulation of the Clip Gain setting.

2.3.2—The Pan Clip Envelope with Draw Mode Is On and Snap to Grid Is Off

This Clip is a little stagnant. Let's give it some motion with the Track Pan.

To access the Track Pan Clip Envelope, do the following:

12. In the Envelope box, click the Device Chooser and select "Show all envelopes" from the drop-down list.
13. Now pull down the same list and choose Mixer as your Device.
14. Pull down the lower Clip Envelope Control chooser and select Track Panning.

Now the dotted line is in the middle of the waveform, which makes sense, as the Track Pan control's default position is in the middle.

Let's try a slightly different use of Draw Mode.

15. Leave Draw mode on, or turn it on if it is not.
16. Do one of the following to toggle Snap to Grid to off:

- Press [cmd-4/ctrl-4].
- Choose Options > Snap to Grid (unchecked).
- Press [Ctrl-click/right-click] and choose Fixed Grid: Off.

17. Now use the Pencil icon to draw a Pan Clip Envelope that is completely free of constraint by the grid.

Nature and music are full of curves. You can draw less mechanical-sounding modulation this way.

You may have noticed that the Track Pan Modulation here is also measured in percentages, just like Volume Clip Envelopes. Pan Clip Envelopes are also a relative adjustment, this time relative to the Track's Pan value in the Mixer. You can still change the Pan value in the Mixer, and the Pan Clip Envelope will continue to adjust the Pan position relative to the new value.

18. Play the CST Clip and look at the Track Pan dial: the dial's value stays stationary, but an orange ring denotes the current modulation value.
19. Move the Track Pan dial to some other value, either left or right. The modulation continues, still relative to the new Track Pan dial position.

However, I'd like to show you a different method in the next exercise to demonstrate Session View automation recording, so:

20. Delete the current modulation Envelope by [ctrl-clicking/right-clicking] anywhere on the Envelope and choosing "Clear Envelope" from the contextual menu.

2.3.3—Recording Automation Envelopes in Real Time to Session View Clips

Drawing Envelopes with a mouse is all well and good. But what if you wanted simply to perform the panning in real time and record that? Now you can!

NEW FEATURE! New in Live 9 is the ability to record automation to Session View Clips in real time using either a MIDI controller—which we'll cover in chapter 7—or a mouse.

Pic. 2.29: The Automation Arm button and the Session Record button.

So far we have been working with *modulation* Envelopes, which are an additional adjustment to a parameter *relative* to that parameter's current value. However, in this exercise, we are going to record actual *automation*, where the parameter's *actual value changes* are recorded.

First, I'll need to point out three new controls that we will use for this: the Automation Arm button, the Session Record button, and the Track Arm button.

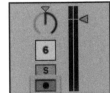

Pic. 2.30: The Track Arm button.

- **Automation Arm**—Sometimes you want to record just audio or MIDI notes without recording the adjustments you make to various Live parameters at the same time. Other times its useful to record everything. Automation Arm toggles whether Live will record parameter automation to Session Clip Envelopes or Arrangement Tracks while recording.

- **Session Record**—This button enables the recording of armed tracks into Session View Clip slots.
- **Track Arm**—Use this button to specify which tracks you intend to record on. By default, Live only allows one track to be armed at a time, but you can change this in the preferences, or override it by holding down [cmd/ctrl] while you click on multiple Track Arm buttons.

Next, let's make a distinction between recording and overdubbing. Recording commits your performance to an Audio or MIDI Clip. Overdubbing is the process of adding additional layers of information to that recording in one or more successive passes. Since we already have the recording of the CST 1 sound file, we are now going to overdub a Track Pan Envelope on top of it.

The process for recording or overdubbing in Session View is essentially the same:

- Decide if you want to record parameter gestures or not, and toggle the Automation Arm accordingly.
- Arm the track(s) you want to record to with the appropriate Track Arm button(s).
- Enable the Session Record button and make your recording into the selected Clip Slot.

DO IT! Let's try it!

21. Select the CST 1 Clip in the Clip grid by clicking on it. If it is selected, you should be able to see it's Clip Properties.
22. Ensure that the Automation Arm button is enabled: we want to record our Track Pan moves.
23. Enable the Track Arm button on the Synth 2 track.
24. Click the Session Record button.

Live starts recording. Since there is already an Audio Clip in this slot, Live begins overdubbing automation Envelopes instead of recording audio. Now, any parameter you move will be recorded as an automation Clip Envelope. And since it is a looping Clip, you can take as many passes as you like to get your Envelope gestures just right.

25. Move the Synth 2 Track Pan dial to pan the CST 1 Clip in an interesting way that moves the sound as it plays, and then let go of the dial as it reaches the end of the Clip and is about to loop.

When you move the Pan dial, you see the resulting automation Envelope recorded to the Clip Envelope editor. If you release the dial, Live begins to play back what you recorded. Move it again, and you overdub that action into the Envelope. The act of clicking on the control toggles you between playing and recording automation.

I went with a right to left panning which looks like this:

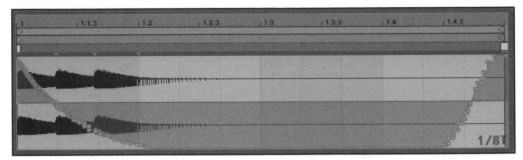

Pic. 2.31: A recorded automation Envelope for the Track Pan Clip Envelope.

26. When you have an automation Envelope you are satisfied with, click the Stop button to exit overdubbing.

27. Disarm the Track Arm button to avoid further accidental overdubbing.

Now you will see that the Track Pan dial has a red square next to it. This square is to let you know that this parameter has automation recorded for it.

When you play back this clip, you will see that the Track Pan dial moves in time with the automation envelope. This is not a modulation Envelope, imposing a moving relative value on the dial's position—it is automation, moving the parameter itself. What happens if we now move the Track Pan dial like we did when it was modulated?

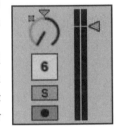

Pic. 2.32: The Track Pan dial with the red automation indicator square.

28. Turn the Track Pan dial to some other value.

Both the red automation indicator and the red Track Pan automation Envelope turn gray.

29. Launch the Clip. The Track Pan dial does not follow the automation Envelope.

Pic. 2.33: The Re-enable Automation switch.

By moving an already automated parameter, you are overriding the automation, once again taking control of this parameter. This allows you to continue to work with the control if you want to, perhaps trying other Pan settings before overdubbing.

Notice the orange, newly lighted switch in the Control Bar: this is the Re-enable Automation switch.

30. To re-enable the automation Envelope, click the Re-enable Automation switch to turn it off.

Now Live goes back to observing the previously recorded Track Pan automation.

So, this should illustrate the differences between parameter modulation and automation. This will get even clearer in chapter 7 when we look at recording automation with MIDI controllers, and in chapter 8's exercises with Arrangement View automation.

2.3.4—The Transpose Clip
Envelope and Breakpoint Editing

The next Envelope we'll look at is the pretty wild: The Transpose Clip Envelope. Get ready to party. And we'll learn a new Envelope editing technique called breakpoint editing in the process.

31. In the CST 1 Clip Envelope box, choose Clip from the Device Chooser, and Transposition Modulation from the Control Chooser.

This Envelope looks and functions a lot like the Track Pan Modulation Envelope in that it starts in the middle, but you will discover that the range of this Envelope is considerably greater.

32. Press [B] or click the Draw Mode switch to disable Draw mode.
33. Put your mouse over the dotted red line that runs down the middle of the Sample Display area: the dotted line turns solid red and a blue circle appears under your pointer. Click the red line. The circle remains in place. You've made what is called a breakpoint.

A breakpoint is like pressing your finger against a rubber band to hold it down on a table: this point on the Envelope will no longer move unless you move it with the mouse.

34. Make another breakpoint somewhere else on the line. Now click-and-drag this second breakpoint somewhere.

You are breakpoint editing. Hoorah! You can use this simple technique to sculpt any Envelope you might need. Notice that you can drag a point "off the screen" of the Envelope editor: The range of possible values for breakpoints is -48 semitones to +48 semitones—that's four octaves up or down—and in order to address that many values, the vertical axis scrolls. Place your pointer over the vertical axis where the transpose value is displayed, and your pointer turns into a hand. Click-and-drag with this hand to scroll the graph up and down.

To remove a breakpoint, do one of the following:

• Single-click on it again.
• Drag a selection across one or more breakpoints and press [delete].

NEW FEATURE! New in Live 9 is the ability to curve Envelopes and automation lines. Place your pointer over a diagonal line between two points, and then hold down [opt/alt]. A small curve appears next to your pointer. Click-and-drag with this new pointer and watch your straight lines turn into beautiful curves.

Experiment with Transpose Clip Envelope breakpoints. Here's what I did: The pitch slides from the first breakpoint at +2 st down to –19 st at the end of the third note at 1.2, and then I applied a small curve to it.

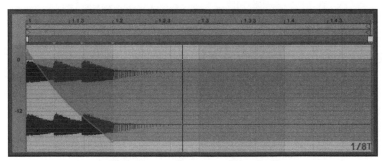

Pic. 2.34: The final Transpose Clip Envelope for CST 1.

> **COOL!** If you want to move breakpoints between semitone values, hold down [cmd/ctrl] while you drag a point for finer resolution. This is useful for making small pitch adjustments such as correcting an out-of-tune vocal phrase.

2.3.5—Unlinked Clip Envelopes, Looping and Non-Looping

In the previous three examples, all of the Clip Envelopes have been exactly as long as the Clip that you were working with. This doesn't have to be the case. Let's make two examples in which the Clip Envelope and actual Clip audio are unlinked from each other.

The first is going to be a short, looping modulation over a longer, non-looping Audio Clip to create a stutter effect. Remember your Atmospheric Clip from the non-looping Clips exercise? One Shots track, Clip Slot 1? Yes *that* one.

35. Click on the Atmospheric Clip to bring up its Clip View Properties, and then click on the Envelope box. You should be looking at the default Clip Volume Modulation Envelope. If not, use the Device and Control Choosers to bring it up.

36. Under Region/Loop in the Envelopes box, toggle the Linked button so that it turns orange and reads Unlinked. Now the Clip and the Clip Envelope can be different lengths.

Pic. 2.35: The Linked Envelope button toggled to Unlinked.

37. Under the Envelope Loop switch, set the Length to 0.0.1, which is a sixteenth note in length. You now have a Volume Clip Envelope that is a sixteenth note in length, and it loops.

38. Set your grid value to 1/32. [Cmd-1/ctrl-1] and [cmd-2/ctrl-2] work well for adjusting grid value size.

39. Turn Draw mode back on by pressing [B], and lower the volume of the second thirty-secondnd note to off by drawing it down at the bottom of the Envelope graph. Play the Intro Scene again. The Atmospheric Clip pulses on and off once every sixteenth note. The Envelope loops,. So this effect continues for the length of the Audio Clip. A bit more interesting, I think.

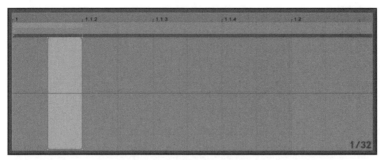

Pic. 2.36: A Looping, stuttering Volume Clip Envelope.

Another combination is a long, non-looping Clip Envelope over a short, looping Audio Clip. Here we go:

40. Remember the shortened version of the MT_Bass Clip you made for the Buildup Scene? It is on the Bass track, and it's in the fourth Clip Slot down. You even changed the Clip's color to signify its uniqueness. Bingo! Click on it.
41. Click on the Transpose button in the Envelopes box.
42. Toggle the Linked Envelope button to Unlinked.
43. This time, also toggle the Envelope Loop button to Off.
44. Just above the Loop button, set the Envelope End value to 6.1.1. Although the Clip Loop Length is a half bar long, the Clip Envelope is now six bars long.
45. Turn Draw mode off.
46. Make a slow, steadily increasing Transpose Clip Envelope that starts at 0 ct at bar 1 and reaches 24 ct by bar 6. That looks like this:

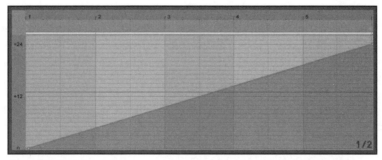

Pic. 2.37: An unlinked, non-looping, steadily increasing Transpose Clip Envelope across six bars.

Play it back. The bass's pitch continues to rise across six bars of the envelope. Granted, it sounds a little cheesy right now, but we'll fix that with Warp Modes and effects soon enough.

47. Save your Set by pressing [cmd-s/ctrl-s].

SUMMARY

- When you import a digital audio file in Live, Live makes an Audio Clip.
- An Audio Clip plays on an Audio Track, which can play back only one Audio Clip at a time.
- An Audio Clip can be either mono (one channel) or stereo (two channels), and an Audio Track can have mono and/or stereo Audio Clips on it at the same time.
- In Session View, Audio Clips are stored vertically in Clip Slots on an Audio Track, and can be played by clicking on their Clip Launch button.
- Clips can be stopped by clicking on an empty Clip Slot's Clip Stop button, the track's Clip Stop button, the Master Track's Stop All Clips button, or by pressing the [spacebar], which stops Live's transport entirely.
- Audio files can be previewed in the Browser, either at the current Set's tempo or at their own original tempo, depending on whether Live is currently playing or not.
- Volume can be controlled at numerous places in Live: a Clip's Clip Gain slider, a Clip's Volume Envelope, a track's Track Volume slider, and the Master Track's Master Volume slider. Each of these adjustments affects all the Devices after it.
- Warped Clips in a Live Set will play back at the Set's master tempo.
- Launching of a Set's Clips will be delayed to the next value set in the Global Quantize box.
- Horizontal rows in the Clip grid are called "Scenes," and can be triggered simultaneously by clicking on that Scene's Scene Launch button.
- Many items in Live—such as a Track, Clip, or Scene—can be duplicated by pressing [cmd-d/ctrl-d] and deleted by pressing the [delete] key.
- Many items in Live—such as a Track, Clip, or Scene—can be renamed with the keyboard shortcut [cmd-r/ctrl-r].
- Many parameters that shape an Audio Clip's playback can be found in that Clip's Clip View, which appears in the Detail View area when a Clip is clicked.
- The Clip View has four separate boxes, entitled Clip, Launch, Sample, and Envelope, respectively, the last three of which can be hidden and shown via their Show/Hide buttons.
- The Sample Display area is used for working with the Loop Brace, Start and End markers, or Clip Envelopes.
- Some Clip View properties can be changed on several Clips at once when multiple Clips are selected.
- You can change a Clip's pitch using the Transpose dial and Detune box.
- A Clip—or a portion thereof—can loop, or not loop. A non-looping Clip is often referred to as a one-shot Clip.
- A Track, Scene, or Clip's color can be changed in the Clip box in Clip View, or by [ctrl-clicking/right-clicking] on a Clip and selecting a new color.
- Follow Actions can control or randomize the order of playback of a series of vertically adjacent Clips.
- Clip Envelopes can modulate or automate many Clip or Track parameters. You can record Clip Envelope automation gestures using the Session Record function.
- Clip Envelopes can be edited using either Draw mode or Breakpoint Envelope Editing mode. In either mode, Snap to Grid can be on or off. Holding down [opt/alt] will allow you to add a curve to your Envelope.
- Envelopes may either be looping or non-looping, and may be linked to the length of the Clip or unlinked and of any length.

Warping, Quantization, and Grooves

Live's digital audio Warping engine is the key technology that makes a majority of the synchronization magic happen so seamlessly. It is what makes possible the ability to take multiple files of differing tempos and keys and use them together. All of the major DAW packages available today have some form of real-time digital audio time-stretching built in, but not only has Ableton been doing it for longer than most of them, in my opinion, they also do it better. Warping in Live is easier to use, and most importantly, sounds better at a wider range of stretching than any other tool I have used. This allows you to use a much wider array of sounds in your sessions.

Whether you realize it or not, you have already used the Warp engine in this Set quite a bit. Your three main Clips—MT_Beats, Lightribal, and MT_Bass—were all created at 125 bpm, but the tempo of our Set is 120 bpm, and they all are playing in sync quite happily. Live's Warp engine "Warps" the 125 bpm Clips to fit the Set's tempo of 120 bpm. If you would like to hear what life would be like without Warping technology, go ahead and turn off the Warp button in the Sample box of one or more of your Clips in this Set, and play back the Scene that contains them. Have you ever listened to a DJ who can't seem to beat-match two tracks together? It sounds like sneakers in a dryer, doesn't it? It's the same thing without Warping technology: total chaos!

But there is far more to Warping than just tempo alignment. Let's have a look.

EXERCISE 3.1—WARP MODES
3.1.1—The Clip View Warping and Tempo Controls

DO IT! Let's work with Warping. Here are two ways to get started:

- You can continue from right where you left off at the end of Exercise 2.3 and use Save As… to save the Set as "My Exercise 3.1.als," or

- You can open Exercise 3.1.als from the supplied Sets in Book Content > Book Exercises Project, and then perform a Save As... and save your Set as My Exercise 3.1.als.

The key to great- and creative-sounding Warping is in the Warp controls for each Clip, which can be found in the Sample box of each Clip's Clip View.

Pic. 3.01: The Seg. bpm controls in Clip View.

This small box actually offers a very wide range of Warping possibilities, so let's take the time to get familiar with all that this area has to offer. To begin, we're going to add a new rhythm Clip for a breakdown section of our evolving Set:

1. Rename the next empty Scene in your Set as "Breakdown." It should currently be named 7.
2. In the Browser, head over to Sounds to Sample > Drum Loops. Find the file named Beat_reaktored_90.wav and click on it. You should hear it preview if the Preview button is turned on.
3. Drag the sample Beat_reaktored_90.wav onto the eighth Clip Slot—in the newly renamed Breakdown Scene—of your first track, the Beats track. This should leave a gap of two empty Clip Slots below the last instance of MT_Beats in Clip Slot 5. Rename the Clip as "Beat_reaktored." Play the Clip by itself by playing the Breakdown Scene or clicking on the Beat_reaktored Clip's Launch button in the Clip grid. It now plays back quite a bit faster, at the Set's master tempo, 120 bpm.

Beats	Perc	Bass	One Shots	Synth 1	Synth 2
▶ MT_Beats			▶ Atmospheric		
▶ MT_Beats	▶ Lighttribal				
▶ MT_Beats	▶ Lighttribal	▶ MT_Bass	▶ The 80s		
▶ MT_Beats Buildup	▶ Lighttribal Buildup	▶ MT_Bass Buildup 1			
▶ MT_Beats	▶ Lighttribal	▶ MT_Bass	▶ The 80s	▶ Postwarvar1	▶ CST 1
				▶ Postwarvar3	
				▶ Postwarvar4	
▶ Beat_reaktored					

Pic. 3.02: The Beat_reaktored Clip in the eighth slot on the Beats track.

You may have noticed that many of the Clips you are working with have a number in their file name, such as the number 125 in s2s_tt_Lightribal_125_lawn3 or the number 90 in Beat_reaktored_90.wav. If you hadn't already guessed this, the number represents the original tempo at which the file was created, and this is the tempo at which the file will play back if you turn off the Warp button in Clip View. It is also the tempo you will hear if you click on the Clip in the Browser while Live's transport is stopped, or if you engage the Raw button in the Preview tab.

4. While the Beat_reaktored Clip is playing, turn the Warp button on and off. The original tempo is quite a bit slower.

You will have to restart the Clip once it gets to the end, because the Warp and Loop functions are linked, and Loop will be turned off if Warp is disabled.

5. Before continuing, ensure that both the Warp and Loop buttons are engaged.

Playing back this 90 bpm Clip at the master tempo of 120 bpm sounds fine, but it is a little frenetic for a breakdown. What if you could hear this Clip playing at half speed instead?

Notice that the area in the Sample box labeled Seg. BPM ("Segment BPM") currently shows a value of 90. This number represents Live's best guess at the Clip's original tempo. In this case, Live has guessed that the Clip's original tempo is 90 bpm, and speeds up the Clip to play it back at 120 bpm when the Warp button is engaged. But what would happen if we told Live that the Clip's original tempo was 180 bpm instead? Live would then slow down the Clip to play at 120 bpm. Let's try it:

6. Underneath the Seg. BPM box there are two buttons: one halves the original tempo, and the other doubles the original tempo. Click on the one to the right, marked *2. The Clip's original tempo now reads 180 and the Loop Length now reads 4.0.0 rather than 2.0.0.
7. Play back the Clip using the Clip Launch button. It plays at half speed, which is equivalent to 60 bpm currently. Much better for a breakdown!
8. Just for fun, go ahead and hit the "halve the original tempo" (:2) button twice, so that the Seg. BPM reads 45. Play it back.

Yowza! One would need several more cups of coffee to appreciate a Clip playing that fast, which is effectively now 240 bpm. Click on *2 twice to put the Seg. Tempo back to 180 before someone goes into cardiac arrest!

9. To get a sense of how this is going to work with the rest of your Clips, remove the Stop button in the eighth Slot on the Synth 1 track just beneath the Postwarvar4 Clip (highlight the empty Clip Slot and press [cmd-e/ctrl-e]).
10. Now go back and launch the fifth Scene, named Main Groove, and let it play for a bar or two. Then click on the Scene Breakdown. You should still hear the three Clips on Synth 1 playing in their looping cycle while the Beat_reaktored Clip plays at half tempo on the Beats track.

So, the Seg. BPM box is key to letting Live know how fast or slow you want a Clip playing back relative to the Set's global tempo.

3.1.2—Warp Modes Overview

Now we are into the juicy stuff! Warp Modes allow you to try out one of several different time-stretching algorithms on a Clip. Each Mode's name suggests the type of sound it was intended for. You can use these different algorithms to help the time-stretching sound more natural, or try out some more adventurous settings to create new and interesting variations of the Clip.

Pic. 3.03: The Warp Mode controls in Clip View.

The default Warp Mode is called Beats, and that is what you will see in the Warp Mode pull-down menu, which you will find directly underneath the Halve/Double Original Tempo buttons. Open this pull-down menu and have a look at the other Warp Modes:

- **Beats**—This mode was created for rhythmic audio, and it is particularly good for drum loops.
- **Tones**—This mode works well on audio with a clear sense of pitch.
- **Texture**—This mode is useful for complex and noisy sounds, such as multiple instruments playing together, a complex synth patch, or the sound of a babbling brook.
- **Re-Pitch**—Re-Pitch works similarly to a record player in that pitch and playback speed are linked together: As the tempo slows the pitch decreases. The inverse is also true.
- **Complex**—This mode is devoted to working with a file of an entire mix, which often contains beat, tone, and texture information in the same Clip. The Complex algorithm uses as much as ten times the CPU load of the other modes, so watch your CPU load meter carefully when using this one.
- **Complex Pro**—As you might surmise, this mode is an extension of Complex mode, and uses even more complex computations and CPU resources. This mode works well with entire mixes whose pitch is also being transposed, and offers two parameters that Complex mode does not, for even finer control over the sound.

IMPORTANT! Learning about how your computer works and how to manage Live's resources is critical to using Live to its maximum potential. See chapter 10, "Best Practices," for more information on this subject.

3.1.3—Texture Warp Mode

Let's try a few of these Warp Modes in action:

The three postwarvar Clips on the Synth 1 track sound a bit grainy, and with all the percussion going on in this track so far, something smoother might sit better in the mix.

11. In the Mixer, click on the Synth 1 track's Solo button ("S"), which will isolate the sound coming from this track.
12. Highlight all three Clips at once by selecting the first one and [shift-clicking] on the last one, or by clicking-and-dragging a box around all of them at once.

In the Clip View you will again see a reduced set of adjustable parameters for multiselected Clips, but the Warp Mode controls are still available.

13. Pull down the Warp Mode selector and select Texture, which makes sense, given the tonality of these Clips.

Already the sound is clearer and smoother. When you choose Texture mode, you will see two new parameters become available: Grain Size and Flux. Click-and-drag these variables up and down and listen to the quality of the sound change. You can also double-click on the boxes and type in values directly. I found a pair of settings that I thought worked well together:

14. Set a Grain Size of 75, and a Flux of 20.
15. Unsolo the track by clicking on the track's Solo button again and listen to the adjustments you made to the Clips on Synth 1 in context with the other Clips.

3.1.4—Beats Warp Mode

Next, let's work on the breakdown drums:

16. Select your newest Clip, the Beat_reaktored Clip on the Beats track.

The Warp Mode is set to Beats. There are a number of parameters to work with here.

First, let's explain the three Transient Loop Modes, the box in the lower-left corner where you can choose one of three icons. When Live has to stretch a rhythmic Clip to a length longer than its original length, the Transient Loop modes provide several ways of dealing with the space that gets inserted between the rhythmic sounds:

- **Off**—The first icon, an arrow pointing to a vertical line, is a mode in which each segment of the sound plays and then silence gets inserted in the gaps.
- **Loop Forward**—In this mode, each sound segment plays and then loops forward if more audio is needed to fill in the gap before the next segment.
- **Loop Back and Forth**—The final mode plays each rhythmic segment and then plays the segment backward to fill in any gaps as needed.
- **The Transient Envelope**—The box to the right of the Transient Loop Modes pull-down controls the size of the crossfades used in conjunction with the different Transient Loop modes. This value can tighten or loosen the envelope of your stretched rhythmic audio. Play with this in conjunction with each of the above Transient Loop Modes.

Pic. 3.04: The three Transient Loop mode icons.

17. Launch the Beat_reaktored Clip, and while it plays back, cycle through the Transient Loop Modes while adjusting the Transient Envelope value and hear the differences. Also, try some radical adjustments to the Transpose dial while doing this to get some wonderfully strange rhythms!

Next, scroll through the Granulation Resolution pull-down options. These control how note values get preserved when applying these stretching algorithms. The default setting of Transients preserves sudden amplitude changes instead of a fixed grid, and often this setting produces the most transparent, natural stretching results for drums. The other settings can create some wild results, especially in conjunction with the Transpose dial.

18. Try each of the Granulation Resolution settings while varying the other settings, including Transpose. Notice which combinations you like.
19. When you have fully explored all that Beats Warp Mode has to offer, set the Warp Mode to Re-Pitch.

3.1.5—Re-Pitch Warp Mode

Re-Pitch mode is a special case among the Warp Modes, because it is not attempting to preserve the pitch while stretching the length. Instead, in this mode pitch and speed are linked much like a record player: When you slow the audio down, the pitch also comes down, and when you speed the audio up, the length gets shorter and the pitch goes up.

In this case, with your Beat_reaktored Clip, the tempo has been slowed down quite a bit, from 90 to 60 bpm (because you doubled the original Clip tempo). With the rest of the Warp Modes, Live must find ways to insert additional samples into the audio and still sound natural (or not) while preserving its original pitch. But with Re-Pitch mode, Live just plays the Clip back slower and lets the pitch follow as needed. Because no new samples need to be inserted, often Re-Pitch mode sounds the most natural and least glitchy. As long as you don't mind the pitch changing, that is!

20. Leave this Clip in Re-Pitch mode when you are done experimenting.

3.1.6—Tones Warp Mode

Next, let's work with the bass sound a bit:

21. Multiselect all the MT_Bass Clips on the Bass track.
22. Change all the bass Clips' Warp Modes to Tones.

The Tones mode has an additional parameter known as Grain Size. Tones mode uses small divisions of the sound known as "grains" for stretching, and varying the grain size will produce different results. In this particular Clip, playing with the grain size can diminish the clicky double attack heard on some of the notes.

23. Try varying the Grain Size value. I liked a setting of 42 for the grain size on this Clip. A medium-small grain size seems to match the quick, sharp attack of these Clips.

In my opinion, none of the Clips we've used so far in this piece would benefit from the Complex or Complex Pro Warp Modes, but go ahead and try them on some Clips to hear what they sound like if you want to. Be sure to revert to the original mode when you are done, because the Complex modes eat up your computer's resources, and we have a lot yet to do in this Project before we are done. Conserve where possible!

24. Save your Set by pressing [cmd-s/ctrl-s].

EXERCISE 3.2—WARP MARKERS

Clip tempo synchronization and transposition are two very cool uses of Live's Warp engine, but they are not the only uses. The following two exercises will show you two more very powerful and very useful techniques that use the Warp functionality to its full potential.

Every musician misses a beat now and again. Maybe you are playing your instrument and your performance is flawless, save for that one wrong note or instance of bad timing. Or perhaps you are trying to work with two drum loops that you like, and they almost go together except for that last fill at the end. Well, using this next tool, Warp Markers, you can stretch and shrink digital audio as though it were a piece of chewing gum. You can use it correctively to fix a performance that isn't quite perfect, or creatively to make a piece of audio do something completely unnatural.

Almost all modern DAWs have some type of audio-stretching tool at this point, but not only was Ableton Live one of the very first not only to have it, but Live also has the easiest-to-use interface and the highest-quality audio-stretching of any DAW I have tried. Warp Markers represent Ableton Live at its best.

In the next three exercises, we are going to explore three techniques of corrective timing: Warp Markers, Quantization, and Grooves.

3.2.1—Warp Markers Defined

DO IT!   Time to work with Warp Markers. Here are two ways to get started:

- You can continue from right where you left off at the end of Exercise 3.1 and use Save As... to save the Set as My Exercise 3.2.als, or
- You can open Exercise 3.2.als from the supplied Sets in Book Content > Book Exercises Project, and then perform a Save As... and save your Set as My Exercise 3.2.als.

Let's fix that sloppy bass line we've been putting up with for several chapters! It has quite a bit of swing, which is fine, but it doesn't fit perfectly with the timing of the two main drumbeats. Let's improve the timing a bit:

1. Click on the first instance of the MT_Bass Clip in the third Slot on the Bass track to bring up its Clip View.
2. Now click on the Sample box's Sample Display title bar to ensure that you are in Sample Display mode and not the Envelope Editor.

Look closely at the waveform in the Sample Editor area. At either end of this Audio Clip you will notice a yellow box in the gray bar above the waveform. These are two Warp Markers, and they are added to any Clip that has Warp enabled in the Sample box. In essence, these two Warp Markers delineate the start and end of the Warped Clip, and allow Live to stretch the Clip to fit the Set's global tempo.

Also notice that directly above the start of each bass note there is a little vertical white line in the gray horizontal bar between the waveform and the Loop Brace. This is known as a "transient," and it indicates a sudden change in amplitude in the waveform. Live designates these as "transients" because transients often present an ideal location to Warp audio from since they typically indicate the start of a new sound.

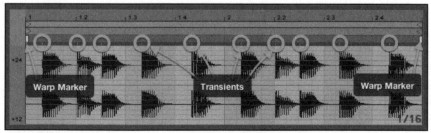

Pic. 3.05: Transient indicators and Start/End Warp Markers.

Place your mouse pointer over one of these small white transient marks. A new gray shape appears above the waveform. This is known as a Pseudo Warp Marker, and its purpose is to suggest where you might create an actual Warp Marker. Let's do that.

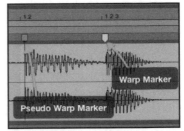

3. Place your mouse pointer over the transient of the third bass note in this 10-note phrase at 1.2.3. When you see the Pseudo Warp Marker appear, double-click on it. It turns yellow. You have just made your first Warp Marker!

Pic. 3.06: A Pseudo Warp Marker and a Warp Marker.

4. Drag this Warp Marker left or right and notice what happens to the audio waveform. Drop the marker somewhere far from where it started, and play back the Clip. You can even move the Warp Marker while the Clip is playing.

More than likely, you have made the timing of the MT_Bass Clip quite a bit more awkward than the way it was to begin with, but you should now have a sense of the power of a Warp Marker. You can pick any point on the waveform and stretch it in either direction, either subtly or to extremes.

Notice that as you move your new Warp Marker, the ends of the Clip do not move because they are anchored to the timeline by their own Warp Markers. Think of the waveform as a rubber band, and each Warp Marker as a pin that you can use to "pin down" the audio, or move to stretch the audio. As you'll see, using multiple Warp Markers together you can correct one section's timing while leaving the rest untouched.

5. Undo your Warp Marker moves by using [cmd-z/ctrl-z] or going Edit > Undo Move Warp Marker(s). Do this as many times as needed until the Warp Marker is back where it started.

3.2.2—Correcting Timing with Warp Markers Snapping to a Grid

This Clip has ten bass notes in it, and the second five are nearly identical to the first five. The first three notes in each bar sound okay, timing wise. It's the fourth and fifth notes that feel a little loose. Before we can move them, however, we need to "pin down" the notes on either side that we don't want to move.

6. We already have a Warp Marker at the third bass note. Double-click on the transient at the beginning of the sixth note as well, so that when we move the fourth and fifth notes that are out of place, the two on either side (whose timing we already like) do not move.

7. Note your Snap to Grid value in the lower right corner of the Sample Editor. Use [cmd-1/ctrl-1] or [cmd-2/ctrl-2] to increase/decrease the grid value until it reads 1/16, which represents a grid size of sixteenth notes. Alternately, you can ctrl-click/right-click on the Sample Editor waveform area and set the grid to Fixed Grid: 1/16.

8. Now double-click on the transients above the fourth and fifth notes in the phrase to create Warp Markers for them. Play with the timing of these two notes by moving their Warp Markers left or right. Notice that the Warp Markers snap to the sixteenth-note grid as you move them.

3.2.3—Correcting Timing with Warp Markers and Snap to Grid Off

While you are moving the fourth and fifth notes, you will still hear the ninth and tenth notes that are out of place. When you find settings that you like for the first half of the Clip, go ahead and correct the second half of the Clip. You could start by double-clicking on the transient above the eighth note to anchor it, the way we did in the first half, but let me show you a great shortcut:

9. Place your mouse pointer above the transient above the ninth note (second from the end). This time, hold down [cmd/ctrl] and double-click.

Live not only creates a new Warp Marker where you clicked, but it also creates one at the transients that are on either side of it. This is a big time-saver when you want to move a single note relative to the notes before and after it. (The end of the Clip at 3.1.1 is already anchored by a Warp Marker, so you do not have to add one after the tenth note.)

10. This time, turn the grid snapping to Off by pressing [cmd-4/ctrl-4] or go Options > Snap to Grid.
11. Move the ninth and tenth notes to timings that you prefer. As you move the Warp Markers this time, you will notice that they do not snap to the grid, and you can choose any locations for the notes freely. The timings you choose do not have to be the same as the timings in the first half of the Clip unless you want them to be.

These are the timings that I chose:

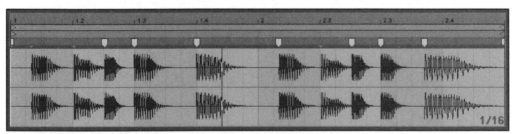

Pic. 3.07: MT_Bass note timings cleaned up with Warp Markers.

Now the MT_Bass Clip sits better with MT_Beats and Lightribal Clips.

12. Undo all your edits until only the starting and ending Warp Markers remain.

We're going to try a different method in the next exercise to achieve similar results.

13. Rename this Clip "MT_Bass Warp 1" and change its color slightly.
14. Save your Set by pressing [cmd-s/ctrl-s].

EXERCISE 3.3—QUANTIZING AN AUDIO CLIP WITH WARP MARKERS

If you have worked with MIDI note data before, you are likely aware of a function called Quantization that moves the recorded notes that you played to the nearest note value of your choosing. But did you know that in Ableton Live you are able to Quantize audio? If your eyes just bulged and your jaw is now hanging open, then you are having the same reaction I did when I saw this next feature in action for the first time.

Quantization is a process of tightening the timings of notes that you played, moving them closer to a predefined grid of your choosing. This was originally a function developed for MIDI note data, but the geniuses over at Ableton have found a way to apply that same concept to digital audio, greatly streamlining the process of tightening up a loose recording. After the last exercise using Warp Markers, this kind of functionality is the next logical step.

3.3.1—Applying Quantization to an Audio Clip

DO IT! Get ready to work with Quantization. Here are two ways to get started:

- You can continue from right where you left off at the end of Exercise 3.2 and use Save As... to save the Set as My Exercise 3.3.als, or
- You can open Exercise 3.3.als from the supplied Sets in Book Content > Book Exercises Project, and then perform a Save As... and save your Set as My Exercise 3.3.als.

Let's clean up another version of that same MT_Bass Clip, this time using Quantization:

1. Select the same MT_Bass Warp 1 Clip we were just working on.

It should only have start and end Warp Markers at this point. If there are any extras, double-click them one at a time to delete them until only the original two Warp Markers remain.

2. To bring up the Quantize Settings, do one of the following:

- Press [cmd-shift-u/ctrl-shift-u].
- Go Edit > Quantize Settings.
- [Ctrl-click/right-click] on the Sample Display waveform area and choose Quantize Settings from the contextual menu.

A small window comes up that asks you which grid value you would like to "Quantize To" and what "Amount" of Quantization you would like to have applied.

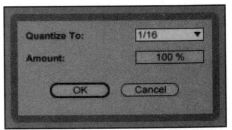

3. Set the Quantize To value to 1/16 and the Amount to 100% (if they are not already set at those values).
4. Press OK.

Pic. 3.08: The Quantize Settings dialog box.

Your MT_Bass Clip now looks something like this:

Pic. 3.09: The MT_Bass Clip after sixteenth-note Quantization.

Live has made a new Warp Marker on every transient and then moved each Warp Marker 100% of the way to the nearest sixteenth-note grid divider. Play the Clip. Each bass note falls more rigidly on the beat. However, I'm not sure I like it that "straight."

5. Undo the previous Quantize function by pressing [cmd-z/ctrl-z] or going Edit > Undo Quantize Audio.
6. Hit [cmd-shift-u/ctrl-shift-u] to bring the Quantize Settings dialog box up again. This time leave Quantize To on 1/16, set the Amount to 50%, and hit OK.

Play the Clip. It definitely has more swing than when the Amount was set to 100%. But the syncopation is still a bit awkward. In the Sample Editor, zoom in on any of the notes. Live has moved each of the notes halfway to the nearest sixteenth-note grid division, which does preserve some of the Clip's swing while still tightening the timing.

7. Undo the last Quantize function by pressing [cmd-z/ctrl-z] or going Edit > Undo Quantize Audio.
8. Hit [cmd-shift-u/ctrl-shift-u] to bring the Quantize Settings dialog box> up again. This time set Quantize To at 1/8 and the Amount at 100% and press OK.

Every note has been moved 100%to the nearest eighth-note grid division. This sounds pretty stiff on the first three notes of the phrase, but the fourth and fifth notes are now more in time with the rhythm Tracks. Can we have the best of both worlds? Yes! Let's try once more:

9. Undo the previous Quantize function by pressing [cmd-z/ctrl-z] or going Edit > Undo Quantize Audio.

This time, before you Quantize, select which notes you want to Quantize.

10. Hover your mouse pointer over the top half of the waveform at 1.3 (bar 1, beat 3). (Clicking in the lower half of the waveform will play the Clip, and we don't want to do that.)

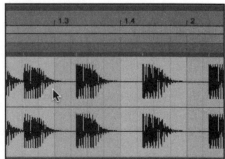

Pic. 3.10: The mouse pointer over the top half of the waveform at 1.3.

11. Click here and drag a selection to the right until you get to 2.1.2. You should have just selected the fourth and fifth notes of the Clip. It should now look like this:

You could press [cmd-shift-u/ctrl-shift-u] to bring the Quantize Settings up again at this point, but we already know that we want to use 1/8 and 100% as our settings:

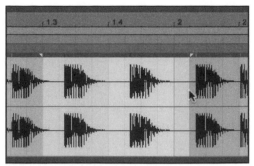

12. To reuse your previous Quantize settings, press [cmd-u/ctrl-u] or go Edit > Quantize.

Pic. 3.11: 1.3.1 to 2.1.2 selected in the Sample Editor on the MT_Bass Clip.

Only the fourth and fifth notes are Quantized because of your selection.

13. Repeat the same two steps for the ninth and tenth (last two) notes of the Clip: select the notes and Quantize them with the same settings.

Play the Clip. This sounds pretty good too. The bass still has a little bounce to it, and yet the loosest four notes are now right on the beat divisions. If you wanted to, you could still nudge the notes off the beat slightly to match the groove of the drums better.

IMPORTANT! Why undo each previous Quantization before entering new settings? Because Quantization is iterative, meaning that if you Quantize a Clip by 50% and then you Quantize it again with the same settings, you have, in effect, Quantized the Clip by 75% (50%, plus 50% of the remaining 50% equals 75%). Additionally, if you Quantize a Clip to sixteenth-note divisions at 100%, and then Quantize again to eighth-note divisions at 100%, this will change the note placements twice, since not every sixteenth note is an eighth note. But if you Quantize to eighth-note divisions first, and then Quantize to sixteenth-note divisions, the notes will not move the second time, because every eighth-note division is already on a sixteenth-note division. Keep practicing with this until it becomes clear in your mind.

14. Undo your Quantization once more until you are back to having the original two Start / End Warp Markers.

We are going to use this same Clip for Grooves in the next section, which I think you will find is be the best method so far for what we are trying to accomplish.

15. Save your Set by pressing [cmd-s/ctrl-s].

EXERCISE 3.4—GROOVES AND THE GROOVE POOL

Thus far you have seen how to Warp an Audio Clip by adding your own Warp Markers for corrective timing, or using Quantization to automatically move your notes closer to an evenly spaced grid value. But what if we wanted to have the rhythmic timings of one Audio Clip move closer to the timings of another Audio Clip instead of a fixed grid? What if you could take one Clip's rhythmic timings and apply it to several other Clips so that their timings would be more alike and sound better together? This is exactly what Grooves are for. If you understand Warping and Quantization, Grooves are, again, the next logical step.

3.4.1—Extracting a Groove to the Groove Pool

DO IT! Are you ready to work with Grooves? I thought so! Here are the usual two ways to get started:

- You can continue from right where you left off at the end of Exercise 3.3 and use Save As... to save the Set as My Exercise 3.4.als, or
- You can open Exercise 3.4.als from the supplied Sets in Book Content > Book Exercises Project, and then perform a Save As... and save your Set as My Exercise 3.4.als.

Since you are by now very familiar with your MT_Bass Warp 1 Clip, let's use it once again. Rather than Quantize the bass Clips with a fixed grid, instead we will apply the Groove of the Lightribal Clip to the MT_Bass Clips. This will ensure that their timings are brought closer together. The congas of the Lightribal Clip have a swing to them that will work well with the bass.

To begin, let's make sure that you are starting from a blank canvas:

1. Once again, bring up the Sample Editor for the same first MT_Bass Warp 1 Clip.
2. Ensure that there are no additional Warp Markers besides the first one at 1.1.1. and the last one. Delete any others that you see by double-clicking on them.

Now, let's extract the Groove from the Lightribal Clip.

3. To extract this Groove, do one of the following:

- [Ctrl-click/right-click] on the first Lightribal Clip and choose Extract Groove(s), or
- Highlight the first Lightribal Clip by clicking on it and then go Edit > Extract Groove(s).

This will take a moment, which a progress bar conveys. When it is finished, do the following:

4. To apply this Groove to all the MT_Bass Clips simultaneously, first multiselect all the MT_Bass Clips in the Clip Grid one of the following ways:

- Click on the first MT_Bass Clip on the Bass track and then [shift-click] on the last of the three Clips.
- [Cmd-click/ctrl-click] sequentially on all the Clips until they are all selected.
- Click-and-drag a box around all of these Clips at once (but be sure not to select any neighboring Clips on other tracks).

The Multi-Clip View will be displayed in the Detail View at the bottom of your screen.

5. In the Clip box—the one all the way to the left—open the Clip Groove Selector pull-down menu and select the Lightribal Groove.

Launch Scene 3, called Add Bass. You will notice that many of the MT_Beats notes are more closely aligned to those of the Lightribal Clip's, but there are some double notes that don't sound great. Toggle the Groove selector back and forth between None and Lightribal to hear the shift.

Pic. 3.12:
The Clip Groove Selector pull-down menu.

You'll continue to refine this in the upcoming Groove Pool section.

3.4.2—Auditioning Grooves from Live's Library with Hot-Swapping

Live also comes with a smattering of Grooves for you to work with that are stored in Live's Library. You could bring up the Library's Grooves folder from the Browser fairly easily, but let me show you an even faster way using a button that you will find throughout the program called the Hot-Swap button.

Pic. 3.13:
The Groove Hot-Swap button in the Clip box.

6. Multiselect all three of your Postwarvar Clips on the Synth 1 track and locate the Clip Groove selector again in Clip View. Instead of selecting a Groove from the pull-down menu, click on the Groove Hot-Swap button (which looks like two arrows chasing each other) just above the pull-down menu.

Clicking on a Hot-Swap button allows you quickly preview a series of presets from the Library in real time while your music is playing. There are many other areas of the program that use Hot-Swap, including Audio Effects, MIDI Effects, Racks, and Instruments. As long as the Hot-Swap button is lit, you can continue to preview presets as much as you like, and they will be Hot-Swapped for the one you had previously selected. When you find the one you want, you simply deselect the Hot-Swap button and keep working. You can even modify the preset from there if you wish—a preset is just a starting point for your creativity.

When you select the Groove Hot-Swap button, Live immediately opens the Grooves folder in the Library where you can audition and select one of the preinstalled preset Grooves that ship with the program. They are broken into folders based on where the Groove came from: some are Grooves from other programs and some are sampled from classic hardware Devices such as the MPC and SP1200 folders. Different genres of music and beat-making hardware machines are known for their unique swing, or groove. Ableton has done the homework to bring all of these Grooves to your fingertips. Thanks, Ableton!

7. Open one of the Groove folders and double-click on one of the Grooves to apply it to the three Postwarvar Clips.

Note that the Hot-Swap button remains lit in the Clip box.

8. Double-click on another Groove file, or use the up/down arrows to select and the [enter] key to apply the Groove to hear its effect on these three Clips.

You can do this while the Clips play to speed up the process. You may want to solo the Synth 1 track so that you can hear the subtle differences. You may hear no change at all when applying some Grooves, since their timings may be quite similar to the Clip you are working with.

9. After you have tried a few Grooves from a few different folders, look in the Logic folder for a Groove called Logic 16 Sub Up 55 and apply it to your Clips.

This one has a nice pulse to it. You will notice that some Grooves, such as this one, contain Velocity information as well as timing information, and you will hear the volume for the Clips change as well as the swing when it is applied. You will learn more about Velocity when we work with the Groove Pool in a moment.

10. Deselect the Hot-Swap button in the Clip box to keep this Groove.

3.4.3—Groove Pool Parameters

There are several more controls for further tweaking these Grooves in the Groove Pool window.

11. To see the parameters for these new Grooves, open up the Groove Pool by doing one of the following:

- Press [cmd-opt-g/ctrl-alt-g].
- Go View > Browser > Groove Pool.
- In any Clip's Clip Groove pull-down selector, choose the last entry, Open Groove Pool.
- Click on the Groove Pool Show/Hide button at the bottom of the Browser.

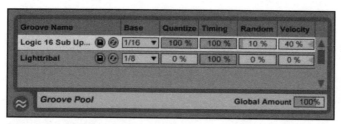

Pic. 3.14: The Groove Pool Show/Hide button in the Browser and the open Groove Pool.

You may have to stretch your Browser divider out a ways to see all of these available columns of the Groove Pool.

The Groove Pool represents a series of controls that globally modify how each of your Grooves is applied in real time. Changing a Groove's settings will affect the playback of all the Clips in your Set that have this Groove applied to it. Very powerful and very cool.

Let's have a look around:

- **Groove Name**—The Groove Name lists all of the Set's current Grooves that you have extracted from Clips or imported from the Library. A Groove that is no longer assigned to any Clips is grayed out, but may still be modified or deleted.
- **Base**—This is the timing resolution that determines which notes of your applied Grooves will be included in the "grooving" process.
- **Quantize**—This control will apply a grid Quantization to the Grooved Clip before applying the Groove timing adjustments. This value is a percentage of Quantization to be applied, exactly like the Quantization Setting's Amount field. The grid value for this Quantization is derived from the Base value mentioned above. By default, 0% Quantization is applied. Sometimes this value can help clean up a very loose performance before the swing of the Groove is applied. If you turn the next field, Timing, down to 0%, no amount of Groove is applied to your Clips, and this field becomes a simple nondestructive grid Quantize amount, which can be quite handy.
- **Timing**—The Timing value represents how much of the Groove's timing is applied to the Clips that reference it. The default is 100%. If applying a Groove seems to distort or diminish a Clip's impact, try taking this value down until you like the sound again.
- **Random**—This interesting control introduces an amount of randomness to your new timings after the Quantization and/or Groove timings have been applied. This can add a bit of "humanness" to your Clips. I like to use this particularly on percussion Clips, such as conga or tabla loops, so they don't feel so stiff and stagnant.
- **Velocity**—Here is another intriguing parameter. Keep in mind that a Groove is simply a MIDI Clip with timing and velocity information that has been played in, or extracted from, an audio recording. You can even drag a Groove file onto a MIDI track and see its timing and velocity values. When a Groove is made from an audio recording, the amplitudes (volumes) of the individual transients that are extracted are translated into MIDI velocity information, so that not only is the amount of swing information preserved, but so are the individual note dynamics. Therefore, the Velocity field in the Groove Pool allows you to impose the velocity information of the Groove onto your Clips. The default is 0%, but when you bring this up to 100%, all of the Groove's velocity information is applied to its associated Clips. Note that this field also goes down into negative values, which imposes inverse velocity information: notes that were loud in the Groove will now be quiet in your Grooved Clips, and quiet notes will be louder. You can achieve a kind of "MIDI sidechain velocity compression" with negative velocity values.
- **Amount**—This is a global value that affects Timing, Random, and Velocity values for all the Grooves in the Groove Pool. The default of 100% simply passes all of the values as they are currently set. A lower value scales all three of those parameters to smaller values. The Amount value also goes up to 130%, scaling and exaggerating all of the Groove's parameters that much more. Want the Groove of your song to increase gradually or suddenly disappear? Automate this parameter! Or assign it to a knob! Fun!

Play with each of these values and notice the subtle timing shifts that occur to the Clips that these Grooves reference. Here are some values I liked that you might try:

12. Set the following values in the Groove Pool:

- Logic 16 Sub Up 55: Base = 1/16, Quantize = 0%, Timing = 50%, Random = 10%, Velocity = 40%
- Lightribal: Base = 1/8, Quantize = 100%, Timing = 100%, Random = 0%, Velocity = 0%

Those settings seems to clean up the double notes on the MT_Bass Clips as well as improve the swing of the notes.

3.4.4—Committing Grooves to Clips

Grooves are applied as timing modifications to a Clip on playback, so you will not see the new Groove's timing information displayed in the Sample Editor when you select a Groove in the Clip Groove selector. However, if you want to apply the Groove to your Clip as a series of Warp Markers, click on the Commit button in the Clip box. Live inserts Warp Markers as needed to achieve the new timings much the way the Quantize Audio function did in the previous section, but this time using the selected Groove's timing grid rather than a fixed, evenly spaced grid. Two things to note when using the Commit Groove button:

- When you use the Commit button (described below) to apply the Groove timings permanently to your Clips and you have set your Velocity value to something other than 0% in the Groove Pool, the Groove's velocity information is translated onto your Clip as a Volume Clip Envelope, which you can than further adjust.
- After committing a Groove to a Clip, the Clip's Clip Groove selector is reset to None, so you are not continuing to additionally apply the same Groove on playback as well. You may still select and commit additional Grooves if you so choose.

Pic. 3.15: The Commit Groove button in the Clip box.

DO IT! Let's try it!

13. Select all of your MT_Bass Clips in the grid.
14. In the Clip box of Clip View, ensure that the current Groove being applied to the Clips is still Lightribal.
15. Click on the Commit button.

Look in the Sample Editor window: new Warp Markers have been added and the timings of the bass Clips have been adjusted. If you switch back and forth between this Clip's waveform and the waveform of the Lightribal Clip, you will notice that the Warp Markers you just applied to the bass Clips match the most prominent amplitudes of the Lightribal Clip's waveform. In essence, you have imposed the Lightribal Clip's timings onto the rhythm of the MT_Bass Clips, bringing their grooves closer together; this is a subtle, but profound, transformation that will go a long way to making your Clips "lock together" and mix more easily. Solo the Perc and Bass tracks and play the Clips together to hear how much closer together they have become.

16. Save your Set!

SUMMARY

- Live's warping engine is what makes Clip tempo synchronization and transposition possible.
- By doubling or halving a Clip's Seg. BPM value, you can instruct Live to play a Clip back at twice or half its original tempo relative to the Set's tempo.

- Live offers a number of different Warp Modes that can either make the Warping of a Clip sound more natural or seriously strange!
- Each Warp Mode has a series of additional controls that can further refine that Mode's Warping tonality.
- In addition to a Clip's Start and End Warp Markers, which are responsible for making a Warped Clip play back at the Set's current global tempo, you can add your own Warp Markers to further modify a Clip's internal timing in the Clip's Sample Editor.
- Live notates a Clip's transients (sudden changes in amplitude) as small, white marks above the Clip's waveform in the Sample Editor. These transient marks are Live's suggestions for logical places to add further Warp Markers.
- When you mouse over a transient, a gray "ghost" of a Warp Marker appears, which is known as a Pseudo Warp Marker. Pseudo Warp Markers can easily be turned into Warp Markers by double-clicking on them or simply by clicking on them.
- Warp Markers will snap to the current grid value if Snap to Grid is on, or move about freely if Snap to Grid is off.
- Audio Clips in Live can be Quantized to a fixed grid value. Quantizing audio will insert a series of Warp Markers on the Clip's transients to facilitate this.
- An Amount value in the Quantize Settings dialog box allows you to move a note a percentage of the total distance to the nearest grid division.
- A portion of an Audio Clip can be selected and then Quantized, which will then affect the timings within only the given selection.
- A Groove is a MIDI Clip that contains timing and velocity information. These Clips can be created by hand in a MIDI editor, played in via a MIDI controller, extracted from the timing and amplitude of an audio recording, or selected from Live's Library of Grooves. This timing and velocity information can then be applied to another Audio (or MIDI) Clip, thereby imposing the timing of one Clip on one or more other Clips.
- Once a Groove has been applied to a Clip, it appears in Live's Groove Pool where various Groove-specific and global parameters can be modified. Grooves extracted from other Audio and MIDI Clips also appear in Live's Groove Pool. These can be saved to Live's Library for future use.
- Grooves affect the timing of a Clip's notes on playback and are nondestructive until they are committed by pressing the Clip's Commit button in the Clip View. Committing a Groove to a Clip will create one or more Warp Markers in that Clip to impose the Groove's timing on the Clip.

Arrangement View 4

Congratulations on making it through Session View and Clip View! You may be feeling overwhelmed with information at this point, but your perseverance is about to pay off as you move into Arrangement View.

Session View is what fundamentally sets Live apart from other DAWs, and if you can get comfortable working with it, you will be capable of improvising arrangements, soundscapes, and even entire DJ sets without a lot of effort. Its power lies in having all those Clip variations right there at your fingertips, ready to be triggered in any order you like with the click of a button.

And yet, there are times when you need to commit to a linear arrangement and sculpt one of those infinite possibilities into a finished product. Maybe that means verses, choruses, and a bridge. Perhaps you need to make a score for a video. Or you could be recording your DJ set to make a promotional demo. When you need to commit to a linear timeline, that is when it is time for Arrangement View. Arrangement View functions just the way the traditional horizontal timeline that most DAWs offer does, plus it has a few unique tricks, as you are about to see!

Understanding Arrangement View and how the two Views work together will be the focus of this chapter.

EXERCISE 4.1—MAKING AN ARRANGEMENT WITH SESSION VIEW CLIPS

This next feature—recording your Session View Clips into an Arrangement—is the feature that made me quit my previous DAWs for good. Prepare for a jaw-dropper!

4.1.1—Preparing to Make an Arrangement

DO IT! Here are two ways to get started:

- You can continue from right where we left off at the end of Exercise 3.4 and use Save As... to save the Set as My Exercise 4.1.als, or
- You can open Exercise 4.1.als from the supplied Sets in Book Content > Book Exercises Project, and then perform a Save As... and save your Set as My Exercise 4.1.als.

When you open Exercise 4.1, you are looking at the (by now extremely familiar) Session View layout of Audio Clips and Tracks, plus a few more that I have added at the bottom. I have been laying these Clips out in this intentional way so that stepping through the Scenes in a top-to-bottom fashion would suggest a rough song structure. However, keep in mind that you can still trigger any Clip you like at any time. Take some time and play through the Clips and Scenes until you are familiar with what they sound like and how they work together.

DO IT! When you feel as though you know your way around the Session grid reasonably well, do the following:

1. Click on the Stop All Clips button to make sure that all of your Clips are stopped.
2. Also, double-click on the square Stop button in the Control Bar at the top of the screen. You will notice that the Bars, Beats, and Sixteenths numbers to the left of the Control Bar now read 1.1.1. These numbers are called the Arrangement Position, and we will delve deeper into what they mean later in this chapter.

Pic. 4.01: The Arrangement Record Button.

3. Now, shift-click on the Arrangement Record button in the Control Bar.

Simply clicking the Arrangement Record button without using shift will engage recording right away, which is not what we want. Using shift-click prepares Live for recording, which will begin when you press the Play button, launch a Scene, or launch a Clip. Done this way, our Arrangement will begin exactly at 1.1.1, which is what we want.

4. Launch the Intro Scene by clicking on its Launch button on the Master Track. You are now recording an Arrangement.
5. Click through the Scenes, or use your [up/down arrows] and the [enter] key, in a way that feels right to you. Feel free to additionally click on individual Clips on the Session View Clip grid as you see fit.

Note the 1 Bar Global Quantize value: New Clips and Scenes will begin at the next bar after you click on them.

6. When you have stepped through all the Set's Scenes, click the Stop All Clips button.
7. Now stop recording—and Live's playback—by doing one of the following:

- Press the [spacebar].
- Click on the Stop button in the Control Bar.

You might be thinking, "I'm confused: I don't see anything new. What did I record just now?" Fear not:

8. Press the [tab] key to switch to Arrangement View, or click on the Arrangement View Selector in the upper right of the interface.

Pic. 4.02: The Arrangement View Selector.

Behold your new Arrangement!

Although you enabled a button called the Arrangement Record button, you did not record any new audio. Instead, Live "recorded" all your Session View gestures into an arrangement here in Arrangement View!

9. Double-click on the Stop button in the transport to return to 1.1.1. in the Arrangement.
10. Press [spacebar] or click on the Play button in the Control Bar to begin playback.

You are now listening to the arrangement you "recorded" from Session View the way you performed it a minute ago. You can still make changes to what you just did, perfecting it, or adding to what is already there. Amazing!

Although we just used this feature to "record" an arrangement of this basic song, you can use this same feature to record an entire Session View performance for as long as you like. Want to capture an hour-long DJ set? No problem: hit Arrangement Record and go! When you finally stop recording, everything you just did will be notated perfectly in Arrangement View down to the subtlest gesture. Did you make a mistake while performing? Of course not, you are a superstar! But if you had made a mistake, you could find it in Arrangement View and correct it. Amazingly powerful.

Also note that the Session Automation we recorded to the CST1 Clip on the Synth2 Track has transferred into Arrangement View automation. Click the Synth2 Track Pan box in Arrangement View to see it. Leave it alone for now; we'll come back to this in chapter 8.

Let's take a look at a few of Arrangement View's unique features:

The Arrangement View Interface

A vast majority of the layout and controls of Arrangement View are replicas of everything you are already familiar with in Session View, but with a slightly different look. Let's get oriented. To have your screen look like the screenshot below, make sure that all of your interface sections are being shown in the View menu. Below is a diagram and list of the areas that are changed from Session View:

Pic. 4.03: Arrangement View with all Show/Hide buttons enabled.

- 1. Overview
- 2. Beat ruler
- 3. Arrangement Loop controls
- 4. Scrub area
- 5. Marker Creation/Navigation area
- 6. Arrangement area
- 7. Track Name area
- 8. In/Out section
- 9. Mixer section
- 10. Track Delay section
- 11. Show/Hide buttons
- 12. Time ruler

Notable Arrangement View differences from Session View include the following:

- The first thing you may have noticed about Arrangement View is that the orientation of your tracks and controls has rotated 90 degrees counterclockwise. The track controls are now on the right instead of at the bottom, and instead of a vertical track full of Clips, tracks now flow from left to right and Clips now have durations on the timeline.
- Each track has a small, triangular Fold/Unfold button in the Track Name box. This is used to minimize or unminimize any track quickly. Tracks may also be manually resized by clicking-and-dragging on the horizontal gray line between Tracks in any of the visible right-hand columns such as the Track Name, In/Out, or Mixer sections.
- The Track Name column has two new pull-down selectors on it. These are used for automation Envelope selection and editing. These features will be covered in chapter 8.

- The Mixer controls, such as Track Volume, Track Pan, and Track Sends are minimized to numerical values to save space. Note that the Sends are now merged with the Mixer controls in Arrangement View, and cannot be hidden unless you minimize the entire track.
- While the Track Sends have been repositioned to the Mixer as numeric boxes, Arrangement View still has Return Tracks that can be shown or hidden, and these tracks function exactly the same as in Session View. You'll learn more about Sends and Return Tracks in chapter 5, "Using Audio Effects."
- The Master Track has the same controls, although the Master Pan and Preview/Cue dials have been reduced to numerical values to save space.
- The Detail View area at the bottom of the screen functions exactly the way it did in Session View, and you can still view and change Clip View properties of any Clips on the Arrangement timeline. Note, however, that once a Clip exists in both Views, they are two separate Clips: adjusting the properties of a Clip in Arrangement View will not affect the same Clip in Session View, and vice versa.

Additionally, there are a few new controls in Arrangement View to be aware of:

- Notice that there is now a Beat ruler and Scrub area at the top of the Arrangement area that functions exactly like the one in the Sample Editor for zooming and scrolling the entire arrangement. As well, there is a Time ruler at the bottom of the Arrangement area, and you can scroll with it, but not zoom.
- Although you have not needed or used it yet, it is useful now to notice the Overview area above the ruler. (Double-check that the Overview is visible by going to the View menu and making sure that Overview is checked). Available in both Views, this miniature representation of your entire Arrangement allows you to both navigate your whole Arrangement and see at a glance which part you are currently viewing via the Zooming Hot Spot black box. The Arrangement Overview functions exactly like the Clip Overview (discussed previously in chapter 2, "Audio Clips and Session View"). Try it!
- The Loop/Punch-In/Out Brace works similarly to the Clip Loop Brace, and its controls are found at the top of your Live interface to the right of transport controls. In addition to allowing you to loop a portion of your arrangement on-the-fly, it has the added functionality of being a punch-in/punch-out range selector for recording to a specific spot or length on the timeline. We'll cover this shortly.
- Although there are currently no Locators in this Arrangement yet, they appear in the Scrub area, and the controls for making and navigating them are above the name of the first track. We'll work with Locators later in this chapter.
- Similarly, although you do not have any Time Signature Change markers yet, they can be inserted into the Arrangement View Scrub area to automate time signature changes.

4.1.2—Using Session View and Arrangement View Together

The Arrangement View is a highly intuitive interface, especially if you have ever worked with another linear timeline DAW application before. You will pick it up in no time. But one of the more challenging concepts to grasp is how the two Views work together. Just because we have recorded our Session View performance into an arrangement in Arrangement View does not mean that we are done with Session View! It is still a creatively fertile environment for exploring new Clips and Scenes. And when you come up with something new in Session View, you can still translate those new ideas into Arrangement View.

IMPORTANT! Fully understanding this next exercise is central to mastering Ableton Live. So take it slow and easy. Don't worry about making a mess of your Set in the following steps—I'm going to have you open an arrangement I've prepared for you in the next exercise anyway. The important thing is that when you are done you understand the relationship between Session View and Arrangement View.

By now your Set should contain a nice assortment of Audio Clips on the Clip grid in Session View and a rough arrangement made from the same Clips in Arrangement View. Let's get reacquainted:

11. Enable the Overview for both Session View and Arrangement View (if it is not already) by pressing [cmd-opt-o/ctrl-alt-o] or going View > Overview in each View. Note that while the Overview functions the same way in both Views, you have the option of independently hiding or showing it in each View.
12. In the Arrangement View, disable the following sections to reclaim some screen real estate: Track Delay, In/Out, and Returns.
13. Double-click on the Zooming Hot Spot box on the Overview to zoom all the way out so you can see your entire arrangement. You could also use the minus key [-] or the magnifier on the timeline to achieve the same thing.
14. Double-click on the Stop button to return the Arrangement Position (in the Control Bar) back to 1.1.1. This assures that you will begin playback from the first bar of your timeline.
15. Press the [spacebar] to begin playback.

In Arrangement View the playback indicator moves along the timeline showing you where you are in the arrangement. Similarly, the Overview presents a miniature version of the same thing.

16. With Live sill playing, press [tab] to switch to Session View.

In Session View, the Overview shows you a similar story, but besides that, nothing much is going on: none of your Clips on the Clip grid are playing.

IMPORTANT! While both Views currently share the same Audio Clips, only the ones in Arrangement View are currently playing. Clips played back in Arrangement View will not launch their respective Clips in Session View.

17. Press the [spacebar] to halt playback.
18. In the Browser, navigate into Sounds to Sample > Drum Loops and find the audio file dr_drLoop_ chukfunk_130. Drag this file onto one of the open Clip Slots on the Beats track, preferably below all your other Audio Clips on the track. Rename this Clip as "Chunkfunk."
19. Press the [spacebar] to start playback again. Notice that playback starts at 1.1.1 again from the top of your arrangement.
20. Now, with the arrangement still playing, launch the Chunkfunk Clip on the Beats track in Session View.

When Chunkfunk launches, you will now hear the Chunkfunk Clip instead of whatever was previously playing on the Beats track. While still playing back, press [tab] to switch back to Arrangement View and notice that the Beats track is grayed out. The MT_Beats and Beat_reaktored Clips are still there on the timeline, but the Chunkfunk Clip you launched in Session View supersedes the playback of these Clips in the Arrangement.

IMPORTANT! Clips launched in Session View during playback will supersede any Clips already playing on the same track in the Arrangement View.

21. While still in Arrangement View, press [spacebar] to halt playback.

Note that the Beats track is no longer grayed out.

22. Press [spacebar] again to restart playback.

Note that the Beats track grays out again, and you are still hearing Chunkfunk instead of Beats track Clips in the Arrangement.

23. With playback still rolling, hit [tab] to switch back to Session View.

Notice that Chunkfunk is still playing.

24. Click on any open Clip Slot's Stop Clip button on the Beats track to stop the Chunkfunk Clip's playback.

Now Chunkfunk is no longer playing, but MT_Beats in the Arrangement does not resume playing. Nothing is playing on the Beats track!

25. [Tab] back to Arrangement View. The Beats track is still grayed out, even though nothing else is playing in Session View.

Did you notice that the new orange button appeared at the left end of the Scrub Area? This is the Back to Arrangement button.

Pic. 4.04: The Back to Arrangement button in the Arrangement View Scrub Area.

There is also a Back to Arrangement button in Session View next to the Stop All Clips button.

26. To re-enable the Arrangement View Clips on the Beats track, click the Back to Arrangement button.

IMPORTANT! Launching Clips (or triggering Clip Stop buttons) on a track in Session View will suspend that track's playback in Arrangement View and light the Back to Arrangement button. Arrangement View Clips on this track will not play again until the Back to Arrangement button is clicked. Clicking this button tells Live to resume playing the Arrangement Clips as they are currently laid out on the Arrangement View timeline, and stop any Clips playing in Session View.

The takeaway here is that you can still launch Clips in Session View to try them out with your present arrangement, and they will temporarily take the place of whatever was previously happening on that track. When you are through trying them out, you can resume your previous arrangement with the Back to Arrangement button. Make sense?

4.1.3—Overdubbing from Session View to Arrangement View

Let's say that after auditioning Chunkfunk in the previous exercise, you decided that you liked the new Clip enough to want it in your arrangement. Let's do the same thing as before, but this time actually overwrite our Session View gestures onto the arrangement in Arrangement View:

27. In Session View, click on Stop All Clips.
28. Double-click on the Stop button to return the Arrangement Position to 1.1.1.
29. Shift-click on the Arrangement Record button to prepare for recording.
30. Click on the Play button or press [spacebar] to begin playback.
31. At some point during bar 12 in the arrangement, click the launch button for the Chunkfunk Clip.
32. [Tab] over to Arrangement View and see your new Clip overwriting on the Beats track.
33. When you would like to stop adding the Chunkfunk Clip and return to the previous arrangement's Clips on the Beats track, do one of the following:

   • Click on the Back to Arrangement button to resume the previous arrangement.
   • Click on the Arrangement Record button again to suspend recording.
   • Click on Stop or press [spacebar] to stop playback and recording. You will still need to click the Back to Arrangement button to hear the Beats track Arrangement Clips.

You now have Chunkfunk on the Arrangement View timeline. Because you hit Record before starting playback, Live "overdubbed" your Session View gestures onto the Arrangement.

Let's do this one more time but on a grander scale!

34. Shift-click the Arrangement Record button.
35. Start playback.
36. Launch any Clips from any track on the Clip grid whenever you want to modify the arrangement you are listening to.

Any track that you launch a Clip on will now be overdubbing over the current arrangement.

37. Stop Arrangement Record using any of the previous three methods.
38. Switch over to Arrangement View and check out the results.

Everything you just did was recorded into the Arrangement. Click somewhere in the Scrub area to play back what you just recorded.

Are we having fun yet, or what?

39. If you like what you did, save your Set by pressing [cmd-s/ctrl-s].

EXERCISE 4.2—EDITING IN ARRANGEMENT VIEW

Arrangement View is where you will sculpt the broad overview and subtle nuances of your song. The tools for doing so are easy to learn and work with, so let's jump in.

4.2.1—Adding Locators to the Arrangement

DO IT! For this next exercise, I have made an arrangement that I would like you to use (if you want to come back to your current Set for use with later exercises, that is fine):

• Open the Set Exercise 4.2.als from the supplied Sets in Book Content > Book Exercises Project, and then perform a Save As... and save your Set as My Exercise 4.2.als.

Arrangements will get increasingly complex as they build in length and number of tracks. The first thing to do is familiarize yourself with this new arrangement I've prepared and put up some "signposts"—known as Locators—to remind you where you are in the song.

1. Play through the entire arrangement and listen for the major musical shifts.
2. When you are done, double-click on the Stop button to return to the beginning of the timeline, 1.1.1.
3. Go Create > Add Locator. A triangle with the number 1 appears in the Scrub area.
4. To rename the Locator as Intro, do one of the following:

• Click once on the Locator's triangle and then press [cmd-r/ctrl-r], as you would to rename any object in Live.
• Right-click on the Locator's triangle and choose Rename from the contextual menu.

Pic. 4.05: A new locator at 1.1.1.

You can double-click on a Locator launch triangle to start playback from that point.

5. [Ctrl-click/right-click] in the Scrub area at bar 5. From the contextual menu, choose Add Locator.

This is another way to add a Locator. Notice that when you do it this way, Live prompts you to rename the Locator right away.

6. Name this Locator as Add Perc.
7. Repeat this process to add a locator called Add Bass at bar 13.
8. Add more Locators at bars 21, 29, 39, 49, and 73.
9. Rename the Locator at bar 21 as "Buildup," but instead of pressing [return], press [tab] instead: Live jumps you to the next Locator for renaming.
10. Rename the Locator at bar 29 as "Main Groove1" and press [tab].
11. Rename the Locator at bar 39 as "Breakdown" and press [tab].
12. Rename the Locator at bar 49 as "Breakdown2" and press [tab].
13. Rename the Locator at bar 73 as "Main Groove2."

You now have Locators defining the major changes in your arrangement.

4.2.2—Working with Clips in Arrangement View

Working with Clips in Arrangement View is almost exactly the same as working with Clips in Session View. Double-click on any Clip on the Arrangement View timeline and Live will present you with the same Clip View properties that you are used to working with from Session View. Let's explore a pair of brief examples to demonstrate these similarities and slight differences.

14. Click on the Lightribal Clip that starts at bar 5 on the Perc track. This brings up the Clip View properties in the Detail View.
15. In the Sample box for this Clip, raise the Clip Gain slider to –3 dB. (You will have to double-click on the gain value and type it in to get it exactly to –3 dB.)

You have raised the gain of this Clip, and this Clip only! All the other Clips on the track—including the one directly after it that is otherwise exactly the same—remain unaffected. This simply reiterates the idea that Clip View properties affect only the selected Clip.

16. Click on the Clip s2s_dt_synth_mornvar1_A#m, which currently begins at bar 57 on the Synth1 track. Now hold down [shift] and click once on the Clip dr_fx_trip string directly below it on the Synth2 track to multiselect them both.
17. In the Clip View properties, you now see the message "2 Audio Clips with Different Lengths Are Selected in 2 Tracks" letting you know that you have multiple Clips selected. Lower the Clip Gain slider to –3 dB. (Again, you will have to type it in to get it exactly to –3 dB.) Both of the Clip's Gain values have been reduced to –3 dB at the same time.

This is simply to show that you can still adjust properties of multiple Clips at the same time in Arrangement View.

Let's try changing two other Clip View properties that work in a logical yet interesting way.

18. Click on the dr_fx_trip string Clip to bring up its properties.
19. Make sure that you are in Sample Display mode (not Envelope Editor mode) by clicking on the Sample box's title bar.
20. Do one of the following to lengthen this Clip's Clip and Loop Length to four bars:

- In the Sample Editor, click-and-drag the Loop Brace's Loop End to 5.1.1.
- In the Sample box, set the Loop Length to 4.0.0 and the Clip End to 5.1.1 by typing in these values in their respective boxes.

As you do this last step, notice what happens to the waveform of the Clip on the Arrangement timeline: the regularity of how often this Clip plays is halved, and it now repeats every four bars instead of every two.

21. Do one of the following to change the Clip's Start point:

- In the Sample Editor, click-and-drag the Clip Start triangle to the right two beats to 1.3.1.
- In the Sample box, set the Clip's Start point to 1.3.1 by typing in this value in the Start boxes.

Notice what this does to the Clip's Waveform in the Arrangement timeline as you move the Clip Start value: the waveform slides backward on the timeline, but the Clip's beginning and ending boundaries remain in place. You are not changing the start time of the Clip on the timeline—rather you are changing the start point of the Clip's playback within the already defined loop. Cool!

4.2.3—Making Edits in Arrangement View

When a sculptor starts a new sculpture, he or she first selects the stone that they want to work with, and then remove the largest chunks with a large chisel before zeroing in on the finer details. I like to think of the previous exercises in a similar fashion: Select the Clips that you want to work with in Session View, lay them out in Scenes, and then record a rough arrangement onto the Arrangement View timeline. This exercise will deal with how to take your rough arrangement and slowly remove and refine what is there, creating new, detailed nuances for your song in progress.

Let's start by learning about a few new intuitive functions that quickly and easily modify your arrangement and how to use the Arrangement Loop settings.

Toward the end of the timeline, the arrangement shifts back into the original motif, but only very briefly. Let's preview this, and then extend it in case we decide to build upon it later:

22. At bar 73, click on the dr_drLoop_chukfunk_130 Clip on the Beats track to select it.
23. Do one of the following to loop the selection:

- Press [cmd-l/ctrl-l].
- Go Edit > Loop Selection.

The Arrangement View Loop Brace moves to surround the selected bars, and the Loop Switch lights at the top of the screen to indicate that Arrangement Looping is now on. Press the Play button to hear these two bars loop repeatedly. Despite the fact that you selected only one Clip region, Looping on the Arrangement View timeline loops all the tracks on this segment of the timeline.

The Arrangement Loop is separate and different from individual Clip Loop settings. The Arrangement Loop is for looping a section of the Arrangement View timeline. There are many reasons you might want to do this: to focus playback on a section of the song you are working on, or perhaps to replay a section of a song while you are playing it live. Since you'll be using the Arrangement Loop repeatedly throughout this section, let's take a moment to understand its controls.

Pic. 4.06: The enabled Loop switch in the Arrangement Loop controls and the Loop Brace.

Notice the numbers to the left of the Loop switch that read 73.1.1. These numbers indicate the start time of the looping region in the Loop Brace—in this case, bar 73, beat 1, sixteenth 1.

The numbers to the right of the Loop switch represent the current length of the Loop Brace, in this case 2.0.0 or exactly two bars.

These three Clips sound pretty good together. We should have them play longer than just two bars in our arrangement. Here are two easy ways to lengthen a series of Clips:

24.   Place your mouse over the right-hand edge of the colored title bar of the dr_drlopp_chunkfunk_130 Clip. You will see your cursor turn into the square Resize bracket, like this:].
25.   When you see the bracket, click-and-drag the right-most edge of the Clip to the right to bar 81.
26.   Click on the Loop switch to disable the Arrangement Loop and play the whole 16 bars you have just created.

You have just resized the length of the Clip on the timeline. Since the Clip has Loop enabled in the Clip View properties, you can extend the length of this Clip indefinitely and it will simply repeat. Note the small, vertical line in the colored Clip name recurring every two bars that indicates where the loop restarts.

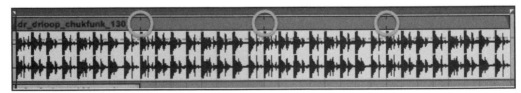

Pic. 4.07: The Loop Start indicator in a Clip on the Arrangement View timeline.

IMPORTANT! Notice that any selection you make or Clip boundary you modify snaps to the current grid value. The controls used for modifying the grid in Sample Edit View work in exactly the same way here:

- Pressing [cmd-1/ctrl-1] narrows the grid, as does choosing Options > Narrow Grid.
- Pressing [cmd-2/ctrl-2] widens the grid, as does choosing Options > Widen Grid.
- Pressing [cmd-3/ctrl-3] toggles triplets on and off, as does choosing Options > Triplet Grid.
- Pressing [cmd-4/ctrl-4] toggles the grid on and off, as does choosing Options > Snap to Grid.
- Pressing [cmd-5/ctrl-5] fixes the grid size, regardless of zoom level, as does choosing Options > Fixed Grid.

Note that the current Arrangement grid size is displayed in the lower right corner of the Arrangement window on the Master Track.

Okay, back to editing: You can do this kind of resizing to multiple Clips at the same time to save time:

Pic. 4.08: The current Arrangement Snap to Grid value.

27. Click on the s2s_fx_Loop_128_crude Clip on the Perc track so that it is selected. Now [shift-click] on the Clip below it, MT_Bass Quant 1, to multiselect them.
28. Place your cursor over the right-hand edge of the Clip name of either of these two selected Clips as you did before. You will see the Resize bracket, which looks like this:].
29. When you see the Resize bracket, click-and-drag the edges out to bar 81 to match the previous Clip on the Beats track.

Here's another way to extend a Clip, or in this case, a series of Clips:

30. Click once on the dr_drlopp_chunkfunk_130 Clip at the top to select it.

Notice that when you click on this Clip the whole eight bars of it is selected, because it is one contiguous, looping Clip.

31. Do one of the following to duplicate the Clip:

- Press [cmd-d/ctrl-d].
- Go Edit > Duplicate.

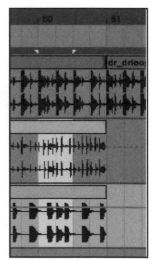

Live duplicates the Clip, creating a copy to the right of it, further down the timeline. Note that it is a discrete, separate Clip rather than an extension of the length of the Clip. Extending a Clip or duplicating it sounds exactly the same when played back. The only real difference is that with duplicated Clips, you can change the Clip View properties of one of the duplicated Clips to differentiate them.

Let's do this to your two other Clips, but in a slightly different way. If you click-and-drag within a Clip, you can make a selection within the Clip instead of selecting the whole thing. You can then perform operations on just that portion of the Clip.

32. Click-and-drag downward in the Beat Time ruler at the top to zoom the timeline view until you can see the numerical divider for bar 80.
33. Put your cursor on the waveform of the s2s_fx_Loop_128_crude Clip exactly at bar 80.

Pic. 4.09: The first two beats of two adjacent Clips selected.

34. Click-and-drag right and down until you have selected the first half of bar 80 on this track and the MT_Bass Quant 1 Clip on the track below. It should look like this:

35. Without changing your selection, execute the Duplicate command nine times (see how much easier the keyboard shortcut is?). It now looks like this:

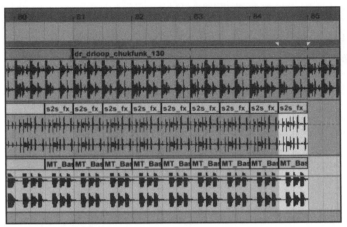

Pic. 4.10: Nine duplicates of two beats of two Clips.

36. Now go through and delete alternating Clips of each to make a checkerboard like this:

Pic. 4.11: Checkerboarded Clips.

As you can see, the Duplicate function works on a selection of Clips, or a selection within Clips. It's a quick way to repeat a phrase. Sometimes extending a Clip is the way to go, sometimes duplicating is more useful if you need individual Clip chunks. You will discover for yourself what works best for what you are trying to do.

4.2.4—Global Timeline Edits

Now let's try our hand at functions that operate on a whole section of the timeline globally. Here's a common situation: Perhaps when recording your Clips from Session to Arrangement View you were a little overhasty when triggering your Scenes, and so a section such as the Main Groove did not get the chance to establish itself fully before you moved on to the Breakdown. This is easily remedied with Duplicate Time.

For the Duplicate Time and Delete Time functions, all you need to do is establish a selection of time that you wish to duplicate or delete, and thankfully you only need make this selection on a single track rather than a gigantic multiselection across potentially dozens of Tracks, which can be cumbersome. Here are two easy ways to accomplish the same thing:

The simplest way is to find a Clip that spans exactly the region you wish to duplicate or delete and click on it to quickly select that time range for your operation:

37. Click on the MT_Beats Clip starting at 29.1.1 and ending at 39.1.1 on the Beats track to select it.

This track conveniently spans one full cycle of the 10-bar Postwarvar synth figure that is looping on the Synth1 track at this point. Repeating this entire section would make a lot of sense.

38. To Duplicate Time across all tracks, do one of the following:

- Press [cmd-shift-d/ctrl-shift-d].
- Go Edit > Duplicate Time.

When you Duplicate Time, Live duplicates the bars on all tracks in the range selected (regardless of whether they are all selected or not) and creates enough time to insert the duplicated bars.

Now we have two identical repetitions of the Main Groove section. I like this better.

Sometimes, however, you do not have a Clip that is exactly the length and placement needed to make such a convenient one-click selection of what you need to duplicate or delete. In these instances, you must make your own selection.

For example, take the Buildup1 section: the bass bends upward in pitch for just under six bars. Yet the Buildup1 section is currently eight bars long, so the bass builds to a crescendo and then just levels off for at least two extra bars, which lessens the excitement that the buildup is trying to create. Let's remove those two extra bars:

39. On any track—even an empty one—click-and-drag a selection from 27.1.1 to 29.1.1. You may have to zoom in a bit to see exactly where 27.1.1 is.

40. To Delete Time and remove these bars across all tracks, do one of the following:

- Press [cmd-shift-delete/ctrl-shift-delete].
- Go Edit > Delete Time.

Delete Time removes the selected bars across all tracks (regardless of whether they were selected) and moves all the later Clips in your Arrangement to the left to fill in the gap.

By comparison, let's make a few standard (nonglobal) deletions:

41. Click on The 80s cymbal crash on the One Shot track at 37.1.1 to select it.
42. To delete it, do one of the following:

   - Press the [delete] key.
   - Go Edit > Delete.
   - [Ctrl-click/right-click] on the Clip and choose Delete from the contextual menu.

The Clip is deleted, and no other Clips are moved as a result. This is the delete function you will likely use most often.

Sometimes it is useful to combine several Clips into one for easier arrangement use. Try this:

43. On the Synth1 track, click-and-drag from bar 27 to 37 to select one repetition of the Postwarvar Clips. To Consolidate these Clips into one big Clip, do one of the following:

   - Press [cmd-j/ctrl-j].
   - Go Edit > Consolidate.
   - Press [ctrl-click/right-click] on the selected Clips and choose Consolidate from the contextual menu.

The three Postwarvar Clips combine into one new Clip.

44. With the new consolidated Clip still selected, duplicate it twice.

Then again, at other times, it is necessary to have a Clip, or a part of a Clip, separated from the rest for processing. This is easily done:

45. On the Beats track, select 55.4.1 to 57.1.1 of the Beat_reaktored Clip. Do one of the following to Split this range of the Clip into a new Clip:

   - Press [cmd-e/ctrl-e].
   - Go Edit > Split.
   - Press [ctrl-click/right-click] and select Split from the contextual menu.

This region of the Beat_reaktored Clip is now its own Clip and has its own Clip View properties. Let's apply a new setting, Reverse, that you have not used until now:

46. Double-click on the new Clip from 55.4.1 to 57.1.1 on the Beats track to open its Clip View properties. In the Sample box, click on the Rev. button, which will reverse playback of the Clip.

Moving right along! Now we will use a combination of the above methods to make several more modifications:

Pic. 4.12: The Reverse button in the Sample box of Clip View.

47. Using the Clip Resize bracket at the edge of the Clip, click-and-drag the beginning of the Beat_ reaktored Clip from 47.1 to 54.1.
48. Click-and-drag a selection on the Beats track from 79.1 to 81.1 (across the end of the Beat_ reaktored Clip) and delete this range.
49. Zoom in on the end of the same Beat_reaktored Clip. Click-and-drag a selection from 78.4 to 79.1 and duplicate this selection (not Duplicate Time!) four times using [cmd-d/ctrl-d].
50. In the same Beat_reaktored Clip, select the snare from 78.3 to 78.4. Copy it using [cmd-c/ctrl-c]. On the same track, click on the grid marker at 80.4 to locate your insert point there, and press [cmd-v/ctrl-v] to paste the snare there.
51. On the Bass track, select bar 66 of the Clip Blu_001_128BPM_Abm and delete it. Delete bar 70 and bar 74 as well.
52. On the Perc track delete bars 79 through 81 from the s2s_fx_Loop_128_crude Clip.
53. On the Beats track, delete bar 26, the last bar of the Buildup section.
54. On the One Shots track, copy the cymbal hit at bar 13. Paste it starting at bar 25. Double-click on this new copy at bar 25 to open its Clip View properties. In the Sample box, click on the Rev. button, which will reverse playback of the Clip.

Now it's taking shape! Let's insert a little space at the end of the Breakdown to ease the transition back to the Main Groove2:

55. Click on any track at bar 81 to set your insert point there. (Using a track with no Clips at that point in the song, such as the One Shots track, might be easiest.) To Insert Time, do one of the following:

- Press [cmd-i/ctrl-i].
- Go Create > Insert Time.

A small dialog box comes up asking you how many bars you'd like to insert.

56. Type a "2" into the second box (or press the [up arrow] twice) so it reads "0.2.0." Hit OK.

Live inserts two beats of silence across all tracks at the insert point.

4.2.5—Automating the Time Signature

Rather than have the Main Groove2 section start in the middle of a bar at 81.3.1, let's change the time signature of bar 81 so that the two new beats you just inserted are their own measure of 2/4.

57. Here are two ways to make a time signature change:

- [Ctrl-click/right-click] on the grid divider at bar 81 in the Scrub area just below the Beat Time ruler and choose Insert Time Signature Change from the contextual menu.
- Click on the grid divider where you want the time signature change to occur on any track in the Arrangement View to locate your insert point, and go Create > Insert Time Signature Change.

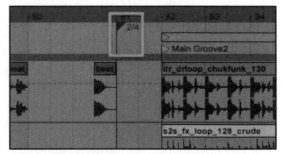

Pic. 4.13: A Time Signature Change marker.

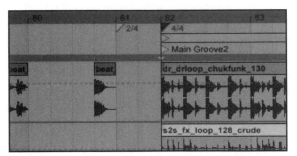

Pic. 4.14: Two Time Signature Change markers.

When you have done either of these, a new time signature change marker appears in the Scrub area, and a small rename box awaits your new time signature value. Type 2/4 into the box and press [enter].

All the bars after the new Time Signature marker will now be counted in 2/4, and that is not really what we want; we want just one bar of 2/4. Repeat the above process at bar 82 to insert a new marker to change the time signature back to 4/4 at that point.

Let's fill in the measure of 2/4 to bring these two parts together:

58. Move the snare on the Beats track from 80.4 to 81.2. (You will have to zoom in to see this level of detail. Adjust your grid to quarter notes if that helps.)
59. Extend the s2s_fx_Loop_128_crude Clip that starts at 82.1.1 back to start at 81.1.1.
60. Extend the dr_fx_trip string on Synth2 that currently ends at 81.1.1 so that it ends instead at 83.1.1.

4.2.6—Automating the Tempo

Virtually every parameter in Live can be automated in Arrangement View. This is done with a simple Breakpoint Envelope editing technique just like Clip Envelopes. We're going to do it to the Tempo parameter right now, but this technique will work on almost any parameter! For more information on mix automation, see chapter 8.

DO IT! Perhaps the breakdown section could use a slight drop in tempo to make it stand out even more:

61. To bring up the global tempo breakpoint envelope, press [ctrl-click/right-click] on the Tempo box and choose Show Automation from the contextual menu.

Pic. 4.15: The Master Track Tempo automation controls.

A dotted red horizontal line appears on the Master Track, and some new controls show up under the track name:

The dotted red line is a graphical representation of the timeline's tempo, with higher tempos at the top of the track and lower tempos toward the bottom. Because the tempo currently does not vary (staying at 120 bpm for the entire song), the line is dotted, flat, and has no variations.

The two new value boxes on Master Track are the Tempo Range Minimum (currently 60) and Maximum (currently 200) fields. These values determine the "bookends" of the editable range of tempos displayed on the Master Track. It is not necessary for you to change these values, but using them to narrow the range of possible tempos can make detailed tempo automation edits a lot easier.

62. Set the Tempo Range Minimum to 115 and the Tempo Range Maximum to 120 to "zoom" the tempo editing range.
63. On the Master Track, drag a selection from bar 57 to 81.
64. Anywhere within the selection, shift-click-and-drag the red Tempo Envelope downward to the bottom of the Master Track but no further, and release it.

Live creates four new breakpoints on the tempo automation envelope.

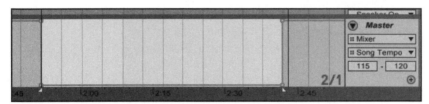

Pic. 4.16: Master Track Tempo automation.

65. Drag the upper left breakpoint at bar 57 back to bar 55, keeping the breakpoint at the top of the visible track range, which is 120 bpm.

This creates a gradual slowdown in tempo from bars 55 to 57 from 120 bpm to 115 bpm. At bar 81, the tempo instantaneously reverts to 120 bpm.

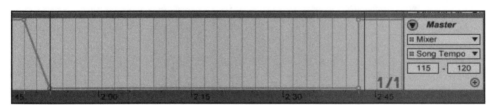

Pic. 4.17: The final Tempo automation breakpoint envelope.

Play through the entire arrangement. You've come a long way! Don't forget:

66. Save your Set!

SUMMARY
- Arrangement View is a horizontal, timeline-centric view, as opposed to Session View's nonlinear approach.
- You can record a performance from Session View into an arrangement in Arrangement View simply by enabling Arrangement Record and then performing your arrangement with your Clips in Session View. Launched Clips and Scenes will take effect on the next Global Quantize value.
- Arrangement View's mixer has all the same controls in a slightly different configuration.
- Clips on the timeline in Arrangement View have Clip View properties just like the ones in Session View.

- The Arrangement Loop Brace functions in a similar fashion as the Sample Editor's Clip Loop Brace, except that its function is to loop a range of time in your Arrangement.
- If you launch Session View Clips while playing back an arrangement in Arrangement View, the newly launched Session View Clips will supersede anything already playing on the same track(s) from Arrangement View. To return to the arrangement as it is laid out in Arrangement View, click on the Back to Arrangement button in the Arrangement View Scrub area.
- Locators may be added to the timeline and renamed. This can be helpful for identifying sections of a song or launching your song from a specific location.
- Clip View properties of Arrangement View Clips may be changed on one or more Clips at a time, much like in Session View.
- Arrangement View Clips may be modified in numerous ways such as Duplicate, Delete, Copy, Cut, Paste, Split, or Consolidate. They can also be resized with the Resize bracket.
- The entire arrangement can be modified globally with functions such as Duplicate Time, Delete Time, Insert Time, Cut Time, and Paste Time.
- The grid in Arrangement View functions very similarly to the grid in the Sample Editor. It can be narrowed, widened, shifted to triplets, turned on or off, and be fixed to a single value if desired.
- A Clip's playback can be reversed by pressing the Reverse button in the Clip View Sample box.
- Tempo and Time Signature (and most other parameters) can be automated to change over time.

Audio Effects

Ableton Live offers a fantastic spread of great sounding audio plug-in effects. Don't let the simple interfaces fool you! These plug-ins can rival many third-party effects. As well, these effects were designed to be used in a live-performance setting and are surprisingly light on your computer's resources, so you can use a lot of them. Now that you have the basics of Live's mechanics under your belt, enjoy diving into these effects. The sound-shaping possibilities here are endless!

TYPES OF AUDIO EFFECTS

There are many ways to categorize types of effects. I like to divide them in the following way:

- Frequency-based effects: equalizers, tone shapers, filters, frequency shifters, resonators, vocoders, and so on.
- Dynamic-range effects: compressors, limiters, gates, expanders, and so on.
- Temporal/spatial effects: reverbs, delays, choruses, flangers, auto panners, and so on.
- Distortion effects: amp/speaker simulators, tube saturators, overdrives, bit/sample-rate reductions, and so on.
- Diagnostic tools: These are not effects so much as tools to visualize and measure audio, but they can show up in your DAW as audio plug-ins, and so people sometimes lump them in with effects. They include level meters, spectrum (frequency) analyzers, correlation/phase scopes, tone/noise generators, and so on.

TWO WAYS TO USE AUDIO EFFECTS

There are traditionally two ways to use an Audio Effect, and this is not just true of Live. These two techniques evolved from years of analog audio engineering throughout the past century of recording, and you will find this methodology replicated in every studio on the planet or DAW on the market.

- You can use effects in series as an insert effect.
- You can use effects in parallel as a send effect.

Insert Effects

When you drop Audio Effects on an Audio Track, they are connected in series. This means that the Audio Clip's signal flows into the first effect on the track, then the effected audio continues into the second effect, and so on down the line. With an insert effect, only the audio playing on the track with the effect gets affected. A good analogy for this would be a guitar player using effect pedals: The guitar outputs the clean sound of the guitar, which then goes through a series of effects that change its sound, and arrives finally at the amp where it gets amplified and sent to the speaker. Each of the effects can be bypassed or their order rearranged to modify the quality of the sound you are seeking. In Live, after audio passes out of the last effect on the track, the audio from that track is mixed together with the audio from the other Tracks at the Master Track, where the audio is output to your sound card and ultimately to your speakers.

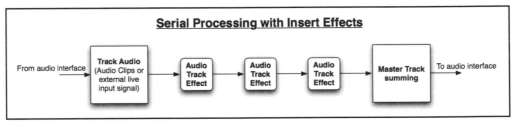

Pic. 5.01: Effects on a track in series using track insert effects.

A typical use for an insert effect would be dropping an EQ or a compressor on a track where it is desirable to color the tone or constrain the dynamics of the entire track's output.

Send Effects

The second method, known as a send effect, sends a copy of any track's signal to what is known as a Return Track. You may then insert effects on these Return Tracks in the same way you would an Audio Track. But the result is different from an insert in series on an Audio Track in several ways:

- You can send a variable amount of signal from any number of tracks to these Return Tracks using a track's Send dial. For example, put a reverb on one of the Return Tracks, and all your tracks can share this reverb in differing amounts at the same time.
- In addition to the amount of signal sent over the track's Send, audio also flows through the track in the usual way, including any effects that may be there. That is why this is known as processing a track "in parallel": two versions of the track are being affected in two different ways at the same time.

The original track and the Return Track's audio are eventually mixed together at the Master Track, where they are then output to your sound card and speakers.

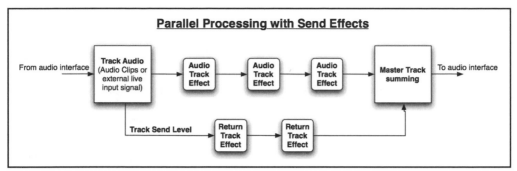

Pic. 5.02: Effects in parallel using a track's Send and a Return Track.

A typical use for a Send effect would be placing a reverb or delay on a Return Track so that you could apply as much or as little of these effects to any track you choose using each track's Send dial.

Master Track Effects

Master Track effects are technically just another use of insert effects, but because they are used on the Master Track, they affect the entire mix. Every sound played through the Master Track will be affected by an effect you put there. It is not uncommon to put an EQ or a compressor on your Master Track to control the overall sound of your entire mix.

I will show you how to apply insert and send effects as you get familiar with a few individual specific Audio Effect Devices.

EXERCISE 5.1—APPLYING AUDIO EFFECTS AS INSERTS ON AUDIO TRACKS

Using Audio Effects is like using spices while cooking: Both are used to enhance flavor, add dimension, and create unique appeal. And just like the use of spices in cooking, there are conventional, traditional ways to use Audio Effects (compressing drums, de-essing a vocal, and so on), and then there are infinite unconventional ways to use (and abuse) them in search of never-before-heard sounds. Both are equally valid approaches, but I believe that knowing some of the rules is helpful when you decide to break them. So we will begin by talking about a few of the more traditional uses of these effects.

In my years of experience as an audio engineer, I have come to the opinion that EQ and dynamic compression are the two most important—and difficult to master—tools in your tool bag. I call them "the salt and pepper" of audio effects. They are the two tools that you will return to every day for the rest of your audio-engineering career, so get to know them well. EQ and dynamic compression are deceptively simple: one adjusts tone, and the other, volume. Yet the more time I spend with EQ and compression, the more secrets they reveal.

Equalization (EQ)

Equalizers, or EQs for short, are tone-shaping tools. They boost or cut the gain of a particular range of frequencies. They can be as simple as the bass and treble controls on a car stereo, or they can be sophisticated algorithms for doing sonic surgery. Returning to the cooking analogy, equalization is the salt of the effects world, insofar as almost any sound could benefit from some of it, yet when overused, it can be harsh and hard to swallow. How much is enough? Like salt, that is a matter of personal taste. But like a great chef, a great mix engineer knows how much is just right.

Live comes with two dedicated EQs: the EQ Three and the EQ Eight. The numbers three and eight refer to the number of frequency bands you can adjust. Let's have a look at both of them.

Pic. 5.03: The EQ Three.

| IMPORTANT! | Note the Device Activator that is present in the upper left corner of every Live Device. Think of it the way you would the foot-activated bypass switch on any guitar pedal: Disabling it bypasses the effect and sends the unaffected audio through with no change to the next effect in the Chain. These switches can be automated in Arrangement View or with a Clip Envelope.

The EQ Three is modeled after the EQ on a DJ mixer, and as such works well as a quick and easy tone shaper for DJ-type applications. The three Gain dials adjust the relative amount of lows (bass), mids (midrange), and highs (treble) in the affected signal. In keeping with the DJ theme, note the three "kill" switches (labeled L, M, and H) that completely filter out (turn off) the lows, mids, or highs, respectively. These are great for making sudden shifts in tone or isolating a particular instrument you want to feature. Want to hear the hi-hat from this beat with the kick drum from that beat? No problem: drop an EQ Three on both tracks, and disable the lows and mids on the first track and the mids and highs on the second track. Easy.

The bonus feature on the EQ Three is something that I have always wished DJ mixers had: two sweepable crossover points. These are adjusted with the two dials at the bottom, FreqLo and FreqHi. These values define the boundaries between low, mid, and high, so you can really tune in the instrument you are after. The 24 and 48 buttons define the slope of the crossover filters. On the 24 setting, the filter slopes downward at a rate of 24 decibels per octave. So if your FreqLo crossover point is 250 Hz (the default) and your mid and high bands are toggled off, the signal's 500 Hz content (one octave above the 250 Hz crossover point) would be turned down by 24 dB, and the 1,000 Hz content (two octaves above the 250 Hz crossover point) would be an additional 24 dB down, or 48 dB lower than normal. At the 48 setting, the filter would slope downward twice as steeply as the 24 dB/octave filter. The slope of the crossover filters will change the sound of the transitions between the bands.

Like all effects, the best way to learn about them is to try them.

5.1.1—Applying an EQ Three Audio Effect to the Beats Track

DO IT! Let's get ready to try out some Audio Effects:

- You can continue from right where you left off at the end of Exercise 4.2 and use Save As... to save the Set as My Exercise 5.1.als, or
- You can open Exercise 5.1.als from the supplied Sets in Book Content > Book Exercises Project, and then perform a Save As... and save your Set as My Exercise 5.1.als.

Let's apply an EQ Three as an insert effect to the Beats track and shape the tone of all the Clips that play on this track. You can do this from Session View or Arrangement View, but since you already have an arrangement made, let's work in Arrangement View for now.

1. Use [tab] to make sure you are looking at Arrangement View.
2. In the Browser, click on the Audio Effects category.
3. Scroll down until you see EQ Three in the list of Audio Effects.

There are three ways to add an Audio Effect to a track. We will try each of them in turn. Here is the first one:

4. Click-and-drag the EQ Three effect from the Browser onto the Beats track. You may drop it anywhere on the Beats track that you like: on the track's name, on any Clip Slot in

Pic. 5.04: The Browser's Audio Effect category.

Session View or on the track's timeline in Arrangement View. When you let go of the effect, you will see it appear in the Detail View at the bottom of Live's interface.

IMPORTANT! Up until now we have only used the Detail View area to display Clip View properties. Its other use is to show the Track View, which is where you will work with Instruments, MIDI Effects, and Audio Effects as we are doing presently. You can switch between these two Detail Views by pressing [shift-tab] or by clicking on either the Clip Overview or the Track Detail tabs below and to the right of the Detail View area. Notice that the Track Detail tab shows the track name (Beats) and a miniature picture of any effects on the track, in this case, the EQ Three you just added.

Pic. 5.05: The Clip Overview and Track Detail tabs.

Okay! We now have an EQ Three on the Beats track. Let's try working with it.

5. Solo the Beats track by clicking on its Solo button in the Mixer section.
6. Click on the first MT_Beats Clip on the Beats track timeline to select it. Press [cmd-l/ctrl-l] to loop this section of the arrangement.
7. Press [spacebar] to begin playback.
8. Adjust the three Gain dials and hear their effect on the sound of the beat.
9. Toggle the three band switches off and on again to hear their effect on the beat.
10. Leave the L button on and turn M and H off. Adjust the FreqLo dial to change the crossover frequency between the lows and mids.
11. Turn the H button on and turn the L and M buttons off. Adjust the FreqHi dial to change the crossover point between the mids and highs.
12. Turn the L and H buttons off and the M button on. Adjust both the FreqLo and the FreqHi dials to hear the range of frequencies in the mids change. Toggle the filter switch from 24 to 48 dB/octave to hear the steeper filter slope.
13. When you are done experimenting, turn all three L, M and H switches on and set the three Gain dials the way you like them.

COOL! Would you like to return a dial to its default value? Click on it once to select it (you will see four black brackets at the corners of the control, or a black box around a value box), and then press the [delete] key. This works on every dial, slider, and value box in Live.

IMPORTANT! Note that adjusting the EQ's Gain dials will definitely affect the track's output gain. Although we think of EQs as "tone adjusters," they definitely affect amplitude (or gain, or volume) of a track as well. If you turn the Gain dials up, you can easily send the track or Master Gain into the red, which means that it is clipping and distorting. Keep an eye on your signal levels as you use any Audio Effect.

5.1.2—Applying an EQ Eight Audio Effect to the Perc Track

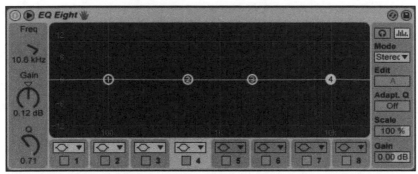

Pic. 5.06: The EQ Eight.

The EQ Three paints with a pretty wide sonic brush, which is fine for broad, DJ-type tonal adjustments across a wide frequency spectrum. When a more precise tonal adjustment is needed, it's time for the EQ Eight.

NEW FEATURE!   The EQ Eight has been retooled for Live 9 with a bunch of great new features.

The EQ Eight is a wonderful sound-sculpting tool, offering up to eight adjustable EQ points, each of which can select between eight available EQ shapes. By combining multiple EQ points and shapes, you can drastically—or subtly—alter a track's sonic characteristics.

DO IT!   To begin with, let's add an EQ Eight as an insert on the Perc track. Here is the second way to add an Audio Effect to a track:

14. Click on the track name that you want to add an effect to, in this case the Perc track, and then double-click on the effect you wish to add in the Browser, in this case the EQ Eight.

An EQ Eight is added to the Perc track, which switches to Track View in the Detail View area and displays the EQ Eight interface.

To begin with, notice the graph across the majority of the EQ Eight. This is a graph depicting frequency from left to right (30 Hz to 22 kHz) and gain from top to bottom (+15 dB to –15 dB). The four numbered yellow circles on the orange line are four of eight adjustable EQ nodes. The other four nodes start in the disabled state by default.

15. In Arrangement View, click on the first Lightribal Clip on the timeline of the Perc track. Press [cmd-l/ctrl-l] to loop this segment.
16. Solo the Perc track.

Notice that the Beats track is unsoloed when you do this. By default, Live allows only one track at a time to be soloed. You can override this functionality in the Preferences on the Record Warp Launch page, or simply by [cmd/ctrl]-clicking on additional Solo buttons. For now, all we need is one track soloed at a time, so the default is fine as it is.

17. Engage playback.

Right away you will notice one of my favorite new features in Live 9: there is now a spectrum analyzer overlaid on the EQ Eight interface. Now you can see what you are EQ-ing! Life is good!

18. In the EQ Eight, click-and-drag the yellow circle node 1 on the EQ graph. Move it up, down, left, and right. Notice its effect on the sound—and the displayed frequency spectrum—and notice the two dials on the left that change as you drag: Freq (frequency) relates to the horizontal axis, and Gain to the vertical axis.
19. With the first node significantly above or below the line, [option-click/alt-click] on it and drag upward and downward. The node stays in place, but the width of the curve widens and narrows. Notice how the dial on the left, called Q, changes with it.
20. Now click on the Audition Mode button in the upper right which—like the Preview button in the Browser—looks like a pair of headphones. Now when you move a filter node, EQ Eight solos the filter you are working with to help you find the frequency range you are listening for. Disable Audition Mode again before continuing.

Each of the eight EQ nodes has these same three controls. If you are familiar with EQs, this interface will be immediately accessible to you. If not, you will quickly discern the following:

- The left side is the low end (bass) of the frequency spectrum, and the right side is high end (treble).
- Above the line adds gain, and below the line cuts gain.
- Q controls the width of the notch.
- You can move the EQ points on the graph, or turn the dials to achieve the same results.
- You can switch between EQ nodes by clicking on their number in the graph or on their Filter Selector numbers below the graph.
- You can turn a particular node on or off using the orange Filter Activator squares below the graph. Use these to enable or disable the nodes you need.

Best of all, the new spectrum analyzer will help you correlate the relationship between your EQ moves and the resulting effect on the sound. You should study this relationship intently, and get to know your frequency ranges as best you can until they are second nature: EQ is the most important tool in a mix engineer's toolbox.

EQ Eight Filter Modes

All eight EQ nodes can select between eight different filter shapes. From top to bottom they are as follows:

- **48 dB/octave Low Cut**—Also known as a "highpass filter," the Low Cut shape is a filter that cuts frequencies below the selected frequency. This version drops off at 48 decibels per octave, which is quite steep. Note that you can additionally affect the slope with the Q dial, and that moving the node up or down on the graph controls Q instead of Gain on filters.
- **12 dB/octave Low Cut**—Similar to the previous filter, but with a more gentle roll-off, resulting in a more subtle filter sound.
- **Low Shelf**—The low shelf is similar to the bass dial on a home or car stereo: the shelf boosts or cuts frequencies below the node. However, unlike the home-stereo bass knob, this shelf has an adjustable frequency dial. Your home or car stereo's shelf is fixed. The slope up or down to the shelf is controlled with the Q dial.
- **Bell**—This filter shape is the default setting, and allows you to boost or cut a given frequency and the neighboring frequencies on either side. Filter width is set with the Q control.
- **Notch**—A notch is like a bell filter, but with an infinite negative gain: it strips out the chosen frequency, and the width of neighboring frequencies is set with the Q control. Note that moving the node up and down controls Q instead of Gain in this setting.
- **High Shelf**—A high shelf is the opposite of a low shelf: it boosts or cuts every frequency above the chosen frequency.
- **12 dB/octave High Cut**—A high-cut filter, also known as a "lowpass filter," is the opposite of a low-cut: it removes all frequencies above the selected frequency. Like the Low Cut filters, they come in two flavors, and the slope is further modified by the Q dial. Note that moving the node up and down controls Q instead of Gain in this setting, just like with the Low Cut filter shape.
- **48 dB/octave High Cut**—A more aggressively sloped version of the 12 dB/octave filter.

Pic. 5.07: The EQ Eight's Filter mode selectors.

You can mix and match as many of each filter mode shapes as you like using different EQ nodes. The effects of two overlapping EQ shapes are cumulative, meaning you can, for example, boost with a shelf while simultaneously cutting a portion of the shelf with a bell.

Before we proceed, let's enable another useful feature:

20. Click the gray triangle in the title bar next to the Device Activator: this is the Toggle Display Location button.

The EQ Eight node graph jumps up into the Arrangement window, increasing in size. As well, the EQ Eight Device now displays Frequency, Gain, and Q controls for every node. Handy!

21. Set node 1 to a 12 dB/octave Low Cut filter, with a frequency of 202 and a Q of 0.68. This strips out some muddiness in the low end that was clashing with the bass and primary drum loops.

Here are some settings that I liked for the EQ Eight on the Perc track's Lightribal Clip:

22. Node 2 is already a bell shape. Set it with a frequency of 725, a gain of 3.10, and a Q of 1.45. This brings out the warmth of the congas and helps it to punch through the drum loops.
23. Node 3 is also a bell with a frequency of 1.58 kHz, a gain of –3.69, and a Q of 1.65. This removes some "honk" in the mids that was annoying and makes room for other sounds in the mix that sound better in this frequency range.

24. Set node 4 to a high shelf, with a frequency of 3.34 kHz, a gain of 2.14, and a Q of 5.92. A little bit of brightness or "air" in the high end gives it some crispness and adds energy to the performance. Although other instruments will also use this range, the congas have short, staccato hits and are panned quite wide, so it doesn't interfere with other sounds all that much.

You might be thinking, "These settings sound good for the Lightribal Clip, but what about when it gets to the s2s_fx_loop_128_crude Clip?" If you did think this, bonus points for you. Indeed, the settings you make on this EQ Eight affect the entire track, and boosting the high end sounds nice on the congas, but it gets a little piercing when it gets to that crispy, crude loop later. Not to worry: if you can put up with it for a few chapters, I'll show you how to automate plug-ins in chapter 8, and we can fix it then.

As you can see, equalizing is a process of removing and bringing out certain aspects of a sound to make it sound better and play well with the other sounds. In general, aim to make sounds more interesting, and keep different instruments from clashing or stacking up poorly in a particular frequency range. This is not something you will master overnight. It will take years of practice. Get started!

Dynamic Compression

Dynamic range is the difference between the loudest sound and the quietest sound in a recording. Dynamic compression reduces the dynamic range of a piece of audio, making the volume more consistent. Often this is done so that you can turn the sound's overall volume up without going into clipping. Like using ground pepper, compression can add punch and impact to your tracks if used correctly. But also like pepper, used incorrectly, it can make a track overwhelming or leave it lifeless. For most people, using dynamic compression well is more challenging than using an EQ.

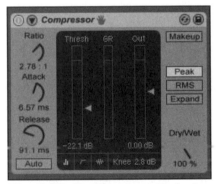

Pic. 5.08: The Compressor Device in Collapsed View.

Imagine listening to a recording of a person who is using a microphone as he gives a lecture. The speaker's volume and distance from the microphone are generally consistent, except in a few places where the speaker coughs. You would like to turn the gain of this recording up, but if you do, the coughing moments will definitely go over into clipping. If you could turn all the loudest parts down—in this case the coughing—you could turn the overall volume up, right? This is exactly what a dynamic compressor does. It reduces dynamic range so you can turn the average volume up.

IMPORTANT! You will notice that I tend to refer to this type of gain-reduction effect as "dynamic compression." I do this not only because that is what it truly is, but also to differentiate it from "data compression," such as making an MP3 or Zipping a file. People often confuse these two types of compression, and they have nothing to do with each other. The first reduces an audio's dynamic range, while the second makes file data smaller.

Live has several dynamics processors, including the Limiter, Gate, and Multiband Dynamics, and even Saturator, Overdrive, and Dynamic Tube do some significant dynamics manipulation. But the one that you will likely use most is the Compressor.

NEW FEATURE! Live 9 sports a brand new Compressor Device with three different views for dialing in your dynamics. The three views each accomplish the same thing, but now you have a choice as to how you would like to visualize your gain reduction. We'll look at all three.

A dynamic compressor works like this:

- You begin by setting an amplitude (volume) threshold. Any signal that passes above this threshold will be turned down—known as gain reduction—thus reducing the signal's dynamic range.
- Signals exceeding the threshold are turned down by a ratio of some number to 1. For example, a ratio of 3:1 means that for every 3 dB the input signal goes over the threshold, the compressor will output 1 dB. This means that if the threshold were –10, and an incoming signal was at –4 (6 dB over the threshold), the compressor would output the signal at –8 dB (2 dB over the threshold, or three times less). The net result is a gain reduction of 4 dB, which is what a gain reduction meter imparts. The larger the ratio setting, the greater the gain reduction for signals over the threshold.
- Since the signal was reduced by 4 dB at the loudest point, you could then safely turn this entire track up by 4 dB without the risk of clipping. The loudest parts got quieter, and the quietest parts got louder—this is dynamic range reduction.

5.1.3—Using a Compressor to Smooth Dynamic Range on the Perc Track

DO IT! To begin, let's add a Compressor Audio Effect to the Perc track. Here's a third way to get an Audio Effect on an Audio Track:

25. Click on the first Lightribal Clip in the timeline on the Perc track in Arrangement View to select it. Then press [cmd-l/ctrl-l] to loop this selection.
26. Solo the Perc track (and unsolo any other tracks).
27. Play the looped range.

Listen to the dynamics of this loop carefully. Several of the conga hits are much louder than the rest, and stick out somewhat. If we used this loop by itself, without other percussion, it might work just fine as it is, but in the context of several other percussive Clips, it's too dynamic. Let's tame it a bit with a compressor.

28. Double-click on the track name you wish to add an effect to, in this case, Perc. This will display the track's Track View in the area at the bottom of the Live Interface. To the right of the EQ Eight is a message that says, "Drag Audio Effects here." Who are we to say no? Drag-and-drop a Compressor from the Browser's Audio Effects category onto this area.

IMPORTANT! You can easily switch the order of effects on a track by simply clicking-and-dragging them by their title bar to where you want them and letting go. You can also choose where in the signal Chain you want to place a new effect by dropping it where you want it when you first add it to the track. In either case, you will see a vertical yellow bar appear that shows you where the effect will be placed if you let go of it. Try reordering the EQ and Compressor on the Perc track a few times to get comfortable with this technique. Obviously, the order in which the effects appear on a track makes a difference as to how the result will sound. For now, place the Compressor after the EQ Eight.

When you first add a Compressor Device, you are looking at the first of the three views, known as Collapsed View. This view benefits from a no-frills, uncluttered look that doesn't take up a lot of space. This is an excellent view to use when you know exactly what you want, but for learning about compression, I'd like to direct you to the third view, known as Activity View.

Pic. 5.09: The Compressor Device in Activity View, and the Show Activity View button.

29. Click the small waveform icon in the lower left corner of the Compressor to bring up Activity View.
30. Start playback. You will see the gray waveform of Lightribal moving in the background. With your pointer, mouse over the orange horizontal line just above the waveform. It turns blue. This is the threshold. Drag this line slowly downward and notice that the value next to "Thresh" adjusts as you do. Each controls the other.

31. When the threshold gets near the top of the moving gray waveform, a second line, this one a lighter orange, begins to move. This line represents gain reduction, the amount that the volume is being reduced over time. Try the entire range of the threshold to hear how the sound changes. The lower the threshold, the more gain reduction you see. When you are done, leave the value at −18.1 dB.
32. Adjust the ratio dial and note the sound of varying amounts of gain reduction. Notice that with a small ratio, there is less gain reduction, which sounds more crisp, pokey and dynamic. Notice how higher ratios create more gain reduction, which sounds flatter and less dynamic.
33. Engage the Makeup button. This will automatically add back any volume lost due to gain reduction. Now, as you lower the threshold or increase the ratio, the output of the signal gets *louder*. This overall increase in loudness is the effect people are often using a compressor to achieve.

Threshold and Ratio are the two most important controls on a compressor, but there are several more controls that also contribute to the overall sound:

- The Attack dial specifies how long it takes for the gain reduction to be applied after a signal has crossed over the given threshold. Higher settings can let a little of the signal's initial transients pass through before it gets compressed, which preserves a punchy attack.
- The Release dial specifies how long the Compressor will keep the gain reduction applied after the signal has dropped back below the threshold. Lower settings allow the Compressor to recover gain reduction more quickly, while higher settings will keep the signal's output gain more consistent. The Auto button will attempt to adjust the release time to fit the source material automatically. Additionally, the Env. button toggles between two release shapes: linear, which seems to work well on less dynamic material like a pad, and logarithmic, which feels a bit more musical on rhythmic sounds.
- A higher Knee value will round out the threshold, causing a more gradual onset of gain reduction as a signal's gain approaches and crosses the threshold. As the Knee setting rises, gain reduction will gradually start to occur further and further below the given Threshold. This can make the gain reduction sound more natural and less aggressive.
- The Output Gain slider allows you to turn the entire output signal up (or down) after the gain reduction has been applied to the loudest parts. The Makeup button does this gain makeup for you automatically. If the loudest signal's gain is reduced by 4 dB, Makeup will add 4 dB automatically. Alternately, you can use the Output Gain slider to set any output value you like.
- The two transient detection modes, Peak and RMS, modify how the Compressor measures input gain, thereby emulating the way that various hardware compressors behave. In Peak mode, the threshold responds well to short, sharp transients. RMS stands for "root-mean-square," and in this setting, the threshold responds to a signal's averaged loudness over time, rather than to transients, which is closer to the way our ears work.
- The Expand button inverts the ratio control so that signals exceeding the threshold get turned up. This is known as upwards expansion, and can be used to add more dynamic range to a performance. Think of it as an un-compressor.
- The Lookahead value allows the Compressor to analyze the signal at 0, 1, or 10 milliseconds ahead of what you are hearing. Increasing this value will often increase the gain reduction as transients over the threshold are detected earlier.

- Finally, there's the Dry/Wet dial. We'll talk about this one in the next exercise. Leave it at 100% for now.

Adjust any and all of these values, and notice what settings make the percussion sound more interesting to you. Take as long as you like. If it isn't entirely clear to you what a setting is doing to the sound, don't worry about it. Compression is a delicate, complex task, and you will get better with practice.

34. Press Play. Apply the following settings while the loop is playing:

- **Peak Detection mode:** These drums have very fast attacks and very little sustain.
- **Attack:** 1 ms—In order to catch these fast attacks, this setting must be quite low.
- **Release:** 129 ms—This is short enough to be fully released by the next beat.
- **Threshold:** -24.1 dB—Achieves enough gain reduction to even out the volume.
- **Ratio:** 3.00—Stiff enough to tame even the loudest hits.
- **Knee:** 10—Creates a rounder, softer gain reduction
- **Output:** +8 dB—This will replace the gain lost from compression and bring up the quieter parts of the loop.
- **Makeup:** Off—We're using the output slider instead to get exactly what we want.

With these settings, the loudest peaks are turned down significantly—note the orange G.R. line showing gain reduction—but the quietest parts are unaffected. The result is a less dynamic track that is more consistent in volume, which allows us to hear more of the quieter parts without the loud parts overpowering. Bypass the compressor while it is playing to hear the difference.

IMPORTANT! You will note that the Compressor registers more gain reduction in the first Lightribal Clip than in the ones that follow. That is because the first Lightribal's Clip Gain is –3 dB and the others are –8 dB. The important thing to understand here is that the Clip Gain adjustment occurs before a track's effects, so any adjustment of the Clip Gain slider will affect the amount of gain going into all the effects on that track. This is especially important with the use of compressors, as their threshold setting is relative to the incoming gain of that track's Clips. If you change a Clip's gain setting, you will also be affecting how much compression is taking place in your Compressor.

Let's see this in action:

35. Engage playback while still looping bars 5 to 13 and soloing the Perc track.
36. Double-click on the first Lightribal Clip that is inside the looping region to bring up its Clip View properties.
37. Reduce the Clip Gain value to –20 dB. The waveform in the Sample editor diminishes to show the reduction in gain.
38. Now press [shift-tab]—this is a very useful keyboard shortcut—or click on the Track View tab in the lower right corner with the miniature EQ Eight and Compressor on it to switch from Clip View to Track View. You will notice that the Compressor is barely registering any gain reduction.

39. [Shift-tab] back to Clip View. Raise the Clip Gain back to –3 dB. [Shift-tab] back to Track View. The Compressor is working quite a bit harder now.

With the Compressor Threshold remaining constant, you are varying the incoming gain to the plug-in Chain, which affects the amount of gain that exceeds the threshold, and therefore the amount of gain reduction.

Now that you understand this, let's take the gain of the s2s_fx_Loop_128_crude Clips down a bit. They are too loud and too compressed for my taste.

40. Click on the first s2s_fx_Loop_128_crude Clip starting at bar 47. [Shift-click] on the last of these Clips, ending at 94.1.1, to select the whole range of them.
41. In Clip View, reduce the gain of all of these Clips to –6 dB.

Now these Clips compress less and are not so overpowering.

IMPORTANT!   Conversely, a track's Volume setting, as determined by the slider/value in the Mixer, occurs after the plug-in Chain: after all the effects have done their jobs, you can set an overall volume for the track. Adjusting this setting will not affect the gain reduction amount in the Compressor, because the adjustment is after the Compressor.

42. Use [shift-tab] to switch the Perc to Track View.
43. Click-and-drag in the track's Volume box to adjust the Track Volume up or down.

The amount of gain reduction in the Compressor does not change, even when the Track Volume is at –inf dB ("negative infinity" decibels).

44. Set the Track Volume back to 0.00 dB.

Hopefully, you are starting to see the interrelatedness of the various gain stages in Live. For Audio Tracks, they happen in this order:

- Clip Gain
- The track's individual Audio Effects gain adjustments (if any) from left to right
- Track Volume
- The Master Track's Audio Effects gain adjustments (if any) from left to right
- Master Volume

5.1.4—Applying a Compressor Audio Effect to the Bass Track to Add Thickness

A compressor can also be used to add some weight, or thickness to a sound.

DO IT!   The primary bass sound is a little wimpy. Let's see if we can add some whomp.

45. Click on the first MT_Bass Clip in the timeline on the Bass track in Arrangement View to select it.
46. Then press [cmd-l/ctrl-l] to loop this selection.
47. Solo the Bass track (and unsolo any other tracks).
48. Play the looped range and listen to the dynamics.

The bass notes all seem to be at about the same volume, so there's no real dynamic range to reduce, but the sound lacks impact. Compression can reduce the attack of the sound and bring out the tail, which is where the meat of the sound is. Or the stalk, if you are a vegetarian.

49. Add a Compressor to the Bass track. Click on the Show Transfer Curve View button.

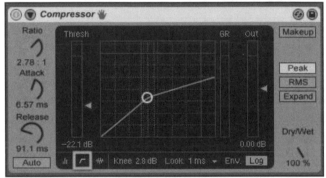

Pic. 5.10: The Compressor Device in Transfer Curve View, and the Show Transfer Curve View button.

This time, let's use the Transfer Curve View, which is the second View. Very similar to the Live 8 Compressor, this view shows a graph that depicts the relationship between input to the compressor, and output from the compressor. Adjust the ratio dial and watch the angle of the line above the threshold change. When the ratio is 1:1, the transfer curve is a straight line, meaning input equals output. As ratio increases, the ouput above the threshold diminishes. Gain reduction is displayed as an orange, downward moving bar in this view.

Here are some settings I like:

- **Threshold:** −17 dB—Flattens the sound nicely.
- **Ratio:** 6:1—An aggressive ratio is pretty unforgiving.
- **Knee:** 6—Rounds the tone a bit, giving it a bounce.
- **Attack:** 2 ms—There are clicks at the start of each note, and I wanted to minimize them.
- **Release:** 9 ms—Lets up quickly so we can hear the tail of each note.
- **Detection:** RMS—I wanted to hear a bit more of the initial pop than Peak allowed.
- **Lookahead:** 0—Same: this lets a bit more pop through.
- **Env.:** Linear—Log seemed too fast.
- **Output:** −3 dB—The Makeup button makes this track a little loud.
- **Makeup:** On.

The final control we've yet to discuss is the Wet/Dry dial. So far we've been using the compressor at 100% wet, meaning we are hearing only the compressed signal. If you dial it back to 0%, you are then hearing only the dry, uncompressed signal, as if you had bypassed the effect entirely. Points between 0% and 100% create a blend of the two, which is known as parallel compression. Blending some uncompressed signal in with the compressed signal allows you regain some of the initial transients (attack) of the sound that the compression may have softened. Try adjusting this value until you get a blend you like. I liked it at 75%.

Ta-da! You've made it through EQ and Compression! Feel free to apply EQs and Compressors to the tracks that you think need them. I cannot stress enough how important these two effects will be to making your songs sound great, so spend as much time as you can with them. They are by far the two most important effects in your arsenal.

5.1.5—Using Other Audio Effects as Inserts on Tracks

If you think of EQ and Compression as salt and pepper, then the rest of Live's Audio Effects are akin to more exotic spices like coriander, turmeric, or chipotle. These effects can be used to give a particular sound a distinctive flavor.

There is no one "right" use or setting for these effects, so I won't go step-by-step through all of them as I did regarding EQ and Compressor. However, one way you can get to know a new effect more quickly is to listen to some of its Presets to hear a range of what it is capable of. A Preset is simply a collection of settings for that Device. Remember when we used the Hot-Swap button to audition Groove templates? Let's use the same technique to preview a few Audio Effect Presets. I'll also show you how to save your own Presets and modify the default settings for a Device.

Loading and Auditioning Presets

50. In the Browser, click on the Audio Effects category to show Live's Audio Effects.
51. In the Audio Effects column, scroll down until you find the Chorus effect in the list.

To the left of the name and icon of every Live plug-in Device, you will see a right-pointing triangle, just like the one you use to navigate folders in the Browser.

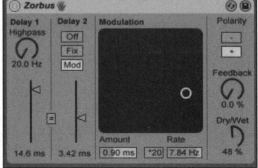

52. Click on the triangle next to the Chorus Audio Effect to open the Device and view its list of available Presets.
53. From the Preset list, click-and-drag Zorbus onto the Synth2 track and drop it.

Live not only applies the Chorus effect to the Synth2 track, but also applies the Zorbus Preset to the Chorus effect all in one action. Nice!

54. Use the Loop Brace to Loop bars 47 through 57.

Pic. 5.11: The Chorus effect with the Zorbus Preset.

55. Solo the Synth2 track and play the loop.
56. Enable and disable the Chorus plug-in's Device Activator switch in the upper left of the Chorus's title bar to compare the track with the Chorus on and off.

This makes the CST1 Clip seem quite a bit more interesting. But let's see what else the Chorus effect has to offer. In the upper right corner of the Chorus plug-in's title bar, you will see two buttons: the Hot-Swap Presets button and the Save Preset button.

Pic. 5.12: The Hot-Swap Preset and Save Preset buttons in an Audio Effect.

57. With Live still playing the loop, click on the Hot-Swap button in the title bar of the Chorus effect.

Live jumps the focus to the Chorus Presets in the Browser, where a new message is displayed, alerting you that you are now in Hot-Swap mode.

While in Hot-Swap mode, you can double-click on any of the current Effect's Presets to apply them and hear what they sound like. You can also use your [up/ down arrow] keys to select a Preset, and the [enter] key to apply it:

Pic. 5.13: The Hot-Swap mode indicator in the Browser.

58. Press [arrow up] to select the Yo Man! Preset, and then press [enter] to apply it.

Notice how the Chorus plug-in's settings change. Wow, that is quite a different sound! Try another one:

59. Press the [up arrow] to select another Preset, and [enter] to apply it.

Step through all the Presets. When you find the one that you like, do one of the following to exit Hot-Swap mode:

- At the top of the Browser, click on the X button to the right of the orange Hot-Swap mode message.
- In the Chorus plug-in on the Synth2 track, click on the Hot-Swap button again.

Hot-Swap mode is disabled. Just as an experiment, do the following:

60. Double-click on another Chorus Preset (while not in Hot-Swap mode).

Live adds a second Chorus Device on the current track with the Preset that you double-clicked on! Not what we want. To remove the second Chorus Device, do one of the following:

- Press [cmd-z/ctrl-z] or go Edit > Undo to Undo the previous action.
- Click in the Device's title bar to select it, and then press [delete].

You're back to just the one Chorus Device.

Note that you can still make changes to any Preset after applying it. Go ahead and do this. This will not alter the Preset's original settings.

Saving Presets

You will probably find some settings that you really like in various Live Devices as you work with them. If you think you will want to work with those same settings again on another track, or even in another Live Set, consider saving your settings to the Library as a Preset.

61. In the same Chorus Device, click on the Save Preset button. You are immediately taken to the Live Device Browser, inside the Chorus Preset list again, but this time there is a new Preset icon, and the Preset's name is highlighted and ready for you to rename it. Give your new Chorus Preset a name, perhaps "CST1 Chorus." Hit [enter] when you are done.

You have saved these settings to the Library for future use. You can recall the Preset in another Chorus Device by using Hot-Swap mode or simply dragging the Preset from the Browser onto the Chorus Device you wish to apply it to. Simple.

Save as Default

A Device's default settings are usually not what you want, and sometimes you will find yourself applying the same kind of settings repeatedly, wishing that the default settings were more useful to your regular needs. Thankfully, this is easily remedied. Every plug-in has a Save as Default function.

For example: In the EQ Eight, I like to start with node 1 as a low-cut filter and node 4 as a High Shelf. Let's make it so that all your EQ Eights will be this way when you load the default EQ Eight Device:

62. Double-click on the EQ Eight in the Live Device Browser to apply it to the Synth2 track that you are currently working on. It can be before or after the Chorus—you choose.
63. Click on the Low-Cut Filter Mode button (the leftmost filter mode) to change node 1 to this shape.
64. Select node 4 by clicking on the associated number 4 on the left of the Freq, Gain, and Q dials. Change the filter mode to High Shelf (fifth from the left) to set this mode for node 4.
65. [Ctrl-click/right-click] on the EQ Eight's yellow title bar and select Save as Default from the contextual menu.

Now, whenever you load an EQ Eight—not a Preset, just the Device by itself—it will start with these settings. If you want to change the default settings to something else, just repeat this process with the new settings. This works for any Live Device.

Don't forget to:

66. Save your Set!

EXERCISE 5.2—
APPLYING AUDIO EFFECTS AS A SEND EFFECT

So far, we have only applied Audio Effects directly to tracks in series (one after another), in a method I described as an insert effect. Let's try the second method, parallel processing, known as a send effect.

The beauty of a send effect is that the effect can be shared among some, or all, of your tracks in differing amounts. This saves precious CPU power, and gives the tracks that send to this effect a similar sound. The most traditional use of a send effect is a reverb effect, which simulates the sound of reflections in an enclosed space. Let's start with that.

5.2.1—Applying a Reverb Send Effect

DO IT!   Let's get ready to use send effects:

- You can continue from right where you left off at the end of Exercise 5.1 and use Save As... to save the Set as My Exercise 5.2.als, or
- You can open Exercise 5.2.als from the supplied Sets in Book Content > Book Exercises Project, and then perform a Save As... and save your Set as My Exercise 5.2.als.

Although you can create send effects in either View, we'll be using Arrangement View for this exercise.

Before we get can create a send effect, we must make sure that the Returns and the Mixer are visible. If you opened Exercise 5.2.als from the supplied Book Content folder, I have made sure they are already visible, but let's briefly review these commands from chapter 1 anyway:

1. Make sure that Return Tracks are visible: Look for two tracks, one named "A Return" and the other "B Return," just above the Master Track. If you do not see them, you can make them visible in one of three ways:

- Press [cmd-opt-r/ctrl-alt-r] to toggle them on and off.
- Go View > Returns.
- Enable the Show/Hide Returns button—which is an "R"—on the lower-right edge of the Arrangement window.

2. Make sure that the Mixer is visible: Look for a vertical row next to your tracks that has your Track Activator, Solo, Volume, Pan, and Send controls. If you do not see them, do one of the following:

- Press [cmd-opt-m/ctrl-alt-m] to toggle them on and off.
- Go View > Mixer.
- Enable the Show/Hide Mixer button—which is an "M"—on the lower-right edge of the Arrangement window.

Okay, now you're ready.

Applying a send effect is a two-step process:

- Place the effect you want to share on a Return Track.
- Turn up the corresponding Send dial on the tracks you want to have the effect on.

DO IT! Let's give it a try:

3. In the Browser, click on the Audio Effects category.
4. In the Audio Effects column, scroll down to the Reverb Device.
5. Drag the Reverb Device onto the track A Return and drop it. The Detail View switches to the Track View for the Return Track, which now has the Reverb Device on it, and the track is renamed "A Reverb" as a result.

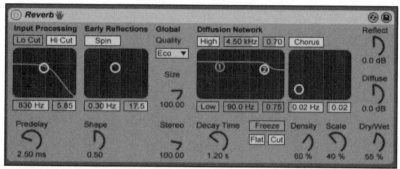

Pic. 5.14: The Reverb Audio Effect.

This is the destination that all of your "Sends" will "Return" to.

6. Find the Send A level in the Mixer for the Perc track. Click-and-drag its value up to –20 dB. You can see an exact value down in the Status Bar at the very bottom of Live's interface as you change the Send level.

7. In a similar fashion, set the Send A level on the One Shots track to –6 dB.

8. Set the Send A level on the Synth2 track to –10 dB.

9. Play back the arrangement.

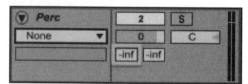

Pic. 5.15: The Send A level box for a track in Arrangement View.

You should hear reverb on the Perc, One Shots, and Synth2 tracks. Solo these tracks if you want to hear them in isolation. You will hear a different amount of reverb on each of these three tracks, because you are sending different amounts of each track to the Return Track with the Reverb

Pic. 5.16: The Status Bar showing an exact value for the Send A level box.

on it. Remember that each track's Send control is sending a copy of that track's sound to the corresponding Return Track (where it gets reverberated, in this case), and that the Send value controls the amount that is being sent from each track. Since there is a Reverb on the A Return track, you can think of each track's Send value as controlling "reverb amount" for that track.

Of course, you can still modify the Reverb's settings or choose a Preset:

10. Double-click on the A Reverb Return Track to show its Track View and the Reverb Device.
11. Click on the Reverb's Hot-Swap button.
12. In the Reverb Device's Preset list, open the Hall folder and double-click on the Large Hall Preset to apply it. Play the arrangement to hear the difference.

IMPORTANT! When using an effect as a send effect in this way, it is traditional to set the effect's Wet/Dry value to 100% wet, or "all effect, no dry signal." This is because you already have a "dry" version of the signal passing through the track to the Master, so the copy that is sent to the Return Track should be 100% effect. If you set the Return Track effect to less than 100%, you would be sending a second dry version of the track to the Master, which will only cause problems when mixing. Note that the Large Hall Preset has the Wet/Dry dial up at 100%. This Preset was intended to be used on a Return Track in this fashion.

5.2.2—Applying a Delay Send Effect

Send effects are a little more advanced than are insert effects, so repetition is good practice. Let's add a Ping Pong Delay effect on our B Return and send some signal to it with a few of our track's Send B values. Also, let's try doing this exercise in Session View to see the differences.

13. Switch to Session View.
14. Make sure that your Mixer, Sends and Return Tracks are all showing. (Check the View menu if you are unsure.)
15. In the Live Device Browser list's Audio Effects folder, scroll down until you see Ping Pong Delay. Drag this Device onto the B Return Track and drop it.

Be sure to have Info View on if you are unsure where some of these controls are or what they do.

Pic. 5.17: The Ping Pong Delay Audio Effect.

16. Turn the Dry/Wet dial all the way up to 100%.
17. Set the Feedback to 40%.
18. Change the Center Frequency to 2.29 kHz.
19. Set the Beat Division to 2.

Now let's send it some signal from our tracks. In Session View, you are given Send level dials instead of numbers. As you rotate a Send dial, the Status Bar displays the exact value.

Pic. 5.18: The Mixer's Send dials in Session View.

20. On the Perc track, turn up Send B to −20 dB.
21. On the One Shots track, turn up Send B to −14 dB.

22. On the Synth2 track, turn up Send B to –6 dB.
23. Play the arrangement from the beginning.

IMPORTANT! Pressing Play in Session View still plays the arrangement you have been working on in Arrangement View unless you also start launching Clips in the Clip grid.

The Ping Pong Delay is delaying only a narrow range of the frequencies it is being sent (which are centered around 2.29 kHz), which is in the upper midrange. This helps to keep it from getting muddy in the bass, and adds a little bit of shimmer on each of your sending tracks.

Try varying the Send A and Send B amounts while the arrangement plays to hear the effect, and then choose your own Send levels.

So now you have been through the two primary ways of applying Audio Effects: using track insert effects and send effects. Both have their many uses. Don't be afraid to experiment—you won't break anything! Live's effects are so plentiful, flexible, and easy to use that they should provide endless new horizons for your music.

You'll notice that we did not yet cover putting Audio Effects on the Master Track. Not to worry: I'm saving that for the next section, when we talk about Audio Effect Racks.

24. Save your Set by pressing [cmd-s/ctrl-s].

EXERCISE 5.3—AUDIO EFFECT RACKS

There are four types of Racks in Ableton Live 9: Audio Effect Racks, MIDI Effect Racks, Instrument Racks, and Drum Racks. I like to call Racks "rabbit hole" Devices, because once you start to explore them, they are truly endless in their possibilities. I have yet to think up a routing that cannot be solved with some combination of Racks, and I have spent long days and nights in the studio trying!

Audio Effect Racks are a unique feature of Ableton Live. They allow you to combine all manner of serial and parallel processing on a single track in ways never before possible. But best of all, they give you a way to gang multiple processing variables together onto eight Macro dials, which allow you to play your effects like a music instrument.

Here are some of the more obvious benefits of using Racks:

- Racks can simplify complex multi-effect processing tasks—such as Master Track processing—into eight streamlined dials.
- Racks can create a signature sound-design transform that can completely reshape a sound with the twist of a single dial.

- Racks can greatly simplify your live or DJ effects setup so that only the controls you want to tweak are showing.
- Racks can save you time by allowing you to save your regularly used Audio Effect Chains as a Preset for quick recall.

Once you become more familiar with what an Audio Effect Rack is capable of, you will likely begin to think up your own Rack recipes to manifest your sound-shaping visions! And just like a chef in training, you should sample great food from around the world to broaden your imagination and inspire new culinary creations! Rather than trying to further explain what Racks are capable of, we're going to try a few of the included Preset Racks before we make our own.

Live includes a sizeable library of Audio Effect Rack Presets for you to try out, and they come sorted into a variety of applications. Some are intended for individual tracks, some for Return Tracks, and some for the Master Track. Some Racks are subtle in what they do and some are anything but! For maximum impact, I am going to have you try out these Racks on the Master Track, where the Rack's effects will affect the entire mix so you can plainly hear what they do.

5.3.1—Audio Effect Rack Presets

DO IT!   It's time to explore the wondrous world of Audio Effect Racks:

- You can continue from right where you left off at the end of Exercise 5.2 and use Save As… to save the Set as My Exercise 5.3.als, or
- You can open Exercise 5.3.als from the supplied Sets in Book Content > Book Exercises Project, and then perform a Save As… and save your Set as My Exercise 5.3.als.

Let's audition a series of Racks on the Master Track.

1. Double-click on the Master Track's track name to bring up the Master Track's Track View, which shows that the track is empty of any Devices.
2. In the Browser, open the Audio Effects category. The first Device in the list is Audio Effect Rack. Click on the triangle to the left of the Device to show its list of Presets.

Notice that the Audio Effect Rack Presets are subdivided into folders to group them by application. There are Preset groups for basses, guitars, drums and vocals, and also for reverb, rhythmic, and mastering. Try these out in your spare time. They will give you a big insight into what Live's effects are capable of and will jump-start your understanding of them.

3. Open the Performance & DJ folder. Scroll down to Cut-o-matic. Double-click on this Preset to add it to your Master Track.
4. Turn up the dial named Rack Wet/Dry all the way.

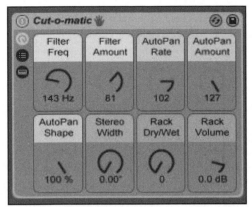

Pic. 5.19: The Cut-o-matic Audio Effect Rack Preset on the Master Track.

This Preset is not overly extreme and will be fairly easy to understand and listen to. All Racks consist of eight Macro dials with names. Play the song and adjust each of these dials to see what they do. Take some time to explore some of the various combinations that can be achieved with just these eight knobs.

When you are ready to go deeper,

5. Click on the Show/Hide Devices button on the left of the Rack.

This button "opens" the Rack so that you can begin to see what is going on "under the hood." You will see that this Rack contains four effects: an Auto Pan, an EQ Eight, a Saturator, and a Limiter.

Pic. 5.20: The Show/Hide Devices button on a Rack.

6. Double-click on the EQ Eight's title bar to unfold it.

> **COOL!** All Live Devices can be folded and unfolded by double-clicking on their title bar or by pressing the [+] or [–] keys when it is selected. This helps save space when you have very long Chains of effects.

Now that you can see the EQ Eight, go back to the Rack controls and adjust the first two dials on the top row and watch what they do. Essentially, these dials work with the EQ Eight's nodes 2 and 3 simultaneously, modifying the Frequency, Gain, and Q dials, respectively.

7. Double-click on the Auto Pan Device to unfold it.
8. Adjust the Auto Pan Amount dial, and notice what it does in the Auto Pan and EQ Eight.

This Macro dial adjusts parameters in two Devices at once. Interesting! You can combine controls on multiple Devices to create complex sonic adjustments. This is the real power of Audio Effect Racks.

Feel free to explore all the dials and their relationships to the Rack's Devices. When you have learned all you can from this Rack,

9. Click on the Hot-Swap button on the Rack's title bar.

Load another Audio Effect Rack Preset and see what it has to offer. Open it up and see how it works. Try Presets from several of the folders. Take a survey of the vast possibilities of Audio Effect Racks.

And when you are done,

10. Delete the Rack from the Master Track by clicking on its name in the title bar and pressing [delete].

Now, let's make one of our own.

5.3.2—Creating a Basic Multi-Effects Rack

You may have noticed that we have not yet attempted to improve or manipulate the sound of your Synth1 track, and it could definitely use some help. That is because I've got something special planned for this track to help it really stand out.

Keep in mind that Racks are definitely an intermediate- to advanced-level concept. If this section seems a bit harder than everything else so far, that's because it is. Stay focused and dive in.

11. Begin by switching to Arrangement View, and looping bars 27 through 57.
12. Solo the Synth1 track, and then double-click on the track name to bring up its Track View, which is currently empty.
13. In the Live Device Browser, inside the Audio Effects folder, find a Device called Audio Effect Rack. Double-click on it to place it on the Synth1 track.

Not very interesting, right? That is because an Audio Effect Rack by itself does not do anything—it is simply a container for placing combinations of effects. See where it says "Drop Audio Effects Here"? Let's do that!

14. In the Audio Effects list, find Auto Filter. Click on the expander triangle next to it to show its list of Presets. Drag the first Preset, Cut-O-Move H, from the Browser and drop it in the empty Audio Effect Rack where it says to do so.

Note that the Rack "bookends" the Auto Filter. This effect is contained within the Audio Effect Rack. That doesn't mean much now, but it will. Let's add a few more effects:

15. In the Audio Effects list, find Chorus. Click on the expander triangle next to it to show its list of Presets. Drag the Preset Resorus from the Browser and hover it over the Track View area, but do not drop it yet.

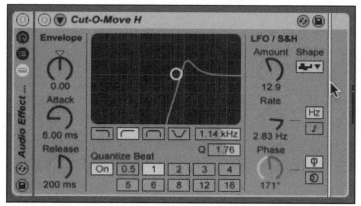

Pic. 5.21: Dropping a second effect after the first, but still within the Rack.

As you drag this second effect over the Track View area, you will see a vertical blue line appear near your cursor, before or after the different Devices there. You saw this before when placing the second Audio Effect on the Perc track. This line is telling you where the Chorus will be inserted if you let go of it there. Currently, there are four possible places you could drop it:

- Far left: Before the Audio Effect Rack entirely.
- Second from the left: Inside the Rack but before the Auto Filter.
- Third from the left: Inside the Rack, after the Auto Filter.
- Far right: After the Audio Effect Rack entirely.

Drop the Chorus at the third location: inside the Rack and after the Auto Filter. It should look like this:

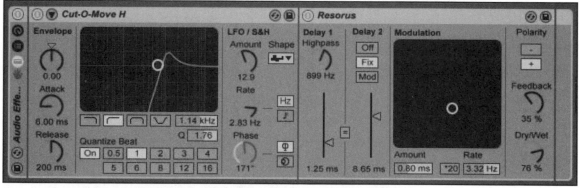

Pic. 5.22: The Auto Filter and the Chorus both inside the Audio Effect Rack.

Continue to add the remaining effects in a similar fashion, dropping them after the previous effect, but still inside the Rack:

16. In the Audio Effects list, find Simple Delay. Click on the expander triangle next to it to show its list of Presets. Drag the Preset Dotted Eighth Note from the Browser and drop it in the Audio Effect Rack after the Chorus.
17. In the Audio Effects list, find Reverb. Click on the expander triangle next to it to show its list of Presets. Open the subfolder Special, and scroll to the bottom. Drag the Preset Wide Ambience from the Browser and drop it in the empty Audio Effect Rack after the Simple Delay.
18. In the Audio Effects list, find Compressor. Click on the expander triangle next to it to show its list of Presets. Drag the Preset Gentle Squeeze from the Browser and drop it in the Audio Effect Rack after the Reverb.

Sounds cool, but so far none of what we have done is any different from simply dropping these five effects on the track in a row without the Rack: the audio from the track goes through the effects in a serial fashion, and we hear the result of these effects in the mix. Let's make it more interesting.

On the far left edge of the Rack you will see three buttons, the bottom of which is lit.

Pic. 5.23: The Audio Effect Rack's three Show/Hide buttons.

- **Show/Hide Macro Controls**—Enable this button. Eight Macro dials appear. These dials are for attaching your favorite effects controls for easy access.
- **Show/Hide Chain List**—Enable this button. The Chain list shows the available Chains for this Rack. Chains are parallel to each other, and can contain Audio Effect Devices.
- **Show/Hide Devices**—Disable and re-enable this button: this button will show or hide the list of Audio Effect Devices on one of the Chains in the previous Chain list.

All three buttons should now be enabled, and you can now see all three sections of the Audio Effect Rack: Macro dials, the Chain list, and Devices. Let's get more familiar with these areas.

5.3.3—Serial and Parallel Processing with the Chain List

Chains are among those features that are more easily shown than described. Walk through the next few steps, and the definition of what a Chain is will emerge.

Currently, your Audio Effect Rack has a single Chain and it is named, not surprisingly, "Chain."

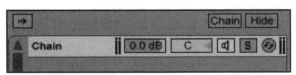

Pic. 5.24: The Audio Effect Rack Chain named "Chain."

Let's begin by renaming it:

19. Do one of the following to rename Chain to "MultiFX":

- Click on the name "Chain" to select it, and then press [cmd-r/ctrl-r].
- [Ctrl-click/right-click] on Chain and select Rename from the contextual menu.
- Click on the name "Chain" to select it, and go Edit > Rename.

Now let's create a second Chain:

20. In the Audio Effect Device list, find Saturator. Click on the expander triangle next to it to show its list of Presets. Drag the Preset Hot Tubes from the Browser and drop it in the Chain list area where it says, "Drop Audio Effects Here."
21. In the Saturator, click on the Soft Clip button to turn it on.

A second Chain appears named, once again, as "Chain."

22. Rename this second Chain as "Crunch," using one of the methods above.
23. In the Audio Effects list, find Redux. Click on the expander triangle next to it to show its list of Presets. Drag the Preset Mirage from the Browser and drop it after the Saturator, but still within the Rack.
24. Adjust the Downsample dial on the Redux to 10.

You now have two Chains: MultiFX and Crunch. Click on the name of the MultiFX Chain and you will see the effects on that Chain. Click on the Crunch Chain and you will see the effects on that Chain. These two Chains exist side by side, or "in parallel." This is much the same as having effects inserted on a track in series, and then having a Return Track with different effects on it.

Okay, definition time: A Chain is a series of Audio Effect Devices within an Audio Effect Rack. You can have up to 128 Chains in a Rack. The track's audio passes into the Rack, where it splits and is processed by all of the Chains of effects simultaneously, and then is mixed back together at the end of the Rack.

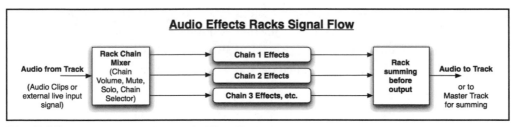

Pic. 5.25: Signal diagram of an Audio Effect Rack.

If there are Devices after the Rack, they are the next recipients of that track's audio, and then it flows to the Mixer section, to the Master Track, and out to your speakers.

In the Chain list, to the right of the Chain name, there are five icons. They are as follows:

- **Chain Volume**—This volume slider controls the amount of signal that goes through this Chain.
- **Chain Pan**—This panner positions the Chain in the stereo field.
- **Chain Activator**—Enables or disables (mutes) the Chain.
- **Chain Solo**—Solos the Chains one at a time.
- **Chain Hot-Swap**—Allows you to swap out the entire Chain with another Chain Preset.

Let's isolate each Chain so that you can hear their effect on the audio individually:

25. Click on the Chain Solo button on the MultiFX Chain.
26. Play the Looped bars of the arrangement.

You hear the first Chain we made, MultiFX, by itself.

27. Disable the Chain Solo button on the MultiFX Chain.
28. Click on the Chain Solo button on the Crunch Chain.

You hear the second Chain we made, Crunch, by itself.

29. Disable the Chain Solo button on the Crunch Chain.

You hear both Chains happening simultaneously, or in parallel.

Voilá: serial and parallel processing all on one track, made possible by an Audio Effect Rack. Make sense?

But wait: It gets better!

5.3.4—Audio Effect Rack Macro Dials

When I was a kid, I had an electric guitar and several effects pedals. I remember vividly, even then, wishing I could have at least ten arms so I could be playing the guitar and tweaking all the effects pedal knobs at the same time.

Presently, we have five Audio Effects on one Chain and two on another. Collectively, there must be several dozen different parameters that we could tweak on those effects. And because they are on different Chains, it's inconvenient to get to the parameters quickly. Macro dials will not give you ten arms, but they will provide a way to adjust a bunch of parameters that we want to have easy access to, easily and simultaneously.

Assigning a parameter to a Macro dial is a simple five-step process:

- Click on the Map Mode button to enter Macro Map Mode.
- Click on the parameter on one of the Devices in one of your Chains that you wish to assign to a Macro dial.
- Click on a Map button underneath the Macro dial you want to assign it to.
- Optionally, adjust the range of values you would like the dial to send in the Mapping Browser.
- Click on the Map Mode button to exit Macro Map Mode.

Let's assign some of your favorite controls to the Macro dials. Then you will see just how powerful Audio Effect Racks are.

30. On the Synth1 track, in the Audio Effect Rack Chain list, solo the MultiFX Chain.
31. Click on the Map Mode button in the title bar of the Audio Effect Rack that we have made.

Pic. 5.26: The Map Mode button in an Audio Effect Rack.

A lot of things just happened:

- Many controls on in the Rack turned green. Green indicates which controls can be mapped to a Macro dial.
- Map buttons appeared underneath each of the Macro dials. This is how you choose which dial you want to assign a control to.
- An area called the Mapping Browser replaced the File/Device Browser. This is where you edit the range of values that a Macro dial will send.

While in Macro Map Mode, you should not attempt to do anything besides assigning effects parameters to Macro dials; otherwise, you may experience some unexpected results.

32. Click on the MultiFX Chain name to show that Chain's Devices.
33. Now click on the Auto Filter's Filter Cutoff parameter below the filter graph—it currently reads 1.14 kHz. When you do, a small black box surrounds it to show that it is selected.
34. Now click on the Map button beneath Macro 1 to assign Filter Cutoff to that Macro dial. The name of that dial is now Frequency.
35. Click on Map Mode to exit Macro Map Mode.

The screen returns to normal.

Play the looped section again and adjust the new Frequency Macro dial. Cool—but no different from adjusting the same parameter in the Auto Filter. Let's add another parameter to the same dial:

36. Enter Macro Map Mode.
37. Click on the Q control just below Filter Cutoff. It currently reads 1.76.
38. Map it also to Macro 1 (currently called Frequency) by pressing the same Map button under the dial as before.

Without exiting Map Mode, adjust the Macro 1 dial (which has been renamed back to Macro 1, now that more than one parameter is assigned to it). As you move it, both Filter Cutoff and Q are adjusted!

Notice that a new entry has appeared in the Mapping Browser up above. Let's explore that.

The Mapping Browser has two entries, one for each Control that we have mapped so far. Each entry lists which Macro dial is assigned to which Device and which Control. And on the far right are two columns: Min and Max.

Min and Max control the minimum and maximum values you want to adjust between. Or, thought of another way, they set the values that turning the dial full left or full right will achieve for that mapped Control. The default is that the Macro dial will control the parameter's entire range of motion. But that is not always exactly what you want.

Presently, the Filter Cutoff ranges from 25 Hz to 19.9 kHz. When the Low-Cut filter is up all the way, it removes so much of the sound that there is nothing much useful left. Let's fix that:

39. Click on the Max box for Filter Cutoff to highlight it. Type in 10000, which sets a value of 10 kHz. Press [enter] to commit to the value.

Now when you turn the dial all the way to the right, the topmost value achievable is 10 kHz.

Similarly, it would be nice if the Q did not disappear so drastically when the knob is turned left.

40. Click on the Min value for the Q entry and drag it up to 1.00.

The Q starts 60% of the way up the scale and increases to 100%. Better.

Just to show you the power of these Macro dials, I am going to map another 10 parameters onto this same dial so it will be controlling a dozen parameters at once. Entering this much data may seem cumbersome, but there is a sizeable sound-shaping reward for you once you are done. Be sure to play the loop and turn the Macro 1 dial periodically while mapping these parameters if you want to hear the complexity evolve. Ready?

41. While still in Map Mode, click on LFO Amount in the Auto Filter, and map it to Macro 1. Set the Min to 15 and the Max to 25.

42. In the Chorus, map Delay 1 Time to the same knob.

Yes, you can map controls from multiple Devices to the same knob!

43. In the Mapping Browser, [ctrl-click/right-click] on the entry for Delay 1 Time and choose Invert Range.

The Min and Max values swap places. You can set a high value to the left end of the dial and a low value to the right end. Nice!

Here's another way to map parameters to Macros that is slightly faster:

44. In the Chorus, [ctrl-click/right-click] on the Delay 2 Time parameter and select Map to Macro 1. Do not modify the Min/Max values.

45. Also in the Chorus, map Dry/Wet. Min: 30%. Max: 70%.

46. In the Simple Delay, map Feedback and Dry/Wet to Macro 1 as well (one at a time). Feedback: Min: 20%. Max: 70%. Dry/Wet: Min: 15%. Max: 55%.

47. In the Reverb, map Stereo Image and Dry/Wet to the same Macro 1 dial. Stereo Image: Min: 20.00. Max: 120.00. Dry/Wet: Min: 30%. Max: 60%.
48. Finally, in the Compressor, map Threshold to Macro 1. Min: −28.0 dB Max: −38.0 dB.
49. Exit Map Mode, and try your creation.

You can see now how powerful a single Macro dial can be! And there are eight of them—just imagine the possibilities!

Remember that the MultiFX Chain is soloed—we haven't even dealt with the second Chain yet. Let's do a few more (much simpler!) mappings to other knobs to finish off this Rack.

50. Unsolo the MultiFX Chain so that both Chains are audible.
51. Enter Map Mode again.
52. Click on the Chain Volume box for the MultiFX Chain in the Chain list, which currently reads 0.00 dB. Map this to the Macro 8 dial. Min: 0.00 dB. Max: −inf dB.
53. Click on the Chain Volume box for the Crunch Chain in the Chain list, which also currently reads 0.00 dB. Map this to the Macro 8 dial as well. Min: −inf dB. Max: 0.00 dB.
54. In the Crunch Chain on the Redux Device, map the Downsample dial to Macro 8. Min: 0. Max: 45.
55. In the Saturator, map Drive to Macro 8. Min: 36.0 dB. Max: 4.5 dB.

Turn Macro 8 (now called Chain Volume) while the loop plays. You now have a crossfader between your two Chains, and the distortion increases as you crossfade.

56. Map the Chain Pan controls for both Chains to Macro 7. Exit Map Mode.

One dial pans both effects Chains. The possibilities are endless!

5.3.5—Renaming Dials and Saving Your Rack Creation

Let's rename our Macro dials so we don't forget what they are. Do one of the following:

- Click once on the Macro 1 dial. The black brackets tell you that it is selected. Press [cmd-r/ctrl-r] to rename the dial.
- Click once on the Macro 1 dial. The black brackets tell you that it is selected. Go Edit > Rename to rename the dial.
- [Ctrl-click/right-click] on the dial and choose Rename from the contextual menu.

57. Rename dial 1 "Smoother" or something equally descriptive.
58. Rename dial 7 "Panner" or something equally descriptive.
59. Rename dial 8 "Crunch X-Fader" or something equally descriptive.

You can also color the dials if that helps you remember what they do.

60. [Ctrl-click/right-click] on the Smoother dial 1. Choose a bluish color from the available color squares in the contextual menu.

61. [Ctrl-click/right-click] on the Panner dial 7. Choose a yellow color from the available color squares in the contextual menu.
62. [Ctrl-click/right-click] on the Crunch X-fader dial 8. Choose a red/orange color from the available color squares in the contextual menu.

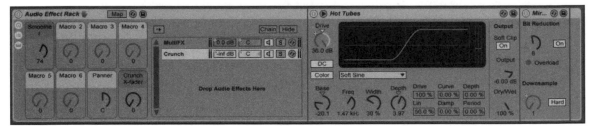

Pic. 5.27: The finished Smoother Cruncher Audio Effect Rack Device.

Finally, do the following:

63. Disable the Show/Hide Devices button and the Show/Hide Chain List button so that you are looking at just the Macro dials.

There you have it—a compact, easy-to-use Rack for transforming your sounds in one particular way.

Best of all, you can save your Rack creations to the Library for future use in other Projects:

64. Click on the Save Preset button in the Rack's title bar.

Live jumps you to the Device Browser inside of Audio Effect Racks and prompts you for a name.

65. Save your Rack as "Smoother-Cruncher" or something equally descriptive.

And finally, don't forget:

66. Save your Set by pressing [cmd-s/ctrl-s]!

THIRD-PARTY EFFECTS

In addition to the wide array of effects that come with Live, you can customize your sound-shaping possibilities by adding third-party effects plug-ins created by other companies. Just the way that every guitar or keyboard or microphone has its own unique sound characteristics, so a third-party EQ or compressor plug-in does its job in a unique way and offers a unique coloration. Live supports Steinberg's Virtual Studio Technology (VST) and Apple's Audio Units (AU) formats (Mac only). Any VST or AU plug-in will work with Live, and most will allow you to map their controls in Racks and automate their parameters. Most third-party effects offer a free trial or demo period wherein you can try their plug-in for free to see if you like it. Additionally, there are hundreds, maybe thousands, of freeware and shareware plug-ins available online. Try searching in your browser for "freeware VST effects" or "shareware AU effects" to find some of the many sites that distribute these.

COOL!   I've gotten permission to distribute installers for several of my favorite third-party effects and Instruments. You will find the installers and instructions in the Book Content Install folder that you downloaded or on your DVD, and a description of these plug-ins in appendix F. Some of them are freeware, so you can use them indefinitely, and others are demo versions that will expire after a trial period. If you try a demo version and like it, I highly encourage you to pick it up from the vendor's website. I chose these particular plug-ins because they will add a unique sonic flavor to your toolbox and because they are some of the best I have found at what they do.

SUMMARY

- Generally speaking, there are two ways to use Audio Effects: in serial as an insert effect, or in parallel as a send effect.
- Live's Audio Effects can be found in the Audio Effects category, and can be applied to any track by dragging and dropping them from the Browser onto the track or by double-clicking on the Device in the Browser to add it to the currently selected track.
- Live's EQ Three and EQ Eight are used for making tonal adjustments.
- Live's Compressor is used for making dynamic range reductions.
- All of Live's Devices have a selection of Presets, which can be browsed and Hot-Swapped. As well, a Device's settings can be saved as a Preset into the Live Library for use in future Sets, or saved as the default state.
- An Audio Effect placed on a Return Track can be accessed from any track for processing with the track's corresponding Send dial.
- Audio Effect Racks offer unique serial and parallel processing combinations, as well as Macro dial assignments for easy manipulation of multiple parameters at once. Racks can also be saved as Presets.
- Live is capable of running VST and AU third-party effects and Instrument plug-ins, which greatly expands Live's already formidable processing possibilities.

Recording Audio with Live

Thus far we have managed to create our song from prerecorded loops, samples, and Presets. It is much easier to learn the mechanics of a new program without the additional challenges of having to be creative on demand and manage performance anxiety. But now that you have a majority of the program's features under your belt, you will no doubt be eager to make your own recordings and samples to put your own unique stamp on your sound. Understanding all of the previous lessons up to this point will allow you to take on the additional technical and musical challenges of making your own recordings with more confidence.

Setting Up for Recording

If you are interested in making recordings with Live, I am going to assume that you have an external audio interface (connected via FireWire, USB, or PCMCIA) and that it was connected and powered on before you booted your computer and launched Live. Before you record digital audio, you should make sure that your audio interface is configured correctly for working with Live. Chapter 10 looks closely at Live's Audio Preferences and discusses methods for tuning your audio interface and system settings. As well, if you are new to audio, digital audio, or computers in general, you will want to read the various appendices on those topics, because this section may use some terminology you are unfamiliar with.

Once you have Live's Preferences and your audio interface configured properly, it's time to have a look at the In/Out section of Live's Audio Tracks.

THE IN/OUT SECTION

Make sure that the In/Out section is visible, using [cmd-opt-i/ctrl-alt-i] to show/hide it. You'll make your first recording in Session View, so let's start there, although the In/Out section is exactly the same in either view.

Pic. 6.01: The In/Out section of an Audio Track.

The top two pull-downs control the Audio From options, while the bottom two control the Audio To options. This simple interface will allow for some fairly sophisticated routing options in addition to allowing recording external sources through your audio interface. The middle three buttons are for selecting monitoring options, which we'll cover last.

Audio from Input Types and Input Channels

Here are the likely input types and their respective input channel options, if any:

Ext. In—Select External In if you want to record an external audio signal (guitar, bass, keyboard, microphone, and so on) in through your audio interface. Input channel options are taken directly from your selections on the Preferences > Audio > Input Config page, and will consist of the various mono and stereo input channels available on your audio interface.

Configure—This is not an input type so much as a handy shortcut directly to Live's audio Preferences for enabling or disabling inputs on your audio interface for use with the External In input type.

Reason—If you have Propellerhead Reason, or another ReWire slave program installed and running, you can select it as an input type here. When Reason is selected, the Input Channels submenu will consist of Reason's 64 Audio Interface outputs in mono or stereo options.

Resampling—Another genius Live feature: When you choose this option, anything playing through your main outputs is additionally routed to the input of your selected track for recording. Want to bounce eight tracks of backing vocals or drums to a single stereo pair? Solo the tracks you want to bounce (or mute the ones you don't want to bounce), select Resampling as the input type, arm for recording, and press record. Does it get any easier? There are no input channel options with Resampling, since the function is hardwired to the Master outputs.

(Track name)—You might be surprised to see the name of every other track in your Set listed here as an input type option. Similar to Resampling, you can record the audio from any other track in your Set. Perhaps you have some amazingly complex audio effects processing on a track that you want to bounce to an audio file. Or perhaps you have a MIDI Instrument that sounds perfect but is taking up too many resources. You could select it as an input and record it to an Audio Track and then delete the Instrument to free up resources. Input channel options for individual track input types are often many and varied here:

If the input track is an Audio Track, you will be presented with three options:

- **Pre FX**—The input is taken from the selected track at a point in the signal Chain before any Audio Effects on that track, which is also before the Mixer.
- **Post FX**—The input is taken from the selected track at a point after any Audio Effects on the track, but before the Mixer section.

- **Post Mixer**—The input is taken from the selected track at a point after any Audio Effects and after the Mixer, which includes any Track Panning and Track Volume settings/automation.

If the input is an Audio Track with an Audio Effect Rack, or a MIDI Track with an Instrument, Instrument Rack, or a Drum Rack, you will be presented with the above three options, plus a potentially very long list of signal access points. For example, if you select the Impulse track as an input source, the input channels include an output from each of the eight sample Slots so you could record any one drum's output to a new Audio Clip. In the case of a Drum Rack input type, you are presented with Pre FX, Post FX, and Post Mixer options for every drum pad and Rack Return in your Drum Rack—a very long list indeed!

Audio To Output Types and Output Channels

Output type and output channel selection are similar to input type and channel selection. Here are the available output types and output channel options:

Ext. Out—Select External Out if you would like to divert the track's output to a different audio interface output from the one assigned to your Master output. You might do this to process the track externally with a hardware processor, to send the track's signal to surround speakers, or to output your various tracks to be mixed in analog on an external mixer. External output channel options are taken directly from the Preferences > Audio > Output Config dialog box, and will consist of the mono and stereo audio interface channel options you select there.

Configure—Again, this is not an output type so much as a handy shortcut directly to Live's audio output channel configuration Preferences for enabling or disabling outputs on your audio interface for use with the External Out output type.

(Track Name)—Here again you will see a list of the various Audio Tracks in your Set, starting with the default output type, Master.

- Tracks set to Master will be summed at the Master Track for output to your audio interface.
- Tracks set to output to another Audio Track in your Set will not be sent to the Master directly, but instead will be sent to the specified Audio Track. Setting multiple tracks to output to the same Audio Track allows for subgrouping of tracks by setting the destination track's Monitor to In, or bouncing tracks to a new Audio Clip by recording the sum of track outputs on the destination track.

Sends Only—This final option mutes the track's main output, but leaves the track's Sends enabled. This allows you to use the Return Tracks as a subgroup or to hear a track only after it has been through a Return Track's effects. One creative use of this feature is for working in surround: make a Return Track for every speaker in your surround setup, put all your tracks into Sends Only output, and use the Send dials to direct a particular track to a particular Return/speaker.

Monitor

The Monitor section allows you choose between hearing the track's input, output, or neither. Whenever a track is monitoring an incoming signal, a small microphone icon appears in the Track Status display.

Note that the Monitor controls are visible only when you have selected an input type other than No Input.

In—When the Monitor is set to In, the track will always relay the incoming signal (set in the Input Type/Channel section) and never relay audio played from a Clip in the track. Here are some scenarios in which you might set the track's Monitor control to In:

- If you have several other tracks outputting to this track and you want to hear the sum of those tracks here.
- If you want to have a persistent live input into Live, such as a microphone or other external instrument.
- If you are sending MIDI to an external MIDI sound source and want to hear the audio output of the Device returned through Live.

Auto—The Auto setting is the default, and likely the one you will use the most, because it is the most adaptable setting. It is great for punching in/out on the timeline in Arrangement View as well (covered in a following section).

- When the track is playing back Clips, the track defaults to monitoring the Clips playing on the track.
- If no Clip is playing, or as soon as track recording begins, the track will monitor the incoming input signal set up in the Input Type/Channel section.
- As well, if Live's transport is stopped, armed tracks set to Auto Monitor mode will switch to input monitoring so you can set levels, practice a part before recording, and so on.

Off—In this monitor mode, no audio from the track (either from the input or Clips on the track) will be heard, regardless of Live's recording status. Here are some scenarios of when you might want to use the Monitor Off setting:

- If you are using external or hardware monitoring, so that you do not hear an echo of your input signal through Live.
- If you are recording input from another track that is also playing back through the Master, so that you do not hear it twice.
- If you are recording something that requires no monitoring through Live, such as a speech or an all-acoustic performance.

RECORDING IN SESSION VIEW

Recording in Session View into Clip Slots is fun and easy, and Live boasts a unique work flow in which you can alternate between playback, recording, and playback again without ever needing to stop the music. You can start with a basic loop, press Play, pick up an instrument, overlay some takes, add new loops for a new section, build an arrangement of Clips, add some more recorded takes, make effects and mix decisions, and you can essentially complete an entire song without ever pressing the Stop button.

The process for making an Audio (or MIDI) Track recording in Session View can be summarized in this way:

1. Arm a track (or tracks) for recording.
2. Select the desired input type, input channel, and Monitoring mode in the In/Out section.
3. Check incoming audio levels and adjust accordingly.
4. If you have a backing Clip or Scene that you want to play along with while you record, launch it. Alternately, enable the metronome in the Control Bar to play along to a click at the current tempo.
5. Choose a Clip Slot for recording and click on its Clip Record button to begin recording at the next Global Quantize value.
6. When you are done—or almost done—do one of the following:

- Click on the Clip Record button again to switch from recording to playback of your new Clip at the next Global Quantize value.
- Click on another Clip Record button in a new empty Clip Slot to stop the current Clip recording and switch to a new Clip recording at the next Global Quantize value.
- Click on the Session Record button to deactivate it, which will stop all Clips recording, and switch to playing them.
- Click on the track's Clip Stop button to stop your Clip's recording at the next Global Quantize value, but continue playback of other already launched Clips.
- Click on the Stop All Clips button to stop recording and stop playback of all other currently playing Clips at the next Global Quantize value, but not stop global playback of the Arrangement Position.
- Click on the Stop button in the Control Bar to immediately stop recording and playback of all Clips and to stop global playback of the Arrangement Position.

Global Quantize and Audio Recording in Session View

The key to successful Session View Clip recording is the Global Quantize setting in the Control Bar. Just as Global Quantize affects the timing of launched Clips for synchronized playback, so too it affects the start and stop timing of recordings for Audio and MIDI Clips in Session View. It takes some practice to get the hang of it, but once you know what to expect, achieving good results should be easy.

Helpful Hints for Recording in Session View

- If you need a count-in before recording starts, you can set one at Preferences > Record Warp Launch > Count-In, or select a value from the new pull-down menu next to the metronome. When you enable this, Live will give you a metronome count-in before recording (and playback of other Clips when recording) begins. I find a setting of two bars to be what I need most of the time.
- Unlike MIDI Clips, which can be created at the length you want and then recorded into, you cannot predefine how long your Audio Clip recording will be before you click on Record. This can create a challenge when you are engineering your own recordings: How do you click on something to stop recording when you are simultaneously shredding a solo on your guitar? Sure you could

finish playing and go back and trim your recordings by hand, but this gets old quickly. Here are two techniques that allow you to stop recording without using your hands:

- Set the Global Quantize value to the length of the Clip you intend to record, and when you go to record, instead of clicking on the Clip Record button once, click on it twice. This will start the Clip recording and stop the recording after the selected Global Quantize value with one action, effectively recording for a specific length. Of course, if you need a value other than 1, 2, 4, or 8 bars, this technique will not work.
- If you own a MIDI footpedal (a sustain pedal works well), you can map it to control a Clip Record/Stop button so you can use your feet to do what your hands cannot.

- By default, launching a Scene will not initiate recording on an armed Audio Track, but there is a toggle switch for changing that behavior on the Preferences > Record Warp Launch page at the very bottom. If you have this enabled and you map a footpedal to the Scene Launch button (which is revealed only when you enter MIDI Map mode in Session View), you can trigger a new Scene or Clip recording with your footpedal. Use this to step through all of your Scenes, recording Clips as you go through your whole song. Alternately, set up a series of duplicate Scenes and record multiple takes to each of the Scenes by stepping on the footpedal. When you are done, delete the Clip takes you don't like.
- Perhaps the technique that requires the least amount of preparation or coordination to pull off is to simply press Record in the Clip Slot of a Scene that loops endlessly, and just keep recording into the single Clip until you have one or more takes you like. You can then use the Clip Start/Stop values to trim your Clip to the take you want to keep. If you want to then get rid of the other inferior takes, simply [ctrl-click/right-click] on the trimmed Clip and choose Crop Clip(s) from the contextual menu. This will save your trimmed Clip, discarding the rest.
- Devices such as Push, the Akai APC40, APC20, and the Novation Launchpad allow for one-button Clip-recording initiation. Although it is not fully hands-free recording, I find it quite a bit easier to press a glowing button than to reach for a mouse or track pad, aim, and click on a tiny button.
- Although it is possible to record to multiple tracks simultaneously in Session View, it is challenging to start and stop recording a series of Clips in the Clip grid at the same time. I find it a lot easier to use Arrangement View for multitrack recording.
- Finally, there is a new button next to Session Record called Prepare Scene for New Recording which will stop current Clips recording, and create a new scene below them ready for a new take.

RECORDING IN ARRANGEMENT VIEW

Making an audio recording in Arrangement View is a much more "traditional" recording experience: You select where the recording will take place on the timeline, and execute the recording. The starting and stopping of recording can be controlled with the Loop/Punch Brace and/or a Count-In. There is no Global Quantize value to worry about, although the Snap to Grid value remains useful.

The process for making an audio (or MIDI) recording in Arrangement View can be summarized like this:

1. Arm a track (or tracks) for recording.
2. Select the desired input type, input channel, and monitoring mode in the In/Out section.

3. Check incoming audio levels and tone, and adjust accordingly.
4. If desired, set Punch-In and/or Punch Out points with the Loop Brace and enable the Punch-In/Out switches. Otherwise, set the Arrangement Position at the location where you would like recording to begin.
5. Enable the Arrangement Record button in the Control Bar.
6. When you are done, press Stop.

Starting and/or Stopping Recording with Punch-In/Out Points

The Loop Brace also serves another key purpose when recording audio or MIDI in Arrangement View: the Punch-In/Out controls. These controls allow you to set a start and end point for your recordings, which can be helpful when you are recording yourself or when you want to overdub a short phrase of a specific length on a track that already contains useful takes you want to keep. Particularly with Audio Clip recordings, which take up valuable hard-drive space, I have gotten into the habit of using the Punch-In/Out Brace to record exactly the length I need and no more. Additionally, you can Loop-record multiple takes with the Loop Brace and then trim the recording to the best take.

Using these controls could not be easier:

Pic. 6.02: The Loop/Punch controls in the Control Bar.

1. Set the Loop Start/Punch-In Point and Loop/Punch Length using one of the following methods:

- Click-and-drag to select a range of bars in the Arrangement that you plan to record to. Press [cmd-l/ctrl-l] to set the Loop Brace to Loop this selection, which is not what you want, but it puts the Loop Brace in the right place. In the Control Bar, deactivate the Loop switch and enable the Punch-In/Out switches.
- Click-and-drag the Loop Brace Start/Stop triangles to the range of bars you want to record to. Enable the Punch-In/Out switches in the Control Bar.
- Type or click-and-drag the desired recording start bar value into the Loop Start/Punch-In Point box. Type in or click-and-drag the desired recording length into the Loop/Punch Length box. Enable the Punch-In/Out switches in the Control Bar.

2. Once you have the Punch values and switches set, place your insert point/Arrangement Position a few bars before the Loop Brace.
3. Enable Arrangement Recording.

When the Arrangement Position reaches the Punch-In point, recording begins. When the Arrangement Position reaches the Punch Out point, recording stops but playback continues until you stop it manually.

Helpful Hints for Recording in Arrangement View

- Note that you do not need to activate both the Punch-In and the Punch Out switches. In other words, you can specify where you want to begin recording without specifying an end point, so you can continue recording as long as you like. Or vice versa: Set a Punch Out point, but start recording right away, without a Punch-In point.
- Even though you set a particular Punch-In point, Live will still record from the point at which you started playback, and simply set the Clip Start at the Punch-In point. This is good, in that any "inspired" moments leading up to the recording take are also captured and retrievable, but most of the time you will end up with several bars of silence at the beginning of your recordings taking up space on your hard drive. You can use the Crop Clip(s) function to solve this after recording.
- You can "Loop-Record" by enabling the Loop switch in the Control Bar. Live will record your looped takes sequentially into one file until you stop recording. Use the Undo/Redo commands to step backward/forward through your takes to the one you want to use. Or, open the Loop-Recorded Clip's Sample Editor to review all of the takes by moving the Loop Brace and Clip Start/End points. When you have selected the take that you want, you can use Crop Clip(s) to get rid of the other unused takes.
- Multitrack recording is as easy as arming multiple tracks for recording before starting to record. You will, of course, have to make all the various logical settings in the In/Out section for each track. There is a setting in Preferences/Record Warp Launch for Exclusive Arming of tracks that you may want to turn off, or you can simply override it by holding down [cmd/ctrl] as you click on the Arm buttons.
- Before recording, decide if you want to have Automation Arm enabled or not. If it is enabled, moving faders and knobs on your controllers or adjusting Live's parameters while audio recording will record your gestures to automation. If this is intentional, then go for it, but I rarely find that I want to record audio and track automation at the same time. Try to focus on getting a good recording of a good performance and worry about mixing details later.

HELPFUL HINTS FOR RECORDING IN EITHER VIEW

- You can choose which file format your new recordings will be written to in Preferences > Record Warp Launch: File Type. The choices are WAV or AIFF. There is no appreciable difference between these file types: files recorded in either type will sound exactly the same and be exactly the same size.
- New recordings made in Live will be saved to your current Project's folder in Samples > Recorded. They are saved with the naming convention of "(recording number) (track name).(extension)," so the fifth recording on a track called Vocals would be saved as "0005 Vocals.wav."
- Be aware that the name of any new recording is taken from the name of the track when the recording was made, and it will affect both the new Clip's name and the file name saved to your hard drive. It is a good idea to get in the habit of naming your tracks before you start recording, otherwise you will end up with a lot of files named "0004 1 Audio.wav" or similar, and when you go searching for that one amazing accordion recording you did last year, it will take you a long time to find it. Better still to rename the track before each new recording so that the filenames are quite specific: "0011 Lead Vocals Verse 2 sm58.wav" is more descriptive than "0011 Vocals. wav." A little planning ahead will save you a lot of time down the road.

- You can save notes about a track/recording: [ctrl-click/right-click] on the track name and select Edit Info Text. I find that saving notes about which microphone/preamp/special settings were used is useful later if you decide to redo or add to a recording.
- There is a Preference for setting the default Warp Mode assigned to new recordings: Preferences > Record Warp Launch: Default Warp Mode. If, for example, you know you will be recording a lot of vocals in a session, set the default Warp Mode to Tones, or perhaps Complex. This way, if the tempo of your Project changes later on, your recorded Clips will likely sound good without a lot of additional tinkering.

See the appendix sections for more information about audio, digital audio, and recording.

SUMMARY

- The In/Out section gives you access to various sound source and destination options, including your sound card's inputs and outputs, as well as track to track recording options.
- The Resampling input type allows you to easily record what you are hearing in your speakers to any Audio Track.
- The Monitor section specifies whether incoming audio is "passed through" to the Master output or not.
- In Session View, new Audio Clips are recorded to Clip slots.
- In Arrangement View, new Audio Clips are recorded to the timeline, and the Arrangement Loop may be used to control recording start, end, and looping points.

MIDI and Controllers in Live

7

This chapter will concentrate on all things MIDI in Live, which contains some of the most sonically creative aspects of the program.

WHAT IS MIDI?

MIDI, which stands for Musical Instruments Digital Interface, is both a hardware specification and a language protocol that digital musical devices use to communicate. You will hear the acronym MIDI used to describe both of these things, which can cause confusion.

MIDI was created in the early 1980s, when the first portable hardware synthesizers had no easy way to communicate with each other. The protocol was adopted fairly quickly, and by the end of the 1980s there were few, if any, synthesizers still being made that did not "speak" MIDI. As well, you could purchase interface cards that enabled early personal computers to also speak MIDI, which began a series of technological innovations that have converged into programs like Ableton Live.

MIDI hardware used to be easier to spot, because such devices always sported a MIDI 5-pin jack. But in the past decade or so, manufacturers have taken to sending MIDI data over the increasingly more abundant USB, FireWire, and Ethernet interfaces—even over Wi-Fi. Yet while the hardware for transferring MIDI data continues to change, the data being sent hasn't changed much. The MIDI specification hasn't been updated since its inception back in the 1980's. Thirty years on, we are still effectively using MIDI 1.0, which is a testament to the clarity of the vision of its creators.

The MIDI protocol was not created to transmit digital audio. Instead, it transmits performance gesture information in the form of short text chunks. You can think of MIDI data as being similar to an old player piano roll: the paper piano rolls had holes punched in them, and when you ran the roll through the player piano, the holes would tell the piano which notes to play and when. The roll captured a performance rather than a recording of a performance. Theoretically, if you could put this roll into a different player piano, you could hear the same "performance" played by another piano.

MIDI data works in a similar way, capturing performance gestures rather than recording audio. These gestures—such as keyboard notes being pressed, knobs being turned, or sliders being moved—can be replayed, edited, and even reassigned to different sound generators. In Live, there are even MIDI plug-ins to transform your performance gestures as they happen. MIDI data is extremely malleable. Every nuance of a MIDI performance can be tweaked and sculpted until it is exactly the way you want it. This is what gives electronic music its precision and limitless possibilities.

Internal and External MIDI

Like a player piano roll, MIDI note data does not make any sound on its own. It needs to feed its information to some kind of sound generator in order to be heard. In the first 15 years of MIDI, this meant using an external hardware device, such as a sampler, drum machine, or synthesizer. These days, sound generators can also be internal, software-based plug-ins—such as Live's own Simpler or Impulse. Although the concepts behind using MIDI internally and externally are essentially the same, the steps for making them happen are somewhat different. I'll walk you through examples of each. In the event that you do not own an external MIDI sound generator, don't worry: you can still learn the concepts with software equivalents of these devices.

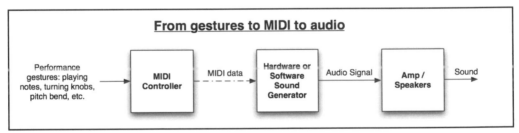

Pic. 7.01: From gestures to MIDI to audio.

SETTING UP MIDI CONTROLLERS

A MIDI controller is a device that generates MIDI messages, such as a keyboard, drum pads, fader bank, or even some DJ mixers. There are even MIDI guitar, saxophone, flute, and violin controllers. A controller may or may not have sound-generating functions of its own: some controllers are just an empty shell that generates only MIDI messages, while others are a keyboard with internal sounds that also transmits MIDI messages. In the past decade, the number and types of MIDI controllers has exploded.

MIDI controllers are used for a lot more these days than just transmitting note data. Knobs, sliders, touch surfaces, and even motion sensors can be mapped to control just about any aspect of Live, such as volume, panning, send levels, transport functions, and nearly any plug-in or soft-synth parameter.

You do not need an external controller to work with MIDI in Live, but having one sure makes it a lot more musical and fun! If you do not have an external MIDI controller, you can skip this next setup section, but you are still not completely out of the game: Live conveniently offers a way to use your computer's QWERTY keyboard as a MIDI input device. I'll show you how to set that up when you get to the MIDI Clip recording stage.

IMPORTANT! Generally speaking, you should try to have all external peripherals, such as sound cards, MIDI interfaces, and USB MIDI devices connected to your computer and turned on before launching Live. This will give Live the best chance to auto-detect them, which will make setup that much faster and easier. The PC version of Live requires this. On Macs, most USB devices will be auto-detected by Live if plugged in while Live is already running. But if they don't, restarting Live—with your devices connected and powered on—will usually solve the problem. If it doesn't, try rebooting your computer and relaunching Live.

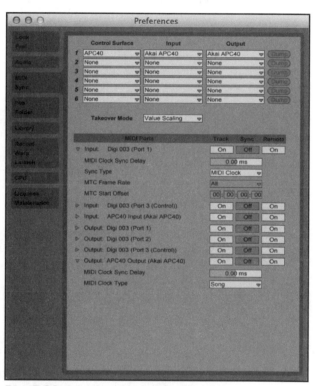

Pic. 7.02: The MIDI/Sync Preferences pane.

Live's MIDI/Sync Preference Pane

Once Live is running, it's time to configure Live's MIDI Preferences. To get to the Preferences on a Mac, go Live > Preferences. On a PC, go Options > Preferences. Then click on the MIDI/Sync tab on the left-hand side.

The MIDI/Sync pane has two sections, and they are not titled, so it is not immediately clear what you are looking at unless you read the manual. Essentially, there are two ways that Live can recognize your external control surfaces:

Natively Supported Control Surfaces are handled by the top section. If your device is listed in the Control Surfaces pull-down list in the top section, then Live natively supports your device. As a result, some or all of your device's controls will already be mapped to logical parameters in Live, such as sliders mapped to Track Volume; knobs mapped to Track Pan; and Play, Stop, and Record buttons mapped to Play, Stop, and Record, and so on. If your device is natively supported in this fashion, simply choose your device from the list and specify the input and output ports you want to use with Live from the columns to the right.

Manual Control Surface Setup is handled by the lower section. If your device is not in the natively supported pull-down list, you will have to set it up manually, and this is easily done. For each MIDI device recognized by Live, you can choose to enable inputs and outputs for Track, Sync, or Remote. Here's what these columns of buttons do:

- **Track (input)**—This button will likely be the most often used of the three. Enabling this button for a device's input allows you to route incoming messages from your device to a MIDI Track in Live, and then record these gestures. As a result of enabling this button, the input will show up in the MIDI Track's I/O as an input option.
- **Track (output)**—If you would like Live's MIDI Tracks to be able to send MIDI messages to this port/device, you should enable the Track button here for each output you plan to address. As a result, enabling these outputs will make them show up in a MIDI Track's I/O as an output option.
- **Remote (input)**—The second most used column, Remote, concerns enabling a port or device for remote control of Live's parameters, such as controlling a plug-in's parameters or transport functions from your control surface. If you plan to map controls on this device or port to functions in Live, enable the button in this column.
- **Remote (output)**—If your device can receive and respond to messages from Live that provide physical or visual feedback, such as moving faders or lit buttons, you will want to enable this button for your device's output.
- **Sync (input)**—The Sync column is for addressing MIDI Beat Clock, which allows Live to sync tempos with other external MIDI devices during playback. Buttons in the Sync column should be engaged for inputs when you wish to receive beat-clock information from another device that is sending it.
- **Sync (output)**—Engage this column for devices or ports that you wish to send beat-clock information, so that they can sync to Live's tempo.

IMPORTANT! **Using the Natively Supported and Manual Setup sections together:** There are a number of instances in which you will need to mix and match settings from both sections of this page. Consider the following points carefully:

- If your device is a natively supported control surface (the Akai APC40 or APC20, for example) and the default mappings work for you, you can set it up in the Native Support section and you won't need to do anything further in the Manual Setup section to start using it with Live.
- If the controller is also a keyboard (an Akai MPK49, for example) and you wish to use it to input notes to MIDI Tracks as well as using the natively supported faders and knobs, you will want to also enable a Track MIDI input in the Manual Control section for the device.
- If you want to add more mappings or override the default mappings for your device, you will want to enable the Remote column for your device's input.

- Likewise, if you want to send customized control information back to your device in a way that is different from the natively supported features, you will need to enable a Remote output port.
- Finally, if you want to send or receive MIDI Beat Clock information for any devices, you will need to enable the corresponding Sync button(s). MIDI Clock is not natively supported for any device.

Using these rules of thumb, you should be able to navigate the settings you need for your specific setup.

Two final settings you should be aware of on the MIDI/Sync Preferences page are:

- **The Dump button**—This button in the Natively Supported Control Surfaces section will send the most recently updated mapping Preset to your device so that it is optimized for working with Live. Ableton updates these Presets to work with the latest versions of Live even if your device's manufacturer does not. Your device must be in SysEx (System Exclusive) Preset Receive mode in order for this to work—refer to the controller's manual to learn how to do this. Once your device is ready to receive SysEx, then click on the Dump button to download the Preset to your controller.
- **Takeover mode**—The Takeover mode setting is quite useful. Imagine that you have a controller with a fader mapped to Volume for a track. Let's say that the fader is all the way down (–inf dB) and the Track Volume is at unity (0 dB) because you moved the Track Volume with your mouse rather than with the fader. Now you move the fader. Takeover mode will control what happens next. Try all three modes to see which one you like the best:

  - **None**—In this mode, as soon as Live receives the new volume reading from the fader, it will jump to that value. This can be troublesome, because then you have a sudden leap in volume.
  - **Pickup**—With Pickup mode, Live will wait until you move the hardware control through the current software value before changing the value. So in the above example, you would have to bring the fader up from –inf dB past 0 dB before it would respond to the fader. This prevents the sudden leap in value that can happen with the None mode.
  - **Value Scaling**—Value Scaling mode is a compromise between the two other modes. With it, the differences between your hardware and software values are averaged until you pass over the software value with your hardware.

Unless you change MIDI device connections to your computer, you shouldn't need to reconfigure the settings on this page very often. However, familiarizing yourself with this page is essential, so that when something unexpected happens—and it will happen—you can troubleshoot quickly and get back to being creative with minimal hassle.

Testing MIDI I/O

Live provides four small indicators for noting the presence of both incoming and outgoing MIDI. These are located in a part of the Control Bar that we haven't covered yet.

Pic. 7.03: The four MIDI In/Out indicator lights in the Control Bar.

In each case, the top box indicates incoming data and the lower box indicates outgoing data. If you have successfully configured your controllers, you should now be able to see these indicators lighting up when you send MIDI data to Live. These are the two you should check presently:

- **Key/MIDI In Indicator**—If you have a natively supported control surface, move a slider or knob on it and you should see this indicator blink.
- **MIDI Track In Indicator**—Press a key or pad on your properly connected and configured keyboard/drum controller, and you should see this indicator blink.

Key Map Mode and MIDI Map Mode

If you are trying to control Live from a non-natively supported controller, or are trying to map a new parameter not covered by your natively supported controller, you must map it manually. Hands down, Live has the easiest and most versatile system for mapping computer keys and MIDI controllers to functions in the program I have ever seen. The process is very similar to mapping Macros in the Audio Effect rack, and is refreshingly simple:

1. Click on either the Key Map mode or MIDI Map mode switch in the Control Bar to enter one of the two mapping modes. Parameters that can be mapped turn orange in Key Map mode and purple in MIDI Map mode.
2. Click on a parameter that you want to control.
3. Press the computer key or move the MIDI control that you want to use to control the selected parameter.
4. Optionally adjust the range of values that will be controlled in the Key Mappings or MIDI Mappings browser.
5. Click on the Key Map mode or MIDI Map mode switch again to exit the mapping mode.

Pic. 7.04: The Key Map mode and MIDI Map mode switches in the Control Bar.

Give this process a try. Once you get the hang of it, you will find yourself shouting "That's it? That is too easy!" Mapping controls in Live allow you to play Live as though it were an instrument itself, which in turn allows for infinite new performance possibilities. I am continually finding new uses for mapped controls. You will, too.

EXERCISE 7.1—MAKING MIDI CLIPS WITH ABLETON LIVE'S INSTRUMENTS

While MIDI Clips are launched and behave in a similar fashion to the functionality of Audio Clips, they are fundamentally different in most regards yet are every bit as powerful and even more flexible to use.

Think of a MIDI Clip as a collection of musical gestures that tell a MIDI device what to do and when to do it. A MIDI Clip can contain note information (keyboards and drum pads); volume, pan, and pitchbend information; and knob twists, fader moves, or any other gesture generated by a MIDI controller.

Every time you press Play in Live, all of these gestures are routed to, and "performed" by, a sound generator of some kind: Live Instrument Devices, third-party software instruments (VSTi), or external MIDI devices. The audio output of these devices can be mixed with Live's Audio Tracks to create your overall song.

What is great about MIDI Clips is that all the gesture information can be easily and endlessly edited, and need never be recorded to an Audio Clip—unless you have some good reason to do so, which I will talk about later in this chapter. It's like having a roomful of musicians who do exactly what you tell them to do, waiting to accompany you every time you press Play. If you want to change what one of these musicians is doing, you simply adjust the MIDI Clip that is telling the instrument what to play.

Creating MIDI Clips

There are three ways to make notes in a MIDI Clip:

1. Create an empty MIDI Clip and use your mouse to enter notes. This may be your method of choice if you are not yet skilled at playing a MIDI controller. You must enter any velocity variation by hand as well, which can be a little cumbersome.

2. Use Live's built-in Computer MIDI Keyboard function to turn your computer's QWERTY keyboard into a MIDI keyboard. This ingenious solution by Ableton allows you to play and record MIDI notes without an additional external hardware controller. You turn this on in the Control Bar by pressing either [cmd-shift-k/ctrl-shift-k] or clicking on the small musical keyboard icon button. The top two rows of letter keys then become keys on a musical keyboard. The downside is that your QWERTY keyboard is not velocity-sensitive, so all the notes that you transmit have a static velocity. This yields fairly unmusical results, unless you are working with a Clip that does not require a lot of velocity variation, such as electronic drums.

Pic. 7.05: The Computer MIDI Keyboard button in the Control Bar.

3. Record your gestures from a MIDI controller into a Clip in Live. In addition to the benefits of real-time recording of notes and velocity, you can record other performance gestures such as pitch bend, modulation wheel, and sustain pedal at the same time. If you are going for a "human feel" in your MIDI Tracks, this is obviously the easiest way to achieve it.

All of these methods can achieve quality results if you know what you are doing—it is simply a matter of finding the method that works best for you. You will try each of these methods in the upcoming exercises. For some of these exercises, I will assume that you have an external MIDI keyboard or drum pads for recording MIDI notes, but if not, feel free to use either of the other methods described above.

7.1.1—Make a MIDI Track with an Impulse Instrument

DO IT!   Let's Make Some MIDI Clips!

- You can continue from right where you left off at the end of Exercise 5.3 and use Save As... to save the Set as My Exercise 7.1.als, or
- Open Exercise 7.1.als from the supplied Sets in Book Content > Book Exercises Project, and then perform a Save As and save your Set as My Exercise 7.1.als.

You will start with using Live's Impulse instrument to generate some additional drum sounds. Here are the steps involved:

1. Make a MIDI Track.
2. Place an Impulse instrument on the MIDI Track.
3. Populate the Impulse with a number of audio samples to play.
4. Create a MIDI Clip in Session View.
5. Place notes in the MIDI Clip that tell Impulse which samples to play and when.

Here we go!

1. In Session View, click on the name of the Beats Audio Track.

New tracks are created to the left of the currently selected track in Session View, and since the track you are making will be a rhythmically oriented track, you should make it next to the Beats track.

2. To create a new MIDI Track, do one of the following:

- Press [cmd-shift-t/ctrl-shift-t].
- Go Create > Insert MIDI Track.
- [Ctrl-click/right-click] on the Beats track and choose Create MIDI Track from the contextual menu.

A new MIDI Track named "2 MIDI" is created to the left of the Beats track. You will notice right away that the meter in the mixer looks different on this new track.

A MIDI Track that does not have an internal instrument on it has a MIDI velocity meter instead of an audio level meter. Let's see this in action:

Pic. 7.06: A MIDI Track in the Session View Mixer.

3. On the new 2 MIDI Track in the Mixer, click on the Arm Session Recording button.

This will route incoming MIDI messages to this track so that you can see the incoming MIDI signal.

4. Play some notes between C3 and C4 on your external MIDI controller, or with the Computer MIDI Keyboard. Pressing [cmd-shift-k/ctrl-shift-k] enables this option.

You should see the track meter displaying the MIDI velocities you play. Now add an Impulse instrument so that you can hear some sounds:

Pic. 7.07: The Arm Session Recording button in the Mixer.

5. Open your Live Device Browser in the Browser. Click on the Instruments category to display a list of Live's Instrument Devices. Drag and drop the Device named Impulse from the Browser onto your new 2 MIDI track.

Several things just happened:

*   The track name changed to 2 Impulse.
*   The meter in the Mixer for this track changed from a velocity meter to an audio level meter.
*   The Impulse instrument appeared in Track View.

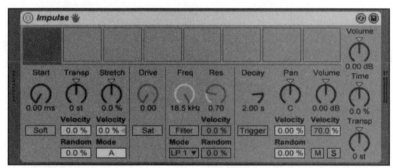

Pic. 7.08: The Impulse instrument in Track View.

You may be thinking to yourself, "What happened to my MIDI Track? Is it now an Audio Track?"

IMPORTANT! Look closely at the meters on either side of the Impulse instrument in Track View: the one to the left (before the instrument) is a MIDI velocity meter, and the one to the right (after the instrument) is an audio level meter. The instrument is the point in the signal Chain at which MIDI gesture data gets turned into an audio signal. It is still a MIDI Track, but since it has an instrument on it, it will output audio—hence the change in meters in the Mixer. You can even place Audio Effects after the instrument to further affect the sound of the instrument, which I will cover later on.

6. Rename this MIDI Track "Impulse Kit."

The Impulse Instrument

The Impulse instrument is a simple multisample player traditionally intended for working with rhythmic samples. Unlike the Simpler instrument, which plays one sample at multiple pitches, Impulse plays eight different samples each at a single pitch.

Right now, Impulse will not make any sound, but go ahead and play your controller's white keys between C3 and C4. A small green triangle flashes in each of the eight squares as you play its corresponding note.

Each of these squares is a sample slot capable of containing an audio file that can be triggered from your keyboard, and each of these slots has numerous parameters in the lower part of the interface that can shape how the sound is played back.

Let's add some sounds to these slots:

7. In the Browser, use the File Browser to find the Sounds to Sample > Kicks folder.
8. Drag the file dr_hit_all round kick.wav onto the leftmost sample slot and drop it.
9. Play C3 on your keyboard to trigger it and hear it.

Fun! Now add some additional sounds to your kit:

10. Also from the Kicks folder, drag s2s_dt_drm_kick10.wav onto the second slot.
11. From the Snares folder, drag dr_hit_old school snare.wav onto the third slot.
12. Also from the Snares folder, drag pd_clap11.wav onto the fourth slot.
13. From the Hats folder, drag Tight.wav onto the fifth slot.
14. Also from the Hats folder, drag Open 909.wav onto the sixth slot.
15. From the Percs folder, drag dr_hit_cr78 lo.wav onto the seventh slot.
16. Also from the Percs folder, drag dr_hit_clikreverb.wav onto the eighth slot.

There. Now you have a full kit of drums to play. Run your fingers up the C3 major scale to hear all these sounds from your keyboard. Alternately, letters A through K on your Computer MIDI Keyboard will do the same thing.

17. In order for these sounds to mix well with your other tracks, find the Volume dial for the Impulse in the upper right corner and take it down to –15 dB.

7.1.2—Making a MIDI Clip for Impulse by Entering Notes with Your Mouse

Unlike an Audio Clip, you can create an empty MIDI Clip and then put notes into it afterward. This can be handy when you want to build a MIDI Clip from scratch, and also when you know exactly how long a Clip you need.

18. Solo the Impulse Kit track.
19. In Session View, double-click on the first empty Clip Slot on the Impulse Kit track to create an empty MIDI Clip.

A new MIDI Clip appears in the grid with no name, and Detail View shows Clip View for your new MIDI Clip.

20. Rename the Clip "Impulse 1."

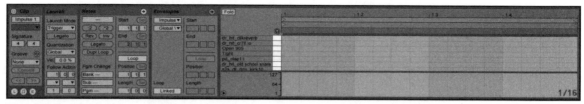

Pic. 7.09: Clip View for a new MIDI Clip.

Clip View for MIDI Clips looks remarkably like Clip View for an Audio Clip. The Clip, Launch, and Envelope boxes look almost identical to their counterparts, and where the Sample box usually is, the new Notes box has the now familiar Start, End and Loop controls on the right, plus some new controls on the left.

Perhaps the biggest change is that the Sample Editor is now replaced with the MIDI Note Editor. This is where you will create and edit MIDI performance data. You will learn about all of its controls as you go, but let's get a quick lay of the land.

Across the top of the MIDI Note Editor you see the now-familiar Beat Time ruler, Clip Start and Stop controls, and the Loop Brace, all of which function exactly the same here as they did in Audio Clips. As well, you will note the Snap to Grid value is set to sixteenth notes. All of the grid controls work exactly the same here as well.

Down the left-hand side of the editor is a column of names of the samples presently in each Impulse slot. The horizontal rows to the right of each slot name is where we will put notes to play each of these samples.

21. Enable the MIDI Editor Preview button—the headphones icon in the editor—so that you will hear notes you make in the MIDI Editor. Then click on one of the white boxes directly to the right of a sample name in the column beneath the headphones button. The corresponding sample plays. Click on the other boxes in the column to hear each of your Impulse drums.

This is a quick and easy way to preview your Impulse sounds before you place them in your Clip.

22. Now double-click on the first box in the timeline in the lower left corner. You hear your kick drum as a blue box appears on the timeline next to that slot.

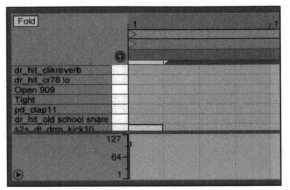

Pic. 7.10: A MIDI note in the MIDI Note Editor.

23. Solo the Impulse Kit track in the Mixer, and launch your Impulse 1 Clip in the Session View Clip grid.

The Clip loops by default, and you hear your kick drum occur on beat 1.1.1 each time it comes around.

24. With Live still playing, double-click to create more notes in the MIDI Note Editor wherever you like, and listen to your first beat emerge.

You can also double-click on a note you have made to delete it, or click-and-drag a note to move it to a different location. Have fun. Be creative!

You can also turn on Draw mode by pressing [B] to draw a series of notes in at one time, such as a hi-hat on every sixteenth note.

You may decide while you are making your beat that you no longer need to hear the notes while you create them. You can turn off MIDI Editor Preview by re-clicking on the blue headphones button. Now you will hear notes only when they are played in the timeline.

Here are a few more ways to select notes. Try them:

- Click-and-drag a selection box around MIDI notes in the MIDI Note Editor to select them.
- Click on the preview box to the right of the slot name again. If the Preview headphones are on, you hear that slot's sound again, but additionally all of the notes on that slot's row are now selected as well. This is handy for making adjustments to all the notes of one sound at the same time.
- Click-and-drag vertically in one of the preview boxes to select multiple rows of notes simultaneously.

Once you have one or more notes selected, you can drag them horizontally to move them all forward or backward in time, or drag them vertically to move the notes to play a different Impulse sound.

7.1.3—Editing MIDI Note Velocity

You may have noticed that all of the notes you are creating are playing back at exactly the same volume. Each MIDI note has a velocity value associated with it that tells the instrument how loudly or softly to play back the note. Like most MIDI parameters, the range of possible values for the Velocity setting is from 0 to 127. When you play a keyboard or drum pad that is "velocity sensitive," you create these velocity values by varying how hard you strike a key or pad. Since you have been creating notes in your Clip with the mouse thus far, Live has defaulted to creating the notes with a velocity of 100. This can sound pretty mechanical. Let's make a little variation, shall we?

Below the MIDI Note Editor is the MIDI Velocity Editor.

Pic. 7.11: The MIDI Velocity Editor.

The Velocity Editor can be resized by vertically clicking-and-dragging the gray divider between the Note Editor and the Velocity Editor. It can also be shown or hidden with the little arrow button in the lower left corner.

The Velocity Editor is a simple graph of each note's velocity from 0 to 127. Under each note you will see a vertical red line with a circle on the top of it. The circle represents the note's current velocity. You can change a note's velocity in one of three ways:

- Click-and-drag the small circle up or down in the Velocity Editor.
- Turn on Draw mode and draw in a series of velocities in the Velocity Editor.
- [Cmd-click/ctrl-click] on any note or selection of notes in the Note Editor and drag up or down.

The third technique is particularly useful when you have a bunch of notes all playing at the same time and you want to adjust the velocity for just one of them.

One quick adjustment you could make is to alter the hi-hat velocity a bit:

25. [Cmd-click/ctrl-click] on one of the notes in the Tight row, and drag its velocity downward to the 80 to 100 range. Do this for each of the Tight notes individually. Try not to make them exactly the same—variation is good.

When you have created a beat that you like, try also soloing the Beats Audio Track and triggering the first MT_Beats Clip to hear how your beat will go with that Clip. Keep it simple for now—you will add to it in the next section. Here is a simple pattern I came up with that works well with the intro section of your song. You should be able to create this pattern fairly quickly if you want to use it.

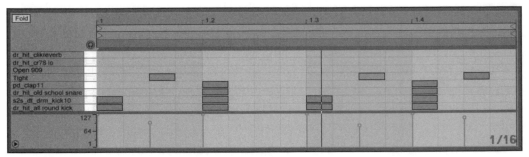

Pic. 7.12: A simple Impulse MIDI Clip beat pattern.

Now you have a good understanding of how the MIDI Note Editor and Velocity Editor work. Now try adding some notes in real time by overdubbing.

7.1.4—Recording MIDI Clips in Session View with the Computer MIDI Keyboard

The second way to make MIDI Clips is to use your computer's keyboard as a MIDI device to play notes in. The Computer MIDI Keyboard is a particularly handy feature of Live when you are using your laptop away from your MIDI controllers and you want to create some MIDI notes in real time. Aside from a lack of velocity sensitivity, pitch bend, or any other controls, the Computer MIDI Keyboard functions in the same way that a basic external controller does, and will serve as a good introduction to MIDI device routing and note entry.

26. To begin, [opt-drag/alt-drag] your Impulse 1 MIDI Clip from Slot 1 in the Intro Scene down to the empty Slot in the Add Perc Scene to copy it. Rename this Clip "Impulse 2."
27. Double-click the new Impulse 2 Clip to bring up its Clip View Properties. In the Notes box, click the Dupl Loop button.

As you might expect, Impulse 2 is now a two-bar Clip, with each of the two bars exactly the same. This function takes whatever is within the Loop Brace and duplicates it.

NEW FEATURE! There are several new MIDI note transform buttons in the Notes box in Live 9. These include a Transpose box, Halve and Double tempo buttons, Reverse and Invert notes buttons, Legatto, and the one we just used: Duplicate Loop button. To use them, you simply select the notes you want to affect and click the button. These are great for quickly adding variation to your MIDI Clips.

Pic. 7.13: The new MIDI transforms in the Note box.

28. Make sure that your track's Arm Session Recording button is still red in the Mixer, and enable your Computer MIDI Keyboard, if it is not already, by pressing [cmd-shift-k/ctrl-shift-k]. While Live is not playing, play the Impulse sounds from your computer's keyboard.

A few details about the Computer MIDI Keyboard:

- Press any of the following keys on your computer's keyboard: A, S, D, F, G, H, J, K. These keys correspond to the note equivalents of C, D, E, F, G, A, B, and C, respectively, and should trigger the drums in your Impulse.
- The W, E, T, Y, and U keys are analogous to the black keys C#, D#, F#, G#, and A#, respectively. They are not assigned to drum slots in the Impulse instrument, so they will not trigger anything right now.
- The O and L keys continue the keyboard into the next octave with another C# and D, respectively. They are also not assigned to drum slots in the Impulse instrument, so they will not trigger anything.
- You can change the octave that your Computer MIDI Keyboard is transmitting downward by octaves by using the Z key, and upward by using the X key. Do not do this right now, because the Impulse receives only notes in the one C3 octave, and you will not hear any notes play in any other octaves.
- The C and V keys respectively decrease and increase the transmitted velocity of the note keys by increments of 20.

Now you are going to add more notes to your Impulse 2 Clip using the Computer MIDI Keyboard. Adding notes to a MIDI Clip in successive passes is called *overdubbing*.

29. Double-click on your new Impulse 2 MIDI Clip in the Clip grid to make sure that you are looking at the Note Editor for that Clip.
30. Click the Session Record Button in the Control Bar.

Pic. 7.14: The Session Record button in the Control Bar.

Live starts playing your Impulse 2 Clip. Notice that the Launch button in the Impulse 2 Clip turns red. This means that you are presently recording/overdubbing to the Clip.

31. With your Impulse 2 Clip looping, play some notes on your Computer MIDI Keyboard.

The new notes are recorded into your Clip. As the Clip continues to loop, you may continue to add more layers of notes. If you don't like what you just played, press [cmd-z/ctrl-z] to undo the notes played in the previous pass of recording. Keep pressing [cmd-z/ctrl-z] to continue removing previous passes of notes you recorded.

Keep experimenting until you have added at least one new element that you like. It doesn't have to be complex or busy.

32. Stop playback.

You've successfully overdubbed some new notes onto your Impulse 2 Clip in real time! Let's clean these notes up.

7.1.5—MIDI Note Quantization

Perhaps some of your overdubbed MIDI notes were a little off the beat. Using the editing techniques from the previous exercise, you could easily move them one at a time onto the grid where you intended them to be. But there is a faster way. Live can Warp and move audio segments closer to the beat using the Quantization menu. Quantization was originally developed for tightening MIDI performances, and of course Live lets you do this.

33. Select any notes in the Note Editor that you would like to Quantize, or better yet, do not select any notes and Live will Quantize all of them.

Notes already on the beat, such as the ones you input with your mouse, will not move as a result of Quantization, as they are already 100% Quantized.

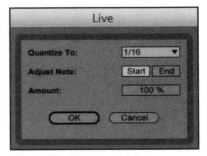

34. Open Quantization Settings by pressing [cmd-shift-u/ctrl-shift-u] or going Edit > Quantization Settings.

The Quantization Settings box allows you to determine the resolution for Quantization, whether the note's start and/or end will be Quantized, and the amount of Quantization to be applied.

Pic. 7.15: The Quantization Settings dialog box.

• 100% Quantization will move affected notes all the way to the value set in the Quantize To field, whereas a setting of 50% will move affected notes halfway to the nearest Quantize To value.
• Note Start times begin when you press the key down, and Note End occurs when you release it. You can choose to Quantize one or both of these.

Quantizing Note End times becomes much more relevant when working with sounds that have a long sustain, such as a string pad or an organ. Most drum sounds, having very short durations, will not benefit from having long note durations unless it is a crash cymbal or something similar with a long duration.

One handy setting in this dialog box is the Current Grid setting under Quantize To, which will Quantize your notes to whatever Snap to Grid value you currently have set in your Note Editor. This way, you can simply set the Note Editor grid how you want your notes to be, and then execute the Quantize function without having to come back to the Quantization Settings dialog box each time you want to Quantize.

Set your settings as follows and press OK:

- Quantize To: Current Grid
- Adjust Note: Start and End enabled
- Amount: 100%

Any notes you recorded that were off the grid are now Quantized onto the grid.

7.1.6—Record Quantization

But what if you knew what resolution of note timings you were aiming for before you ever started overdubbing? Live has a Record Quantization feature that will automatically move your notes directly to the nearest grid value as you record them. (This feature only works with MIDI recordings, not audio.)

To enable Record Quantization, go Edit > Record Quantization, and then choose the resolution you wish to record at. For now:

35. Set Record Quantization to sixteenth notes.
36. With the Impulse Kit Track's Arm Session Recording button in the Mixer still engaged, press Session Record and overdub some additional notes using the Computer MIDI Keyboard.

Notes that you play while overdubbing will now automatically land on the nearest 16th note. Handy!

Now let's put these two new Impulse Clips into the Arrangement. You can certainly record them over with Arrangement Record, but when the Arrangement gets to a more detailed state, such as it is now, I tend to want to just grab them and move them like this:

37. Click-and-drag the Impulse 1 Clip away from its current Clip grid location, as though you were going to drop it somewhere else on the Clip grid, but don't drop it. As you drag it, you see a ghost version of it following your cursor.
38. Without dropping the Clip, press [tab] to switch to Arrangement View. The ghosted Impulse 1 Clip is still following your cursor.
39. Drop the Impulse 1 Clip on the Impulse Kit Track at bar 13. Resize the Clip so that it lasts until bar 21.
40. Switch back to Session View and repeat the process for the Impulse 2 Clip, dropping it at bar 27 in the Arrangement, and extend it until bar 47.
41. Option-drag the Impulse 1 Clip at bar 13 to copy it, and drag it all the way over to bar 82. Extend it to bar 96.

You've now created two new Impulse MIDI Clips in Session View and placed them in the arrangement in Arrangement View.

MIDI Routing and Monitoring

The third method of MIDI Clip creation involves using your MIDI controller. But before you work with your external controller, you need to have a look at MIDI routing in the In/Out section.

42. To make the In/Out section visible, do one of the following:

- Press [opt-cmd-i/alt-ctrl-i].
- Go View > In/Out.
- Click on the Show/Hide In/Out Section button in the lower right corner of the Session Clip grid. (It looks like an "I-O" in a circle.)

The In/Out section handles the routing of audio and MIDI signals coming and going to and from Live's Tracks, as well as a section for selecting between three monitoring options. Whenever you plan to make a recording, whether it is audio or MIDI, you will want to check your settings here to be sure things are configured the way you want them.

The In/Out section has up to four pull-down menus for directing your track's input and output signals. From top to bottom:

Pic. 7.16: The In/Out section for a MIDI Track.

- **Input Type**—This selects what kind of device will be used for input: computer MIDI keyboard, a particular external controller, another track, and so on.
- **Input Channel**—If the selected device has multiple inputs or can transmit on multiple MIDI channels, they are listed and selectable here.
- **Output Type**—This directs the track's output. The default, Master, sends the track's output to the Master Track to be mixed with the other tracks and output to your speakers.
- **Output Channel**—If the selected device has multiple outputs, they are listed and selectable here. For external sound-generating MIDI devices, you can select what MIDI channel you are sending data to here.

The middle section handles monitoring for your Tracks. This was covered in chapter 6 in regards to audio, but there are some subtle differences here for MIDI Tracks, so read this carefully:

- **Auto**—This monitor mode is the default mode, and is the most flexible. While in Auto monitor mode, MIDI notes on your MIDI Track will be audible during playback. When you enable the Arm button on the track, and when you are recording, you will be able to monitor incoming notes played on a controller. This is the mode to use for overdubbing MIDI Clips.
- **In**—Selecting this monitor mode disables your ability to hear Clips played on the track, and instead always favors the incoming signal regardless whether you are in playback or recording. Use this setting when you need a constant input to a track, such as a rehearsal or performance keyboard, a way to put effects on an incoming signal, or for use as an auxiliary input for subgroups and Rewire inputs.
- **Off**—This mode disables monitoring of the track's incoming signal altogether. This is useful when you are monitoring your incoming signal outside of Live, such as when you are playing an external hardware synth, but recording only MIDI. If you had monitoring on, you would likely hear double MIDI notes: one directly from the synth, and one being played back (slightly later) through Live. Turning monitoring off allows you to record the MIDI data but not listen back to it through Live while recording it.

You can learn more about audio inputs, outputs, monitoring modes, and recording in chapter 6.

Let's examine the current settings for your MIDI Track, which are the defaults:

- **Input Type:** All Ins
- **Input Channel:** All Channels

Live conveniently defaults to an input type known as "All Ins" that routes any incoming MIDI signal to any armed Track. This means that if you have a keyboard controller, a drum pad controller, and the Computer MIDI Keyboard all connected and enabled for input in your Preferences, then playing a note on any of these devices will trigger notes on any Record Armed Track, or any MIDI Track whose monitoring is set to In. Most of the time, this will be the simple and easy setting to use for recording from any of your devices to a single MIDI Track one at a time. However, if you wanted to record some MIDI notes for a Simpler on one MIDI Track from a keyboard controller, and simultaneously record MIDI notes for an Impulse on another MIDI Track from a drum-pad controller, you can specify a specific input device for each track so that Live will route incoming notes appropriately.

7.1.7—Recording MIDI Clips in Arrangement View from a Controller

Let's record a performance of gestures from a MIDI controller (keyboard, drum pads, and so on). If you do not own an external MIDI controller, feel free to use the Computer MIDI Keyboard again for this exercise.

IMPORTANT! Also for this exercise I will be using the fantastic TAL Elek7ro-II shareware synthesizer that the geniuses at Togu Audio Line have been generous to let us use. You can find Elek7ro-II and many other great plug-ins at the company's website (http://kunz.corrupt.ch). Please consider making a donation to the company through its PayPal link if you continue to use Elek7ro-II or any other plug-ins from the site. The installation instructions for this third-party VST/AU synth are included in the supplemental materials under Book Content > Install, and a brief review of the included third-party devices is in the Appendix F. If you haven't already installed TAL-Elek7ro-II, take the time now to do so. You will be glad you did. Be sure to save your Set and quit Live while installing any new plug-ins. After installing it as instructed, reopen Live and this Set and continue with the exercise. If for any reason you can't get the Elek7ro-II to work, feel free to use another third-party soft synth that is compatible with Live.

43. Switch to Arrangement View.
44. Click on the Synth1 Track name to select it. Create a MIDI Track directly after it by pressing [cmd-shift-t/ctrl-shift-t].
45. Rename this new track "PannerPad."

46. Arm the track so that you will be able to play the Elek7ro-II you are about to place there.

47. In the Browser, choose the Plug-ins Category. Open the VST folder from the second column. You should see a device named TAL-Elek7ro-II. Double-click on it to place it on your new MIDI Track.

Pic. 7.17: The TAL-Elek7ro-II synth interface.

You should now see the Elek7ro-II interface.

Click on the keyboard with your mouse or play a few notes on your MIDI controller to hear the default Preset. With your mouse, turn a few knobs while you play to hear what they do. When you have experimented for a while, close the window with the Elek7ro-II in it.

In the Track View area, you will now see the generic third-party Live device interface.

The third button in the generic device's title bar looks like a wrench and is called the Plug-in Edit button. Click on this to get back to the Elek7ro-II's interface at any time. Below that is a VST Preset pull-down menu that currently reads BS Startup, the name of the Elek7ro-II's default Preset.

48. Click on the VST Preset pull-down, and scroll down the list to select PD Panner XS. Play some notes on your keyboard to hear what this Preset sounds like. If your MIDI controller has a modulation wheel, move this control while you play the notes.

Pic. 7.18: The generic third-party device interface in Track View.

The modulation wheel controls the panning rate. Sweet!

49. Play the arrangement back from the beginning, and play this patch along with what you are hearing.

The main section of the song is in A minor, so sticking to the white keys should work with what you already have.

One idea I liked the sound of was to double the Postwarvar progression between bars 27 and 57 with the new PD Panner XS Preset. It's a pretty simple two-note progression for the most part. Here is what one ten-bar progression looked like after I recorded it.

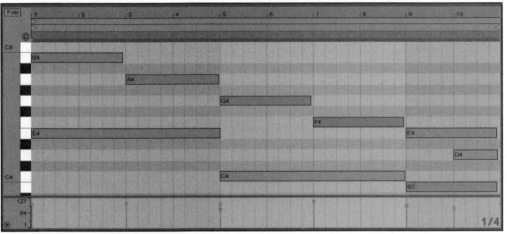

Pic. 7.19: The notes for doubling the Postwarvar progression with the PD Panner XL Preset.

Learn this if you want to, or make up something else that you like for this section. When you have something repeatable, continue with the next section to record it.

50. Place the Arrangement Loop Brace to start at bar 27 and end at 57. Instead of enabling the Loop switch in the Control Bar, enable the two switches on either side of it: the Punch-In switch and the Punch-Out switch.

The Punch switches allow you to control where recording will begin and end. You will start recording a few bars before and record until a few bars after, but the resulting MIDI Clip will be exactly 30 bars long.

51. Click in the arrangement on bar 25 of your PannerPad Track to place the playback point there, or type "25.1.1" into the Arrangement position in the Control Bar.
52. Your Record Quantize value is probably still set to sixteenth notes. If you want to change this or turn it off, go Edit > Record Quantization and select a Quantization size or No Quantization. Quarter note quantization seems like the best choice for recording the pattern pictured above.
53. Click on the Arrangement Record button, which is also engaged by pressing F9 on your computer keyboard, and get ready to record in eight beats when you reach bar 27.

When you are done, stop playback. You have just made your first MIDI recording!

If you do not like what you played, press [cmd-z/ctrl-z] to undo your last take and try again. When you have something you like, continue to the next section.

54. Double-click on the new MIDI Clip on the PannerPad Track between bars 27 and 57 to bring up the MIDI Note Editor.

Notice that instead of Impulse slots listed on the left-hand side of the Note Editor, there is now a keyboard. You can resize and scroll the keyboard by clicking-and-dragging in the Note Ruler to the left of the vertical keyboard. Your cursor changes into a magnifying glass when you put your cursor over this area.

55. Click on the Fold button in the upper left corner of the Note Editor.

The keyboard disappears and is replaced with a list of only the note names used in your Clip. This can be a handy view for editing notes. Take a moment to clean up any performance errors you may have made.

Here are a few more handy editing tricks for working with melodic content:

56. Place your cursor over the beginning of one of the notes in the Note Editor. It turns into an open square bracket, like this: [. Click-and-drag the note's start point left or right to change it.
57. Place your cursor over the end of one of the notes in the Note Editor. It turns into a closed square bracket, like this:]. Click-and-drag the note's end point left or right to change it.
58. Play back what you have.

7.1.8—Overdubbing and Editing MIDI Performance Gestures: Modulation Wheel

Let's overdub some modulation wheel gestures to this Clip to make it more interesting. To overdub MIDI notes or performance gestures in Arrangement View, there is a dedicated switch we must use called—not surprisingly—the MIDI Arrangement Overdub switch. Without this enabled, new MIDI recordings overwrite previous ones already in the Arrangement.

Pic. 7.20: The MIDI Arrangement Overdub switch in the Control Bar.

59. Click on bar 25 again on the PannerPad Track to place the Arrangement position there.
60. Make sure that the MIDI Arrangement Overdub switch is on to enable MIDI overdubbing.
61. Enable Arrangement Record.
62. When you get to bar 27, move the modulation wheel in interesting ways. It can be as subtle or as crazy as you like.

63. After you pass bar 57, recording punches out and stops. You can now stop playback as well.

Your modulation wheel moves are merged with your notes in the PannerPad MIDI Clip.

64. To view and edit this mod wheel data, double-click on the MIDI Clip you just overdubbed to bring up the MIDI Clip Note Editor, and then click on the Envelope box to make it active.

You should now be looking at a MIDI Clip Envelope that graphs the modulation wheel moves you just recorded. If you do not see the mod wheel data, do this:

65. In the Envelope box, click on the Device Chooser pull-down menu and select MIDI Ctrl.
66. Click on Control Chooser just below it and select 1 - Modulation.

The bottom of the graph represents the bottom of the mod wheel range of motion, and the top of the graph represents the top of its range. All the Breakpoint Editing techniques that work in Audio Clip Envelope editing apply here as well. You can edit the data by adding, moving, or deleting breakpoints on the Envelope, or you can switch to Draw mode and draw in any corrections you like. Be sure to turn off Snap to Grid if you want to draw smooth, non-Quantized lines.

You now have three separate ways to create MIDI Clips: with a mouse, with your Computer MIDI Keyboard, and with your external MIDI controller. You can mix and match these techniques to fit your creative needs and ability. In most other regards, MIDI Clip View parameters are much the same as their Audio Clip cousins.

7.1.9—Making MIDI Clips from Audio Clips

But wait: There's more!

Have you ever wanted to take a recorded performance of, say, a bass line, a piano riff, or a drum fill, and re-create it using a different sound or drum kit? How about the ability to sing a musical idea into a mic and then turn that into MIDI notes for playing with a synth?

NEW FEATURE! New in Live 9 is the ability to make MIDI Clips from Audio Clips! If you have used the ever-so-useful Slice to New MIDI Track feature from Live 8—which we will cover in depth later in this chapter—then these three additions will seem like the next logical step. Live can now take an audio recording and attempt to extract pitch, velocity, and timing information from which to make a new MIDI Clip. Once you have the extracted MIDI notes, you can assign any MIDI device you like to play it back.

The Convert Audio to New MIDI Track function comes in three flavors:

- **Convert Melody to New MIDI Track**—This works best on monophonic (capable of only one note at a time) instrument recordings such as a trumpet, flute, bass, or human voice.
- **Convert Harmony to New MIDI Track**—This is suited for polyphonic (capable of multiple notes at a time) instrument recordings, such as piano, guitar, organ, or a choir.

- **Convert Drums to New MIDI Track**—When working with percussion recordings, this is the best algorithm to use, and Live will do its best to put each rhythmic instrument—kick, snare, toms, hi-hat, etc.—on its own note lane so you can replace each drum individually.

Let's see it in action.

The more that we work on this song, the more I feel the need to do something to improve the MT_Bass loop. The rhythm of it is fine, but the tone is not doing it for me. Audio effects can only do so much. Let's extract the timing and pitches of the MT_Bass Clips, and have our TAL Elek7ro-II replay them using a better sound in the next Exercise.

67. In either View select the first bass Clip, MT_Bass Warp1 and do one of the following:

- [ctrl-click/right-click] on the Clip and select Convert Melody to New MIDI Track.
- Go Create > Convert Melody to New MIDI Track.

The Melody algorithm is the logical choice here, as the MT_Bass Clip has only one note playing at a time.

Once executed, you will see several things happen:

- Live creates a new MIDI Track called 5 Melody to MIDI.
- The new Track contains a MIDI Clip of the same length as the MT_Bass Audio Clip. If you look at it in the MIDI note editor, you will see note, timing and velocity information Live extracted from the Audio Clip.
- Live created a new Instrument Rack on the new MIDI Track to play the new MIDI Clip.

68. Solo and play the newly created track and Clip. For comparison, hold down [cmd/alt] and click solo on the Bass Track as well to hear both together.

Here's what Live came up with:

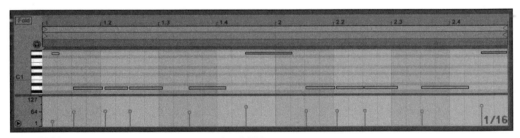

Pic. 7.21: The MT_Bass pattern converted to MIDI.

The pitches, timings, and velocities seem pretty close to the original. In the next exercise, we'll make a better bass patch to play these notes. But before we do that:

69. Delete any "extra" notes that you don't like, such as the first note in the upper left corner.
70. Rename this new MIDI Track to "Bass 2 Redo." Rename the new MIDI Clip to "MIDI MT_Bass."

71. [opt-drag/alt-drag] the MIDI MT_Bass Clip to bar 25 to copy it. Lengthen this new Clip to Bar 57. Do the same thing to copy the original Clip to bar 82, and then lengthen it to Bar 93.3. Select and delete the second half of each bar starting at bar 89 to match the MT_Bass Audio Clips above it.
72. Save your Set by pressing [cmd-s/ctrl-s].

EXERCISE 7.2—INSTRUMENT RACKS

There are four types of Racks in Ableton Live: Audio Effect Racks, Instrument Racks, Drum Racks, and MIDI Effects Racks. Racks make possible an exceptionally diverse array of creative processing, and are the key to using Live to its fullest potential.

Instrument Racks allow you to work with multiple instruments and effects together, mixing and matching all manner of devices to create complex, one-of-a-kind instruments.

With Instrument Racks, you can do the following:

- Create complex MIDI instruments with complex effects processing that can be saved as Presets for instant recall.
- Layer and split keyboard sounds from different devices.
- Map Macro controls to your favorite instrument and effects controls for real-time playability and exotic transformations.

7.2.1—Creating a Layered Instrument with Instrument Racks

DO IT!   Let's make a layered Instrument Rack!

- You can continue from right where you left off at the end of Exercise 7.1 and use Save As to save the Set as My Exercise 7.2.als, or
- You can open Exercise 7.2.als from the supplied Sets in Book Content > Book Exercises Project, and then perform a Save As and save your Set as My Exercise 7.2.als.

1. Double-click on the name of your newest MIDI Bass 2 Redo to bring up its Track View.
2. Click the title bar of the Instrument Rack in Track View—named Melody to MIDI—to select it, and then press [delete] to delete it. We are going to make our own bass Instrument Rack shortly.
3. In the Browser, click on the Plug-ins Category.
4. In the VST folder, double-click on the TAL-Elek7ro-II device to add it to your Bass 2 Redo MIDI Track.

You might be thinking, "But wait! Why didn't we start with an empty Instrument Rack from the Device Browser?" That's because I am going to show you a new shortcut:

5. Click the TAL Elek7ro-II's title bar to select it, and do one of the following to Group the device into an Instrument Rack:

- Press [cmd-g/ctrl-g].
- Go Edit > Group.
- [Ctrl-click/right-click] on the device's title bar and select Group from the contextual menu.

Group is a command that you can also perform on a series of tracks—you'll learn about that in chapter 8. But in this case, Group takes one or more selected devices and contains them in an appropriate Rack type—in this case, an Instrument Rack.

6. Make sure that the last two buttons on the left-hand side of your rack, Show Chain List and Show Devices, are enabled.
7. In the new device in Track View, click on the VST Preset pull-down menu. Select "BS Back in the 80's."
8. In the Chain list, there is currently one Chain named "TAL Elek7ro-II." Rename this Chain "Back in the 80's."
9. Solo Bass 2 Redo and play one of your MIDI bass Clips to hear this sound in action.

Rumble! Not too pretty. That is because the notes the TAL Elek7ro-II is playing are too low. Let's fix that with one of the new MIDI Note box functions:

10. Double-click the first MIDI MT_Bass Clip (not the Audio Clip above it!) on the Bass 2 Redo track to bring up its Clip View properties.
11. In the Notes box, you will see a white box with A0-G1 in it. This is the Transpose box.

Pic. 7.22: The Transpose box in the MIDI Notes box.

The Transpose box allows you to adjust the pitch of selected notes, or, if no notes are selected, the pitch of every note in the Clip. The current value, A0-G1, is telling you that this Clip's notes currently range from A0 to G1. You can adjust this range in one of several ways:

• Click-and-drag the value up or down with your mouse.
• Click on the box and type in a semitone transpose amount such as +12 for up an octave, and -24 for down two octaves.
• Click on the box and type in a new value for the lowest note in the range, such as C4, which will move the lowest note in the selection to C4 and adjust the rest of the notes accordingly. Alternately, type in a new value for the top note in the range preceded by a dash [-], such as -C7, which would set the highest note in the range to C7 and move all other notes relative to that Transpose Amount.

For our purposes:

12. Click in the transpose box and type in either +24 or A2 which will transpose all the notes of this Clip up two octaves into a more useful range.
13. Do this to all the other Bass 2 Redo MIDI Clips on the timeline one at a time, practicing all three of the transpose methods described above.

While still soloed, play the newly transposed bass Clips to hear the difference. Ah. Much better! That's a bass tone we can work with.

If you unsolo the Bass 2 Redo Track, you will then be listening to both the Audio and MIDI versions of this bass line, and they do not play well together. I'd like to hear just the new MIDI bass line from now on, but deactivating the entire Bass Track won't do, because there are other Clips on the track that I still want to hear, namely the buildup bass at bar 21, and Blu bass in the breakdown at bar 57. I could delete the MT_Bass Audio Clips from the timeline, but in case we need them again in the future, let me show you how to deactivate them instead.

14. Click on the first Audio Clip on the Bass Track which is named MT_Bass-Warp1 and then do one of the following to deactivate it:

- Press the zero [0] key on your computer keyboard.
- [ctrl-click/right-click] on the Clip and choose Deactivate Clip(s).
- In the Clip box, deactivate the yellow Clip Activator in the upper left-hand corner.

15. Deactivate the rest of the MT_Bass Audio Clips that are duplicated by MIDI Clips using one of the methods above. The timeline should now look like this:

Now only one bass sound is playing at any given time. Good.
Back to making our layered Instrument Rack:

16. From the Plug-in Device Browser, drag a second TAL-Elek7ro-II device onto the Chain List area and drop it where it says, "Drop MIDI Effects, Audio Effects, Instruments or Samples Here." A second Chain, named TAL Elek7ro-II, appears.
17. In the new Elek7ro-II device, choose the Preset "BS Rotund XS." Rename this Chain "Rotund XS."
18. Play one of the MIDI MT_Bass Clips to hear how they sound together.

Now you have two Elek7ro-II instruments stacked on top of each other, both responding to the same incoming MIDI. The two instruments stacked up make for a big, full sound. Stacking sound generators in this way is known as making a layered instrument, and it is a common technique for making complex sounds.

Let's make a few more little adjustments:

19. In the Chain list, Pan the Back to the 80's Chain to 20L, and the Rotund XS Chain to 21R using the Chain Pan boxes. This will give the sound some width.
20. Click on the Audio Effects Category in the Browser. In the list of Audio Effects, find the Saturator. Open the device to show its Presets. Double-click on the Preset Soft Shaper.

The Saturator is added *after* the entire Instrument Rack. Audio effects applied to a Chain affect only that Chain. Audio effects applied after the entire Rack affect the Rack's entire combined signal, which is what we want in this case. The Soft Shaper is adding some harmonics and controlling the overall dynamics slightly.

7.2.2—Split Keyboard Instruments and Simpler

One technique you will see performing keyboardists use is a keyboard that's split so that the lower half plays one sound played by the left hand, and the upper half plays another sound played by the right hand. Instrument Racks allow for this kind of functionality quite easily. Let's try it:

21. Make sure that your Instrument Rack on the Bass 2 Redo Track is visible.

22. In the Browser, bring up your File Browser and navigate to Sounds to Sample > Stab One Shots. Hold down [cmd/ctrl] and click on all four of the following files to multiselect them:

- s2s_stb_oneshot_2v3_Cm
- s2s_stb_oneshot_9v5_Cm
- s2s_stb_oneshot_11v1_Cm
- s2s_stb_oneshot_14v1_Cm

23. Drag these four files to your Instrument Rack and drop them on the Chain List where it says, "Drop MIDI Effects, Audio Effects, Instruments or Samples Here."

Four new Chains are created. Rename them as follows:

- 2v3
- 9v5
- 11v1
- 14v1

Click on the first of the new Chains, 2v3, to show its device.

When you drop a WAV file onto an Instrument Rack, it creates a Simpler device to play back that file. A Simpler is Live's basic sample-playback instrument, and despite what its name implies, it is quite capable.

Simpler will allow you to take a sound file and play it across the keyboard at different pitches. If you play a C3 note on your keyboard, you will hear the sound as it was originally recorded. Notes above C3 will play the sound higher and faster, and notes below C3 will be lower and slower, repitching sound much the way a record player does, but one note at a time. Additionally, Simpler has a whole host of variables for changing the playback of the sound each time it is triggered.

If you play back your looped Clip, you will hear a great big mess as your bass line is now played by six Chains at once! Not what we want.

Above the Chain List are four buttons: Key, Vel, Chain, and Hide. These each reveal (or hide) a Zone Editor.

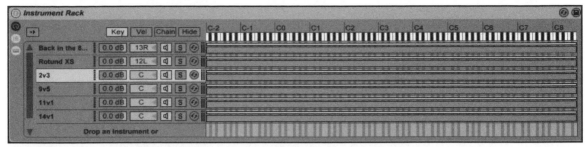

Pic. 7.25: The Key Zone Editor in an Instrument Rack.

24. Click on the Key button, which is the Show Key Zone Editor button.

The Key Zone Editor displays which Chains respond to which range of incoming MIDI notes. Currently, the six green bars impart that all six Chains are set to receive incoming notes across the entire keyboard range. Let's change that:

25. Click on the Back to the 80's Chain name in the Chain List to select it. Shift-click on the second Chain name, Rotund XS, to multiselect them both.
26. In the Key Zone Editor, put your cursor over the right-hand edge of the green bar. Your cursor should change into a closed Resize Bracket, like this:]. Click-and-drag the end of the green key zone to the left until it reads B4.
27. Click on the 2v3 Chain in the Chain List. Shift-click on the last Chain, 14v1, to multiselect the last four Chains.
28. In the Key Zone Editor, place your cursor over the left-hand edge of one of the lower four green bars. Your cursor changes into the open Resize Bracket: [. Click-and-drag the lowest four key zones from C2 to C5.

By doing this, the first two Chains—the bass Instruments—will respond only to incoming notes from C–2 to B4, and the last four Chains—the stabs—will respond only to incoming notes from C5 to G8.

29. Play one of your MIDI MT_Bass Clips again.

Now only the bass Chains play again. Note that the Key Zone editor's mini keyboard shows which notes are being triggered to help you visualize your key zones.

Let's add some notes for the One Shots to respond to:

30. Double-click the MIDI MT_Bass Clip starting at bar 13 to bring up its Note Editor.
31. In the Note Editor, add a C5 note at 1.4.4 and a C6 note at 2.4.4, like this:

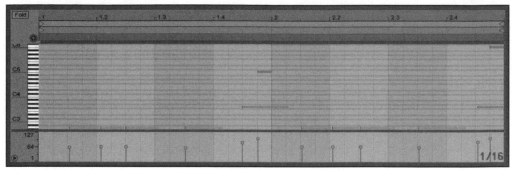

Pic. 7.26: Two new One Shot notes in the Note Editor.

32. Play the Clip.

These two new notes play the Simplers in Chains 3 through 6, while the A2 and G3 notes are played by the Elek7ro-II Chains. You now have a keyboard split that allows you to play different Chains with different parts of the keyboard.

However, while the new notes are in the range of the Simplers, the stabs are pitched up very high and sound thin. You can change which octave the Simpler notes play in using the Simpler's Transpose parameter:

33. First, hide the Key Zone Editor by clicking on the Hide button above the Chain List. This will give you more room to work on your Simplers.
34. Click on the 2v3 Chain to show its devices. Find the Transp (Transpose) value box in the Chain's Simpler. (It is above the Detune box and beneath the Sustain dial.)
35. Click-and-drag in the box to adjust it, or click on it and type in a value of –24 st (semitones). This will make the Simpler transpose its sound down two octaves from the note it receives.
36. Do this for the three remaining stab Chains: 9v5, 11v1, and 14v1.

Okay! Now the incoming notes from the MIDI Clips at C5 and C6 play these sounds as if they were at C3 and C4. They sound fuller in this range.

COOL!   If you extrapolate from here, you can imagine making an Instrument Rack having 128 different keyboard zones, one for each note, where each zone would play one or more Chains. You could make that, but you will soon learn that Drum Racks do exactly that. More on that in the next exercise.

7.2.3—Velocity Splits

In the same way that you just split your incoming notes by key zones, you can also split incoming notes by velocity zones, where notes of a certain velocity range are played by one or more Chains, and the rest by one or more other Chains. Let's do this:

37. In the MIDI Note Editor of the first MIDI MT_Bass Clip, decrease the velocity of the C5 note at 1.4.4 to something less than 64.
38. Press [shift-tab] to switch to the Track View, where your Instrument Rack is.
39. Press the Vel button above the Chain List, which is the Show Velocity Zone Editor button.

The Velocity Zone Editor works in a similar way, but this time with regard to incoming note velocities. Currently, all six zones respond to all 128 different velocities. Let's make it more interesting:

40. Adjust the red bar on the 2v3 Chain so it responds only to velocities 64 to 128.
41. Adjust the red bar on the 9v5 Chain so it responds only to velocities 1 to 63.
42. Adjust the red bar on the 14v1 Chain so it also responds only to velocities 1 to 64.
43. Play the Clip.

Now you hear three of the Chains play on the first note and two play on the second.

COOL!   This is a fairly simple use of velocity splitting, but you can do a lot with this feature: imagine that you have 16 recordings of the same kick drum played at 16 different intensities, from soft to hard. You can make an Instrument Rack with 16 Chains of Simplers that play the first sample at velocities 1 through 15, the second sample at velocities 16 through 31, and so on. This makes for a very convincing kick drum instrument that responds to how hard you play it, just the way a real kick drum does. This technique is called *multisampling*. You can buy multigigabyte sample libraries of multisampled pianos, for example, that have each note sampled at 128 different velocities! Who says MIDI can't sound realistic?

Let's add a Ping Pong Delay Device to one of the Chains for interest:

44. Click the Hide button to Hide the Velocity Zone Editor.
45. Click on the 2v3 Chain to display its devices. Navigate to the Ping Pong Delay device in the Audio Effects Category of the Browser. Drag the Ping Pong Delay from the browser and drop it after the Simpler on the 2v3 Chain. Adjust the device's parameters like so:

- Center Frequency: 1.50 kHz, Bandwidth: 1.50.
- Click on the Sync button to change it to Time, and set the Ms Delay time to 381 ms.
- Feedback: 75%, Dry/Wet: 75%.

46. Using the magnifier on the Beat Time Ruler, Zoom all the way out to see your entire timeline.
47. [Option-drag/alt-drag] the MIDI MT_Bass Clip to the right to copy it. Drop it so that the duplicate starts at bar 27. Lengthen this new duplicate to end at bar 57, overwriting the previous MIDI Clip exactly.
48. [Option-drag/alt-drag] the same MIDI MT_Bass Clip at bar 13 all the way over to bar 82. Shorten it to end at bar 89.3.

As I listen back to bars 27 to 57, however, I am not liking the One Shot stabs there: they seem to clash with the Postwarvar Clips. As it turns out, you can deactivate notes as well as Clips:

49. Double-click on the MIDI Clip from bar 27 to 57 to show its Clip View properties and the Note Editor.
50. [Ctrl-click/right-click] on the C6 note at 2.4.4 and choose Deactivate Note(s) from the contextual menu.

If you want to deactivate a series of notes on the same key, you can do the following:

51. Click on the C5 note in the vertical piano roll of the MIDI Note Editor to select all the C5 notes (just one in this case). Now [ctrl-click/right-click] on the same C5 note in the piano roll, and select Deactivate Note(s) from the (very small) contextual menu.
52. Play the Clip.

Bingo. Now you have the bass notes playing without the One Shots for the entire Clip.

7.2.4—Configuring Third-Party Instrument Device Parameters

With Instrument Racks, using Macro control dials becomes even more fun than with Effects racks, because you are augmenting the performance capabilities of your instrument. Given that you can map just about any parameter from any device in your rack, you can dramatically increase the playability of your instruments.

Mapping parameters to Macro dials is exactly the same in an Instrument Rack as it is in an Audio Effect Rack. The only new twist you need to learn about is how to map controls of a non-Live-specific third-party VST instrument, such as the TAL-Elek7ro-II. Looking at the Elek7ro-II plug-in interface, there are a plethora of knobs to play with, but the generic third-party VST Device seems to have only an *x-y* controller. How would you go about assigning more of the Elek7ro-II's controls to a Macro dial? Fear not: there are a few additional steps, but it is still quite straightforward. Let's take it one step at a time.

We'll go through the following steps:

- Configure a third-party VST parameter for control in Live.
- Assign two controls to the device's *x-y* controller.
- Map parameters to Macro control dials.

Let's get started:

53. View the Instrument Rack on the Bass 2 Redo Track. If either the Key Map or the Velocity Zone Map is showing, click on the Hide button to hide it.
54. Click on the Back to the 80's Chain in the Chain List to show its Elek7ro-II device.

Of the three buttons in the Elek7ro-II's title bar, you've already used the Plug-in Edit button that looks like a wrench, and the one to the far left you already know is the Device Activator. The middle button that looks like a triangle is the Unfold Device Parameters button.

55. Click on the Unfold Device Parameters button in the Elek7ro-II's title bar.

You are presented with a new button, Configure, and a message that says "To add plug-in parameters to this panel, click on the Configure button." Sounds like a plan!

56. Click on the Configure mode button in the Elek7ro-II's title bar.

The Elek7ro-II interface pops up and the Configure button turns green. Any parameter in the Elek7ro-II that you click on will appear in the device's sidebar and will then be available for control in Live.

57. Click once on the following controls in the Elek7ro-II to add them to the device's sidebar:

- Filter: Cutoff, Resonance
- Mixer: Tune, Noise
- LFO 1: Rate, Intensity
- LFO 2: Rate, Intensity
- Sub: Semi

58. Click on Configure again to exit Configure mode.

Pic. 7.27: A third-party device's parameters configured for automation or Macro assignment.

You now have nine controls available for manipulation, automation, or mapping to Macro dials. Let's try the simplest, and one of the most fun mappings, to the assignable *x-y* controller.

Beneath the assignable *x-y* controller are two pull-down menus of any control you configured to the sidebar in the previous step.

59. Click on the left pull-down menu and select Cutoff from the list.

This assigns the *x*-axis parameter to Filter Cutoff.

60. Click on the right pull-down menu and select Resonance from the list.

This assigns the *y*-axis parameter to Filter Resonance.

61. Play your Clip and move the yellow dot on the *x-y* controller up, down, left, and right with your mouse.

Easy and fun! You can do this with any two parameters you like. Third-party effects plug-ins work the same way.

62. Now, repeat the same configuration steps above for the Rotund XS Elek7ro. You do not need to assign any controls to its assignable *x-y* controller—just configure the same nine parameters.

When you have configured the nine same controls for the second device, continue to the next step.

7.2.5—Instrument Rack Macro Control Mappings

Time to configure your Macro controls! Ready?

63. Show the Macro controls with the Show/Hide Macro Controls button on the far left side of the Instrument Rack. It is just beneath the Rack's Device Activator button, and should be the only button that is still deactivated at this point.
64. Now that it is visible, click on the Map Mode button in the Instrument Rack's title bar.

The Map Mode button and many of the available controls turn green and are ready for mapping. Instrument Racks use the same process as Audio Effect Racks:

- Click on a green control.
- Click on the Map button under the dial you want to map it to.

Here is our list of mappings. It will be faster and easier to map all of one Elek7ro-II's controls, and then go back and do the second one in exactly the same way, rather than switch back and forth for each Macro mapping:

- Map Cutoff to Macro 1 on both Elek7ro-II devices.
- Map Resonance to Macro 2 on both Elek7ro-II devices.
- Map LFO1 Rate and LFO1 Intensity to Macro 3 on both Elek7ro-II devices.
- Map LFO2 Rate and LFO2 Intensity to Macro 4 on both Elek7ro-II devices.
- Map Master Pitch to Macro 5, and make the Min: 0.50 and the Max: 1.00 on both Elek7ro-II devices.
- Map Noise Volume to Macro 5, and make the Min: 0.00 and the Max: 0.40 on both Elek7ro-II devices.
- Map OSC3 Tune to Macro 5, and make the Min: 1.00 and the Max: 0.00 on both Elek7ro-II devices.
- Rename the Macros Dials by clicking on their name and then pressing [cmd-r/ctrl-r] and naming them "CUTOFF," "RESO," "LFO 1," "LFO 2," and "MIND BENDER," respectively. Color the Dials if you like by [ctrl-clicking/right-clicking] on each one and selecting a color from the contextual menu.

Whew!

65. Play the Clip and turn some Macro dials!

And for serious playability, tweak the Macro dials with knobs on your controller. If your controller is a natively supported device, you should not need to do any additional mapping: just click on the title bar of the rack to select it and turn knobs on your controller. They should map automatically to any selected device. If your controller is not natively supported, enter MIDI Map mode and map the Macro dials to knobs or faders on your controller first.

Super cool. And this Instrument Rack does not even have any effects mapped yet! Nor did you map any of the Simpler's controls! I'll let you explore those possibilities…

66. Save your Set by pressing [cmd-s/ctrl-s].

EXERCISE 7.3—DRUM RACKS

A Drum Rack is like an Impulse and an Instrument Rack mashed together into one. If you know what an Akai MPC2000 is, a Drum Rack is like one of those—on steroids!—with all the convenience of a plug-in. Drum Racks are the ultimate drum machine, but they can be used for all kinds of things. And if you own any kind of MIDI drum pad controller, prepare to be very excited!

7.3.1—Making a Basic Drum Rack

DO IT!   Drum Racks, Here We Come!

- You can continue from right where you left off at the end of Exercise 7.2 and use Save As to save the Set as My Exercise 7.3.als, or
- You can open Exercise 7.3.als from the supplied Sets in Book Content > Book Exercises Project, and then perform a Save As and save your Set as My Exercise 7.3.als.

For starters, let's make a basic Drum Rack.

1. Select the Beats Track by clicking on its name.
2. Create a new MIDI Track.
3. Open the Instruments Category in the Browser, and double-click on Drum Rack to place it on the new MIDI Track.
4. Rename the track "Perc Rack."

You are now looking at a four by four grid of Drum Rack pads. Each pad represents a single MIDI note, the name of which appears on the pad. On the left-hand side of the interface is the Pad Overview: the black square indicates the current octave. Click-and-drag the black square and the pad names change to the currently selected octave. In all, you have

128 drum pads to assign sounds to. So, a Drum Rack is like an Instrument Rack with a different sample or synth on every note! Let's add a few sounds:

5. In the Browser, head over to Sounds to Sample > Percs.
6. Multiselect "pd_perc_3.wav" through "Washy 5.wav," ten samples in all.
7. Drag the multiselected list of samples onto the Drum Rack pads, and hover over pad

Pic. 7.28: An empty Drum Rack Device.

C1. You will see an orange outline specifying which ten pads the samples will occupy when you drop them. Drop them onto the C1 pad.

The ten samples occupy the first ten pads from C1 on up to A1. Each occupied pad now has a mute, preview, and solo button, and if you put your cursor over the pad, a Hot-Swap button also shows up.

Let's play your Drum Rack from a controller:

8. Arm your Perc Rack MIDI Track with the Arm for Arrangement Recording button so that you can send some MIDI notes to the track.
9. Play your Drum Rack with your MIDI controller, or use the Computer MIDI Keyboard. (Press the [z] key twice to put the Computer MIDI Keyboard in the C1 octave to play the Rack. You will see the corresponding pads in the Pad Overview light up as you play.)

You now have an instrument that will play your sounds. It's that simple. It's a lot like an Impulse so far, right? But wait: there's more! Let's see what is going on beneath the hood:

10. Enable the Show/Hide Chain List and Show/Hide Devices buttons on the left-hand edge of the Drum Rack.

Much like the Audio Effect Rack and Instrument Rack, a Drum Rack utilizes multiple parallel Chains. In the case of a Drum Rack, each pad has its own Chain. Select any pad or Chain, and you are presented with a Simpler instrument with that pad's sound file loaded. Much like an Impulse Instrument, you can tweak parameters for each sound individually. Let's do something you can't do with an Impulse:

11. In the Browser, go into Audio Effects and find the Grain Delay. Open it, find the Preset Minor Third Up, and drop it onto the Washy 4 pad.
12. Play the A3 key from your controller or click on the Washy 4 preview button to hear it.

Ah ha! Every pad can have its own set of Audio Effects! That is because every pad has its own Chain. But wait: there's more!

13. Switch to Session View, and find the Perc Rack Track.

14. Next to its name in the Track title bar you will see a little arrow. This is the Chain Mixer Fold button. Click on it.

Wow! The Drum Rack Track unfolds, and now you have a channel strip for every pad. All the basic adjustments like volume, pan, and solo/mute control the same parameters in the Chain List, so this is just another (very cool) way of visualizing that information. Feel free to adjust the Chain Volume and Chain Pan settings for each Chain as you see fit. I left the volumes alone but randomized the pans for all of the Chains.

But wait! There's even more! (Does it feel like a late-night television commercial yet?)

On the left-hand side of the Drum Rack, you may have noticed that there are a few new buttons at the bottom that were not on the Audio Effect Rack or the Instrument Rack. These four buttons consist of the following:

- **IO: Show/Hide Input/Output section**—Yes, a Drum Rack has its own In/Out section. Use this section for routing incoming pad notes to play a particular note on that pad's device.
- **S/R: Show/Hide Sends, Show/Hide Returns**—Yes, a Drum Rack has its own Send and Return effects loops.
- **Dashed Arrow: Auto Select**—When this button is engaged, playing any pad will also select its Chain in the Chain List and show its devices. This is handy for doing some quick pad-by-pad device editing.

Let's make an effects loop on the Drum Rack:

15. Enable the R button to show the Drum Rack's Return Chains area.

A new area appears in the lower half of the Chain List. This is the Return Chain List. Let's do as it says and drop an Audio Effect here:

16. In the Audio Effects Category in the Browser, find the Reverb Device, open it, open the Room folder, drag the Wooden Room Preset, and drop it on the lower half of the Chain List, known as the Return Chain List area, in the Drum Rack.
17. Enable the rack's Show/Hide Sends button (S) to see the Chain Send level on each Chain.

You have a new Chain Send Level column in the Chain List, and a new Chain Send Level box in the Sends section of the Session View Mixer. Let's set all of the Chain Send levels at once:

18. In the Session View Mixer, click on the Track title bar of the first of the Drum Rack's Chains, pd_perc_3, to select it. Shift-click on the Washy 4 Chain Track title to multiselect all of the Chains. (Do not include the Wooden Room Chain—that is the Return Chain.) Click in the Send Level box and type in –10, or click-and-drag in the box to change the value. All of the Send values change at once.
19. Play your controller to hear the reverb on the percussion samples.
20. When you are done, disable the Perc Rack's Chain Mixer Fold button so the track is back to a single column.

Not bad!

You may have noticed that you have not created a pattern to play the Drum Rack yet. You will do that in the last section of Exercise 7.3.

7.3.2—Slice to New MIDI Track (Drum Rack)

Yet another jaw-dropping feature of Live is the Slice to New MIDI Track feature. Let's say you have a drum loop that you like the groove of, but you don't like all of the sounds. What if you could replace one or more of the sounds in the loop? Or better yet, what if you could make a drum kit out of all the sounds in the drum loop and make your own beat out of it? Slice to New MIDI Track to the rescue! You are going to do all that and more!

I like the beat_reaktored_90 Audio Clip a lot, but it gets a little boring after 16 bars or more. Let's glitch it out a bit.

21. In Arrangement View, find the beat_reaktored_90 Audio Clip on the Beats Track that starts at bar 57 and ends at bar 78. Select it by clicking once on it. It turns blue.
22. [Ctrl-click/right-click] on the beat_reaktored_90 Audio Clip, and choose Slice to New MIDI Track from the contextual menu, or go Create > Slice to New MIDI Track.

A dialog box appears. This is one of those dialog boxes that will be easier to understand the second time you see it. For now:

23. Set the Create One Slice Per pull-down to Transient, and the Slicing Preset to Built-in. Press OK.

After displaying a quick progress bar, Live creates a new MIDI Track below the Beats Track named beat_reaktored_90, and there is a new MIDI Clip on the track from bar 57 to 61, which is one loop length of the beat_reaktored_90 Clip.

24. Rename the new sliced MIDI Clip as "beat_reaktored_sliced." While you are at it, rename the new MIDI Track as "Sliced."
25. Double-click on the new beat_reaktored_sliced MIDI Clip to bring up its Note Editor.

It looks like the following:

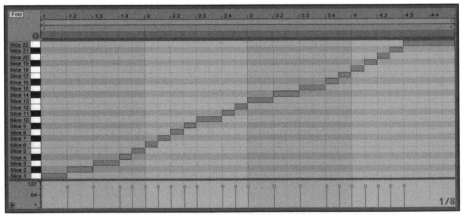

Pic. 7.29: The beat_reaktored_sliced MIDI Clip's Note Editor.

"What the heck is that chromatic scale all about?" Wait for it…

26. Solo the new Sliced MIDI Track.
27. Select the new beat_reactored_sliced MIDI Clip on the timeline and press [cmd-l/ctrl-l] in order to loop bars 57 to 61, and play the new MIDI Clip.

"Hey! That sounds just like the original beat_reacktored_90 Audio Clip!" Yes it does. Let's find out how Live did that.

Notice that the keys of the Note Editor piano roll are named as Slices 1 through 22.

28. Press [shift-tab] to switch from Clip View to Track View.

Now you are looking at a Drum Rack populated by 22 slices—the same slices you saw in the piano roll.

29. Play the Clip and watch each of the slices/Drum Rack pads get triggered sequentially.
30. Double-click on the Slice 1 pad to bring up its device Chain.

As before, you see a Simpler device, and it has the entire beat_reaktored_90 sample loaded, but this pad's Simpler has the start and end times set so that it plays only the first kick drum of the sample.

31. Click on the Slice 2 pad.

You see the very same thing on this pad, except that it plays only the second kick drum in the sample. The third slice/pad plays only the snare, and so on throughout the entire beat, creating 22 slices and pads.

So, this should all be starting to make some sense now: Slice to New MIDI Track takes an Audio Clip and slices it up by its various transients—since Transient is what you chose in the Slice to New MIDI Track dialog box—into a new Drum Rack of Simplers, each one playing its own chunk of the overall sample. Additionally, Live makes a new MIDI Clip that plays each of those Drum Rack pads in order, thereby re-creating the original beat played by Simplers. All very cool.

But here is where things really start to get interesting! Because each of the transients can now be triggered individually, you can make any beat you want with these samples. You can rearrange some of the MIDI notes to create some variation or make a new beat entirely.

7.3.3—Glitching up a Slice to New MIDI Track Beat

Now let's try three simple ways to restructure your beat_reaktored_90 beat to get your creative juices flowing. We'll do the following:

- Manually move the MIDI notes around and use some of the new MIDI Notes box transforms.
- Adjust the Drum Rack's Macro dials.
- Add a Beat Repeat Audio Effect after the Drum Rack.

But before we do:

32. In the Arrangement View, [ctrl-click/right-click] on the original beat_reaktored_90 Audio Clip on the Beats Track and choose Deactivate Clip(s).
33. Click on the beat_reaktored_sliced Clip on the Arrangement timeline to select it. Duplicate the Clip four times by pressing [cmd-d/ctrl-d] four times.
34. Extend the last duplicate's length by two bars so that it ends at bar 79.
35. Multiselect the five MIDI Clips from bar 57 to 79 with [shift-click]. Press [cmd-l/ctrl-l] to loop these bars in the Arrangement.

Okay. Now we can try some glitching methods. Here we go.

Method 1:

36. Double-click on the first beat_reaktored_sliced MIDI Clip starting at bar 57 to bring up its Note Editor. In the second half of the Clip, move three notes of your choosing up or down by a random amount to assign them to another Drum Rack pad/slice.
37. Double-click on the second MIDI Clip starting at bar 61. Click on one of the notes in the middle and duplicate it four times using [cmd-d/ctrl-d]. Do this again to two more random notes.
38. Double-click on the third MIDI Clip starting at bar 65. Select any four notes by dragging a box around them. In the Clip View Notes box, click the Play at Double Tempo button (:2). Immediately after doing this, duplicate the (still selected) double-speed notes to fill in the gap.
39. Double-click on the fourth MIDI Clip starting at bar 69. Select the second half of the pattern, and then in the Clip View Notes box, click the Invert Notes button (Inv).
40. Double-click on the fifth MIDI Clip starting at bar 73. Select a chunk of eight random notes, and click the Reverse Notes button (Rev) in the Clip View Notes box.
41. Play back the entire range of Clips from 57 to 79.

Moving notes to different slices will obviously change which pad plays. The rhythm is maintained, but the drum is different. Duplicating a note makes a little stuttering roll on that slice. The three transforms in the Notes box are fairly self-explanatory.

Method 2:

Did you see that the beat_reaktored_90 Drum Rack has Macro control dials already mapped? These dials are mapped to the same parameter in every Simpler in the rack, so adjusting the dial adjusts the parameter for every Simpler. These controls make for some amazing transformations.

42. While the five Clips play, adjust the Macro dials. Try all the combinations you can think of.

Method 3:

43. In the Browser, in Audio Effects, find the Beat Repeat device, open it up, and drag the Semisubtle Preset to the space *after* the Drum Rack.
44. Play the Clips.

The Beat Repeat device is great for adding some randomness to a Clip, particularly to a drumbeat. Feel free to play with the device's settings to see what it does. You can always return to the Semisubtle settings by dragging the Preset from the Browser onto the Beat Repeat Device, or by using Hot-Swap to reselect the Preset.

7.3.4—Play the Percussion Drum Rack with Another Track's MIDI Clip

You may recall that you never came up with a MIDI Clip to play your percussion Drum Rack that is now on Track 3. Sometimes creative opportunities present themselves in unexpected places. Try doing the following:

45. Find the first beat_reaktored_sliced Clip at bar 57 on the Sliced Track. [Opt-drag/alt-drag] the Clip directly down to the Perc Rack Track below to copy it.
46. Rename the new duplicate Clip "Perc_reaktored_sliced." Change its Clip color.
48. Double-click on the Clip to bring up the Note Editor. Move the Clip Start marker to the right by an eighth note, to 1.1.3. Bring the Loop End marker to 2.4.1
47. Extend the length of the Clip to bar 79.

By moving the start marker by an eighth note, the Perc_reaktored_sliced samples are now syncopated against the beat_reaktored_sliced notes, and by shortening the loop length to seven beats in length, the Perc Rack pattern will rarely repeat in the same way against the Sliced pattern. This makes it sound a bit more interesting, more like a tabla would be played, and allows it to compete to a lesser degree with the heavy-hitting drum slices.

Drum Racks are a wonder, aren't they?

48. Save your Set by pressing [cmd-s/ctrl-s].

EXERCISE 7.4—MIDI EFFECTS

You've looked at Instrument Devices and Audio Effect Devices. The only one left unexplored at this point is MIDI Effects.

When you look at a MIDI Instrument Device, you will notice that the left, or incoming, level meter on the device is a MIDI velocity meter, and that the meter on the right, or outgoing, meter is an audio level meter. This is because the instrument is the point at which the MIDI data is turned into audio. If the MIDI Track outputs to an external hardware MIDI sound generator, then the point of transformation from MIDI to audio happens there, but the idea is the same.

Therefore, MIDI Effects must go on a MIDI Track *before* a MIDI Instrument Device, or on a MIDI Track that outputs to an external MIDI device, while the signal is still MIDI. The MIDI Effect manipulates the MIDI data from a MIDI Clip before it reaches the sound generator, thus altering what the instrument is instructed to play. Conversely, Audio Effects go after an instrument, and they affect the instrument's output audio.

Once you understand this, MIDI Effects are fairly straightforward to use. You simply drop them on a MIDI Track—before an Instrument—to modify what your instrument will play. Let's try a few.

7.4.1—Adding a Random MIDI Effect to the Sliced Track to Create Variations

DO IT!   Time to rock the MIDI Effects!

- You can continue from right where you left off at the end of Exercise 7.3 and use Save As to save the Set as My Exercise 7.4.als, or
- You can open Exercise 7.4.als from the supplied Sets in Book Content > Book Exercises Project, and then perform a Save As and save your Set as My Exercise 7.4.als.

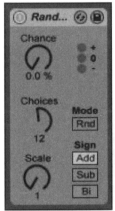

The first thing you will do uses a simple MIDI Effect called Random, and you will use it to further randomize the notes played by the beat_reaktored_sliced MIDI Clip. Can you ever have too much glitchiness? I think not.

1. In the Browser, find and select the MIDI Effects category.
2. Drag the Random device from the Browser and drop it anywhere on the Sliced Track.

The Sliced Track View opens and the Random Device is inserted before the Drum Rack.

The Random MIDI Effect is a pretty straightforward device that has just a few controls, and it can be used subtly or it can turn a performance completely inside out.

Pic. 7.30: The Random MIDI Effect.

- Like Beat Repeat, it has a chance percentage dial that dictates the probability that a particular MIDI note's pitch will be randomized.
- If a note is chosen for randomization, the Choices dial determines how many random choices there are to choose from. A setting of 1 will allow only the original pitch as a choice, whereas a setting of 10 allows for ten multiples of the Scale setting to be chosen.
- The Scale dial determines the scale interval of the random notes available. A setting of 1 means that the steps are chromatic, while a setting of 12 means octaves of the incoming note are the only available scale choice. A Choice of 3 and a Scale of 12 would allow the incoming note, a note one octave in difference, and a third note two octaves in difference to be the available random note options.
- Add, Sub, and Bi determine if the random pitch jump is upward, downward, or either.
- Rnd mode selects notes randomly from the available random pitches, and Alt selects them sequentially.

Here are some settings I thought worked well for the Sliced Track:

- Chance: 20%, Choices: 6, Scale: 1.
- Mode: Rnd, Sign: Bi.

This means that there is a 20% chance that a note one to six slices above (ahead of) or below (behind) the current slice will play instead of the one indicated in the MIDI Clip. This gives the Clip an additional amount of variation that is still within the realm of something a drummer might play. Crank the Chance dial up to 100%, and suddenly you've moved from Dubstep to Free Jazz!

7.4.2—Adding an Arpeggiator to the PannerPad Track

An Arpeggiator takes incoming MIDI notes or chords of notes and plays rhythmic and melodic variations of them in a pattern. It can add movement to an otherwise stagnant melody or series of chords. Arpeggiators are a staple of dance music.

Take the Postwarvar Clip on the Synth 1 Track: this was almost certainly made with an Arpeggiator triggering sixteenth-note pulses of the same held chords you used on the PannerPad Clip. The two sound good together, but let's add some pulse to the PannerPad to make it even tighter with the Postwarvar Clip.

3. In the Live Device Browser, open the MIDI Effects folder, find the Arpeggiator device, and open it. Drag and drop the Classic UpDown 8th Preset onto the PannerPad Track.
4. Solo only the PannerPad and Synth 1 Tracks.
5. Loop bars 27 to 57.
6. Play it.

Pic. 7.31: The Arpeggiator MIDI Effect.

It sounds okay. You'll need to make a few revisions to this Preset and to the PD Panner XS Preset to make it more like the Postwarvar Clip:

7. In the Arpeggiator's Style pull-down, select the Thumb Up style. (It currently reads UpDown.)
8. Set the Rate dial to 1/16. This will make the repeating notes happen every sixteenth note instead of every eighth note.
9. Set the Gate dial to 70%. This controls the length of each triggered note—in this case the note length will be 70% of a sixteenth note.
10. Under the Retrigger section, select the Note button. This will make the Thumb Up pattern start over every time a new note is played.

The attack and the release for this Elek7ro-II Preset are long and pad-like. Let's shorten both to get more of a pulse and less of a wash:

11. Click on the Plug-in Edit button in the title bar of the TAL-Elek7ro-II instrument. It is the one that looks like a wrench.
12. In the Elek7ro-II's interface, find the Envelopes section. Turn the Attack and the Release knobs counterclockwise as far as they can go, down to off. Set the Decay and Sustain knobs at about half, or straight up. While you're at it, in the synth's Mixer section, turn the Volume knob up to about 11 o'clock to balance it with the Synth1 track.

Ahh. That's better!

7.4.3—MIDI Effects Racks and the Chain Selector

Here we are at the last of the four rack types: MIDI Effects Racks. Now that you have made it through the other three types of racks, MIDI Effects Racks will seem quite familiar to you. However, there is one feature of Audio Effect Racks and Instrument Racks that I did not cover previously—the Chain Selector—that I will cover now in MIDI Effects Racks that will allow you to use all three of these racks in a whole new way. It is a slightly more advanced concept, and I wanted to cover the core concepts of racks a few times before I threw Chain selection into the mix. Be assured that the way you use Chain selection here works exactly the same way with the other two racks that support it, and can be used with those devices in a similar fashion.

For this MIDI Effects Rack, you are going to make several different Chains with different Arpeggiators on them, and then use a Macro control to switch between the Chains in real time.

13. Double-check that bars 27 to 57 are still looping in the Arrangement.
14. Now find the MIDI Effects Rack device in the Live Device Browser, inside the MIDI Effects folder. Drag this device onto the Bass 2 Redo Track and drop it.

The empty MIDI Effects Rack is automatically inserted before the Instrument Rack that is already on the track, since that is the point in the signal Chain where the signal is still MIDI data.

15. Turn on all three Show/Hide buttons on the left-hand side of the rack so that you can see the Macro dials, the Chain List, and each Chain's Devices.
16. In the Chain List, there are currently no Chains. [ctrl-click/right-click] in the Chain list area and Choose "Create Chain." Use [cmd-d/ctrl-d] to duplicate this Chain three more times so that you have four Chains in the Chain List. Rename the first Chain "Straight."
17. In the Browser, in the MIDI Effects Category, open the Arpeggiator device's Preset list. Drag-and-drop the Preset Classic UpDown 8th onto the second Chain in the MIDI Effects Rack's Chain List. In the new Arpeggiator device, click on the Sync button to change it to Free, and set the Rate dial to 249 ms. Rename this second device Chain as "Funky."

18. From the Live Device Browser, drag-and-drop the Arpeggiator's Housier Than Thou Preset onto the third Chain in the Chain List. Rename this Chain as "Housey."

19. Drag-and-drop the Arpeggiator's Ubiquitous Preset onto the fourth and last Chain in the Chain List. Rename this Chain "Ubiquitous."

If you play the Bass 2 Redo Clip from the timeline, the MIDI notes will play through all four Chains and be arpeggiated by three of them in different ways simultaneously. What you want is to be able to select from each of the different Arpeggiator Chains one at a time. To do this you will use the Chain Selector.

20. Above the Chain List, click on the Chain button, which is the Show Chain Select Editor button.

It is directly to the right of the Key and Vel buttons, which you have used previously. Enabling this button opens the Chain Select Editor.

Pic. 7.32: The Chain Select Editor.

This editor looks very much like the Key Zone Editor and the Velocity Zone Editor from an Instrument Rack. Those editors allowed you to divert incoming MIDI data to different Chains based on keyboard note ranges and velocity ranges. Similarly, the Chain Select Editor allows you a way to select which Chain from the Chain List is presently active, but this time it will be based upon the twist of a Macro dial. Instead of notes or velocities selecting a Chain, you will select the Chain in real time.

Above the Zone Editor you see the familiar Zone ruler defining a zone range of 0 to 127. New to this Zone Editor is the vertical orange bar, presently sitting at value 0. This orange bar is known as the Chain Selector, and it selects which Chain is presently active.

21. Click-and-drag the orange Chain Selector to the right to a value of 16 and drop it there.

If you try to play the loop now, you will not hear any Bass 2 Redo notes playing. That is because the Chain Selector has been moved to a value that does not intersect any Chain zones. Currently the Chain Select Editor graph shows that all four Chains have the same zone value of 0, and *only* 0. Let's fix that.

22. Place your cursor over the right-hand edge of the small zone bar at 0 for the Straight Chain. When you see it turn into a closed, square bracket like this:], click-and-drag the zone boundary to the right to lengthen it to cover 0 to 24.

23. Play your loop again.

Now you hear the notes playing normally through the Straight Chain, because the zone selector value of 16 intersects the Straight Chain zone of 0 to 24. Make sense?

Your goal here is to make four equally sized, nonoverlapping zones for our four Chains. You can resize them all one at a time, but there is a faster way to do it:

24. Continue to lengthen the Straight Chain zone bar all the way to 127 so it covers the entire range of values.
25. Now [ctrl-click/right-click] anywhere in the Zone Editor and choose Distribute Ranges Equally from the contextual menu.

The zones spread out to cover the entire range of values without overlap.

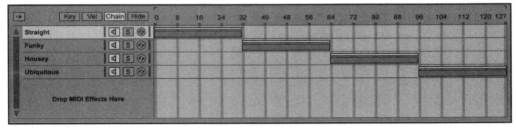

Pic. 7.33: Zones distributed equally in the Chain Select Editor.

26. Start playback.
27. Drag the orange Chain Selector bar to different values on the Zone ruler.

You should hear no arpeggiation when it intersects the zone between 0 and 31, because that selects the Straight Chain, which has no MIDI Effect on it. You should hear a different arpeggiation when you intersect each of the remaining three zones, which in turn activates each of the respective Chains with Arpeggiator devices on them.

So far, so good! Now you need a way to control Chain selection with a Macro dial:

28. Click on the Map mode button to enter Map mode.

Note that the entire Zone ruler turns green, indicating that it is a control available for mapping to a Macro dial.

29. Click on the green Zone ruler to select it.
30. Click on the Map button under the Macro 1 dial to assign it to that dial.
31. Click on the Map mode button again to exit Map mode.
32. While the loop plays, turn the Macro 1 dial, which is now named Chain Selector.

Pretty fun! With the turn of a dial you can select an arpeggiation style in real time! You made only four Chains for this rack, but you can use the Chain Selector to select up to 128 combinations of Chains.

Of course, there are a zillion other uses for Chain selection. In an Audio Effect Rack, you can make a multi-effects device that allows you to switch between as many as 128 different effects Chains with the turn of a Macro dial. You could make an Instrument Rack with a different Chain for each of the different keyboard sounds you planned to use in a performance and use a Macro dial to switch between them onstage.

I'll leave the subject of Racks with one final teaser that will make your brain hurt: Did you know that it is possible to put a Rack inside of another Rack? Try it! You can then assign Macro knobs of the internal Rack to the Macro knobs of the outermost Rack. A Rack controlling other Racks! Wow. Think of the possibilities.

33. Save your Set by pressing [cmd-s/ctrl-s].

MIDI CLIPS WITH HARDWARE SYNTHS (EXTERNAL MIDI)

Working with external hardware synths can be a little more complex to deal with, but the results can be excellent. I still find that certain hardware devices create more character and dimension than most software synths. The same is true for some samplers and drum machines. Because the device's keys and pads were designed to work with their own internal sound generator, they can often be more responsive and musical to play. And there is the added benefit that they almost never crash.

If you have one or more external MIDI devices, there are a number of ways that you can incorporate them with Live. Read through this entire section a few times, and then mix and match the techniques that best fit your setup.

The following setup sections refer to devices with traditional MIDI ports and cables, rather than USB connectivity, which is comparatively simple. However, once you have your devices hooked up, the rest of the work flow is the same for either connection type.

MIDI Cables, Ports, and Channels

All MIDI connectors on a standard MIDI cable are the same, and there is no directionality when plugging them in. However, when a cable is connected between two devices, MIDI information always flows in only one direction over any given cable. That is because there are multiple types of ports on a MIDI device that either send or receive MIDI data. While this creates the need for more cables than a USB setup requires (which can send and receive on the same cable), it does allow for more elaborate routing options.

MIDI ports come in three kinds:

- **MIDI Out**—The MIDI Out port transmits data and gestures created on that device.
- **MIDI In**—This port receives data and gestures coming from another external device.
- **MIDI Thru**—This port sends out a copy of whatever came in the MIDI In port, and this allows for daisy-chaining multiple devices together.

Each MIDI cable/port is capable of carrying a total of 16 channels of MIDI data. Different devices will be able to transmit and/or receive on one or more MIDI channels. A device that is capable of producing more than one sound at a time is known as a *multitimbral* device, and different MIDI channels can be assigned to play the different sounds simultaneously. Some multitimbral devices also have multiple audio outputs, and different internal sounds can be routed to different physical audio outputs for individual mixing and processing.

MIDI Signal Routing

Although there are an infinite number of possible MIDI setups and routings, I find that these three basic configurations give enough conceptual detail to allow you to extrapolate how to configure your own particular combination of devices.

IMPORTANT! Two MIDI routing rules that must be observed: 1) "Never make a circular MIDI loop between more than two devices." So you could go out of device A into device B, and out of device B back into device A, but you would never want to go out of device A into device B, out of device B into device C, and then out of device C back into device A. You won't break anything, but you can make data collisions that will prevent any further data from flowing. 2) "Avoid daisy-chaining more than three devices together." Again, you will not break anything, but devices further down the chain will begin to have noticeable *latency*, which is a delay between when you strike a key and when the device sounds.

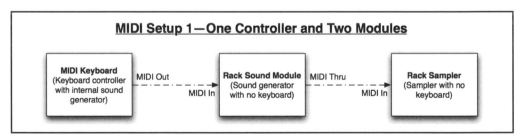

Pic. 7.34: MIDI Setup 1: One controller and two sound modules.

1. **One controller and two sound modules**—This setup does not have a computer and is geared more toward use during a live performance. The idea here is that your primary controller can play its own internal sounds and can trigger sounds in the remaining devices downstream. This can be achieved by setting each device to receive on its own range of unique MIDI channels. In the example shown, the controller could receive (its own notes) on MIDI channels 1 through 8,

the sound module on channels 9 through 12, and the sampler on channels 13 through 16, and then you could choose which device is sounding by varying the controller's transmit channel. If you intentionally set two or more devices to receive on the same channel, notes transmitted on that channel will sound all receiving devices, creating a layered sound. Note that any gestures created directly on the sound module (or sampler) will not reach either of the other two devices, as nothing is connected to its MIDI Out port. Essentially, there can be only one controller in this setup.

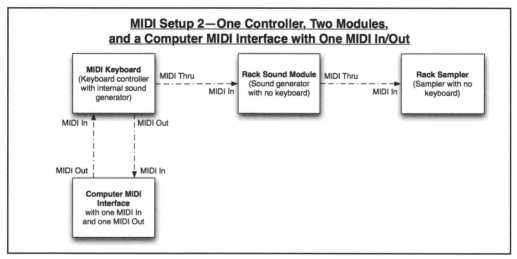

Pic. 7.35: MIDI Setup 2: One controller, two sound modules, and a computer MIDI interface with one MIDI In/Out.

2. **One controller, two sound modules, and a computer MIDI interface with one MIDI In/Out**—This is a typical home-studio setup, since most audio interfaces have only one MIDI In port and one MIDI Out port. Routing is quite similar to the one depicted in the previous diagram, except for the loop to and from the computer and the move of the cable from the MIDI Out port of the controller over to the MIDI Thru. There are several particulars about this setup that need to be noted and observed:

- How does a signal get from the controller to the sampler? Follow the signal: assuming a transmit channel of 13 through16, note messages will go out of the controller into the computer, out of the computer back into the controller. The incoming MIDI signal will be immediately replicated to the controller's MIDI Thru port and sent to the sound module. The sound module will replicate the signal again to its own MIDI Thru port, which relays it finally to the sampler.
- In order for the signal described above to pass directly through the computer, you must turn on a setting in your DAW or audio/MIDI interface known as "MIDI Thru" or similar. This allows signals sent to the computer to be echoed out of the interface's MIDI Out port so that they will reach their downstream destinations.
- Another important setting you will want to investigate is a setting in the controller known as Local: Off. The Local control enables or disables the connection between the controller's keys and its internal sound generator. If you leave Local enabled, you will hear double notes playing out of the

controller: one note is triggered by the keys directly, and a second note on message will go out the MIDI Out port, through the computer, and back into the controller's MIDI In port, where it will also sound. By turning Local off, you will hear only the note that traveled through the computer.

- While you can use the controller and the computer to record and address notes and gestures intended for all the devices in this setup, you can still have only one controller in this setup, as there is only one MIDI In port on the audio/MIDI interface. This means that you cannot record any gestures from the sound module or sampler without first repatching your MIDI cables. As well, you can still address a total of only 16 MIDI channels shared among all of your devices, because there is only one MIDI Out port on the audio/MIDI interface.

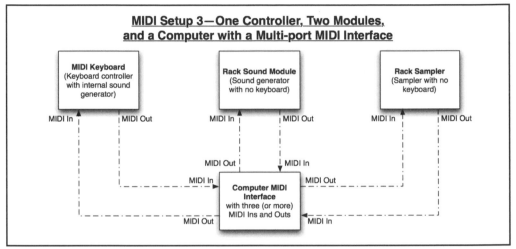

Pic. 7.36: MIDI Setup 3: One controller, two sound modules, and a computer with a multiport MIDI interface.

3. **One controller, two sound modules, and a computer with a multiport MIDI interface**—In a studio where you want to use more than one controller at a time and address up to 16 MIDI channels on each device, you will need a multiport MIDI interface, separate from your audio interface. These come in various configurations, but eight MIDI Ins and eight MIDI Outs is common. With this much I/O, setup and routing is greatly simplified. Each device has its own MIDI loop to and from the interface, so any device can be a controller, and every device can be addressed on its full range of MIDI channels. Note that if you needed to, you could still use any device's MIDI Thru to daisy-chain additional devices.

MIDI Device and Channel Routing in Live

Routing external MIDI signals in and out of Live follows the same procedures described previously for soft synths.

1. In the In/Out section, select an input device and input MIDI channel for that device. If you leave this on "All Ins" and "All Channels," the MIDI Track will accept any incoming MIDI signal on any port of any device, so long as it is configured properly in Preferences > MIDI Sync.

2. You will then want to configure an output device and output MIDI channel to route the information being recorded to the proper device/channel.

3. Finally, you will want to set a suitable monitor mode, depending on your needs. Most of the time, Auto will suffice. Remember, this is MIDI monitoring at this stage; monitoring audio coming from your external devices is another subject entirely, discussed in the next section.

Once you have the In/Out section configured, arming Tracks, recording, editing, and playback work exactly the same as working with an internal soft synth, discussed earlier in this chapter.

Monitoring External Devices

So far, we have been discussing only MIDI signal routing, recording and monitoring, and have not touched on what to do with the audio produced by these devices. In many ways, monitoring your external MIDI hardware is similar to any other external input, such as a microphone or guitar. Essentially, you can use an external mixer, or use Live as your mixer.

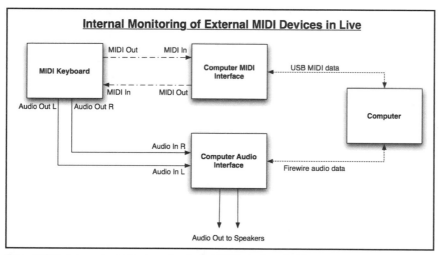

Pic. 7.37: Internal monitoring of external MIDI devices in Live.

In this setup, external devices' outputs are routed into inputs on your audio interface and into Live. If you have enough inputs on your audio interface, you can simply leave all your devices connected to your interface and make a separate Audio Track for each device. If you do not have enough audio interface inputs, you could submix some or all of your external device's audio in a mixer before it was sent to your interface.

Once your external sound generator's audio is routed into Live, you could then use either an Audio Track or the External MIDI Instrument Device to allow you a persistent audio input that can be mixed in real time with your other Live Tracks:

- Using an Audio Track as your input to Live gives you the benefit of being able to record any of your incoming sounds to the Audio Track quickly and easily. The downside is that you now have two tracks for one sound generator: a MIDI Track for triggering the external device, and an Audio Track for monitoring and recording it's sounds in Live.
- Using an External MIDI Instrument Device solves the above problem, combining MIDI output and audio input into one track, but you can only record MIDI on the track. Of course, routing the audio output of this track into another track for recording audio is easily done, but you still end up with two tracks. In my opinion, this is the better, more streamlined solution.

There are several benefits of routing your external sound generator's audio signals back through Live in this way:

- If you want to record any of your external device's outputs as audio in Live, this is easily done.
- You can even put Audio Effects on an incoming signal without recording it to audio. Simply place the desired effects on the Audio Track with the incoming audio from your external MIDI devices.
- You do not ever need to record them as audio for their signals to be included in your final mix: when you use the Export Audio/Video command with an Audio Track monitor set to In, Live will actually render your audio in real time, including any incoming signals from your external devices. Recalling the exact state of your Set later is somewhat harder, but with a little documentation, it is very possible.

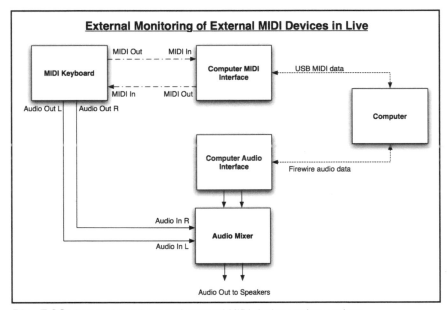

Pic. 7.38: External monitoring of external MIDI devices using a mixer.

In this setup, all sound sources, including Live, pass through an audio mixer before arriving at your speakers. The primary benefit of this method is that you don't have to deal with the audio latency incurred by passing the signal through the computer, which can be challenging. To record any external device's audio output with this setup, it is a simple matter of routing a mixer's channel(s) to your audio interface. I have used the mixer's aux sends or bus/group outs for this purpose. Some mixers, such as Mackie's small-format mixers, have a function that routes muted channels to a secondary pair of outputs called "Alt. 3–4." This is quite handy for this purpose, because it mutes the device's output to the speakers while simultaneously routing it to Live. If your recording track's monitor is set to In, or Auto, you will hear the incoming sound to be recorded through Live's Master Outputs back in the mixer. Perfect.

SUMMARY

- The term MIDI stands for Musical Instruments Digital Interface, and the acronym refers to both a protocol and the hardware specification.
- MIDI sound generators can be either internal to your computer (software synths) or external (hardware synths) devices.
- A MIDI "controller" is a device that generates MIDI messages, such as notes, pitch bend, modulation wheel, sustain, as well as knobs and faders. A MIDI controller may or may not also generate its own sounds.
- The Live Preferences MIDI/Sync pane is where you configure your MIDI controllers and interfaces to work with Live. MIDI controllers are either natively supported, or set up manually on this page.
- Live gives you four MIDI indicators in the Control Bar to indicate incoming and outgoing MIDI messages.
- Live allows you to easily map your MIDI controller's knobs, buttons, and sliders to parameters in Live via the MIDI Map Mode.
- By turning on the Computer MIDI Keyboard, you can use your computer's keyboard as a makeshift MIDI keyboard.
- Note messages can be created in Live's MIDI Clips by drawing them in with a mouse, or recording them with the Computer MIDI Keyboard or an external MIDI Controller.
- The Impulse Instrument Device is a useful drum machine-like soft synth. Although similar in some ways, Drum Racks are far more customizable.
- The MIDI Editor in MIDI Clip Properties allows you to edit MIDI notes, as well as velocity and continuous controller information. The Fold button will restrict the number of note lanes in the editor to only the ones that are currently in use.
- You can "overdub" MIDI data, layering multiple passes of performance onto a single MIDI Clip.
- MIDI Clip notes can be quantized, moving each note closer, or onto, a user-specified grid. Alternately, Record Quantization can quantize a performance in real time, while it is being recorded, for instantaneous results.
- Incoming and outgoing MIDI, as well as signal monitoring, can be configured for each MIDI Track in the In/Out Section of the Mixer.
- New in Live 9 is the ability to extract a MIDI performance from an Audio Clip. There are three algorithms for doing this: Convert Melody, Harmony, or Drums to New MIDI Track.
- Instrument Racks, Drum Racks, and MIDI Effect Racks are versatile tools for sound design, allowing you to save complex layered instruments and their associated effects to a preset for repeated use. Eight Macro knobs can be configured to make a multitude of adjustments to the Devices contained in the Racks, opening up new automation and modulation possibilities.

- Live 9's new MIDI editing functions in the Notes box give handy access to useful tasks like note transposition, inversion, reversal, duplication, and legato.
- Chains in Instrument Racks and MIDI Effect Racks can be selected via keyboard splitting, velocity switching, and the Chain Selector.
- Simpler is a straightforward device for sample playback and manipulation.
- Third-party Instrument and plug-in parameters can be mapped to Macros for playability, modulation, and automation purposes. The Third-Party Plug-in Device interface includes an x-y pad for easily manipulating two plug-in parameters.
- Slice to New MIDI Track will cut an Audio Clip into slices and spread it across a Drum Rack where it can be replayed via MIDI and manipulated in an endless variety of ways.
- MIDI Effects and MIDI Effect Racks manipulate incoming MIDI data before it is played by an Instrument.
- External MIDI hardware can be controlled by Live, and the audio output from such devices can be routed back into Live for further transformation.

Mixing and Automation in Live

This chapter will walk you through the wonders of automation and give you some tips for making your mix dreams come true.

EXERCISE 8.1—MIX AUTOMATION IN ARRANGEMENT VIEW

By far the most powerful aspect of the modern DAW is the ability to automate just about every parameter of a mix. The term *automation* refers to the program's ability to record and play back, not just audio and MIDI data, but also all your mix gestures, such as changes in volume, panning, send levels, and even Audio Effect plug-in settings over time. Want to slowly add some distortion to a sound across eight measures? Want a sound to fade out? Want a sound to pan from left to right? That is all automation. Automation is like having dozens of extra hands on a giant mixing console that do exactly what you tell them to every time you play your mix back. And since that automation is editable down to a very fine level of detail, you can make just about any sound transformation you can imagine with only your mouse! And like so many other features of Live, the way Ableton has implemented automation is simple, elegant, and immensely powerful.

8.1.1—Recording Basic Automation Gestures

DO IT!   Two Ways to Get Started:

- You can continue from right where you left off at the end of Exercise 7.4 and use Save As to save the Set as My Exercise 8.1.als, or
- You can open Exercise 8.1.als from the supplied Sets in Book Content > Book Exercises Project, and then perform a Save As and save your Set as My Exercise 8.1.als.

Remember how we recorded Track Pan automation to the CST Clip in Session View in chapter 2? And do you recall how, when we recorded our Session View performance into Arrangement View in chapter 4, the Session View Track Pan automation was carried over into the new Arrangement? Well, now we are finally going to work with Arrangement View track automation.

The process of recording automation in Arrangement View is similar to recording automation in Session View:

1. Enable the Automation Arm button in the Control Bar.
2. Enable Arrangement Record in the Control Bar.
3. Make the desired mix gestures.
4. Stop playback.

The next time you press Play you will hear the parameters re-enacting your previous performance. It's that simple.

The most obvious use of automation is to vary volume over time to balance the levels of your tracks throughout your song or to create dynamics changes.

DO IT! Let's make some Track Volume automation moves. To begin, let's fade in the Atmospheric Clip on the One Shots Track at the very beginning of the song.

1. Enable the Automation Arm button in the Control Bar if it is not already.
2. Double-click on the Stop button in the Control Bar to make sure that the Arrangement position reads 1.1.1.
3. Locate the orange and white Track Volume box for the One Shots Track, which currently reads 0. Click-and-drag this value down as far as it will go to –Inf.

Pic. 8.01: The One Shots Track Volume box.

4. Click on the Arrangement Record button in the Control Bar, or press the F9 key to enable Arrangement Recording. While Live plays the Intro section of your arrangement, click-and-drag the Track Volume value for the One Shots Track upward. Ideally, by the time playback reaches bar 13, you should be at 0 dB in the Track Volume box.
5. Press [spacebar] again or click on Stop to halt recording.

You should now see a red line that is dotted with circles overlaid on top of the Atmospheric Clip on the One Shots Track that appeared while you were recording the Track Volume fade-in. This is known as an automation Breakpoint Envelope.

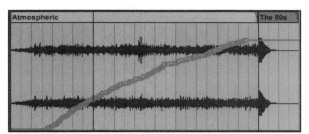

Pic. 8.02: The dotted red Track Volume Breakpoint Envelope.

6. Return to the beginning of the timeline and play back what you did. Watch the Track Volume slowly increasing in the Track Volume box while it plays.

Note the small red square in the upper left of the Track Volume box that indicates that this parameter has been automated. All automated parameters will display this indicator.

Pic. 8.03: The Track Volume box with a red, square automation indicator.

Note as well that you are hearing the Clip's looping Volume Envelope that you made earlier, which provides the stutter effect and the gradual fade-in of the Track Volume automation working together.

If you think you can improve this automation move on a second try, press [cmd-z/ctrl-z] to undo what you just did and repeat the above steps to have another pass at it. Practice makes perfect!

8.1.2—Track Panning Automation and the Automation Control Chooser

Ready for more? Let's add some panning automation to the same section:

7. Double-click on the Stop button in the Control Bar to make sure that the Arrangement position reads 1.1.1.
8. Locate the white Track Pan box for the One Shots Track, which currently reads "C" (for "center").
9. Click on the Arrangement Record button in the Control Bar, or press the F9 key to enable Arrangement Record.
10. While Live plays the Intro section again, click-and-drag the Track Pan value for the One Shots Track up and down slowly. See if you can make the Atmospheric sound sweep slowly back and forth across the stereo spectrum a few times by the time playback reaches bar 13.
11. Press [spacebar] again or click on Stop to halt playback.

Pic. 8.04: The Track Pan box.

As you record your panning automation, a new red envelope showing panning automation overlays on the One Shots Track. Where did your Volume automation go? Have no fear: it is still there.

Notice the two pull-down menu boxes under the Track Name to the left of the Mixer column: the top one reads Mixer and the second reads Track Panning. These are the Device Chooser and the Automation Control Chooser, respectively.

These two pull-down menus allow you to select which automation envelope is currently overlaid on the track. In this case the Device Chooser and the Automation Control Chooser are telling us that we are looking at the automation envelope of a parameter in the Mixer called Track Panning. They are very similar to the Clip Envelope Control/Device Choosers from chapter 2.

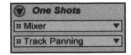

Pic. 8.05: The Device Chooser and Automation Control Chooser.

12. Click on the lower pull-down menu to see a list of other parameters available for automation in the Mixer: Speaker On, Track Panning, Track Volume, X-Fade Assign, A Return, and B Return.

Note that two of them, Track Panning and Track Volume, have the red, square automation indicator next to their names to impart that this parameter has been automated.

13. Select Track Volume from the Automation Control list.

You are once again looking at the Track Volume automation envelope.

This pair of pull-down menus will show you which automation is currently on display as well as allow you to choose another automation type for viewing.

But there is an even faster, easier, and more intuitive way to switch the views. Simply click on the control of the automation that you want to view.

14. Click on the One Shot Track's Track Panning box in the Mixer.

The automation envelope for Track Panning is displayed.

15. Click on the One Shot Track's Track Volume box in the Mixer.

The automation envelope for Track Volume is displayed! Easy.

8.1.3—Adding Automation Lanes

I know what you are thinking: "What if I want to see both the Volume and the Panning automation envelopes at the same time?" You can do that, too, of course:

Just below the two automation pull-down menus in the Track Name area there is a circular button with a plus symbol on it. (You may have to stretch the Track divider downward to see this button on other tracks, but it is there.) This is the Add Automation Lane button. Click on it.

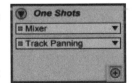

Pic. 8.06: The Add Automation Lane button.

The Track Volume automation envelope moves down onto its own lane, with a ghost of the track's Clips behind it.

16. Now click on the Track Pan box in the Mixer.

The Track Panning automation envelope is now displayed over the main Clips lane, and you can now view (and edit) both envelopes at the same time.

8.1.4—Editing Automation Envelopes with Draw Mode Off

Sometimes you will find that you need to adjust or correct an automation envelope, or that it is simply more expedient to create an automation move with your mouse than it is to record it. There are several ways to go about executing these tasks. Editing of the red automation breakpoint envelopes overlaid on a track works in a similar way to Clip breakpoint envelopes. Again, there are two modes for working with them: Draw Mode On, and Draw Mode Off. The following edits will explore both of these modes.

17. In the Control Bar, make sure that Draw mode is set to Off, which is indicated by the pencil icon button being gray.

Remember that Draw mode can be toggled on and off with the button, or by pressing [B] repeatedly.

Note the series of small, red circles on the automation envelope that give it its shape. These are the breakpoints.

- To create a new breakpoint on the envelope, click anywhere on the automation line.
- To move a breakpoint, click-and-drag it.
- To move a line between two breakpoints, or a selected range of breakpoints, put your cursor near to the line: when it turns blue, click-and-drag it up or down.
- To curve a diagonal automation line, put your cursor near the line, and when it turns blue, press and hold [opt/alt], and then click-and-drag.
- To delete a breakpoint, click on it.

Using these five simple techniques, you can create any automation envelope shape you can imagine.

One thing you may have already noticed is that when you pressed Stop after creating your Track Volume automation pass, the Volume for the remainder of the Track dropped back down to −Inf. By default, when recording stops, Live returns a parameter to the value it had before automation recording began. As you may recall, you brought the Track Volume all the way down (to −Inf) before you started to record, so that is where Live returned it when you hit Stop. If you leave it like this, you will no longer hear the crash cymbals that occur later on the One Shots Track. Let's fix that:

18. Find the last breakpoint on the Track Volume lane for the One Shots Track. It will likely be soon after bar 13, where you stopped recording your Track Volume automation pass. Click on the breakpoint to delete it.

Sometimes it can be hard to delete breakpoints that are at −Inf. You will know that your cursor is directly over the breakpoint when it turns blue and its value, −Inf, is displayed next to it.

When you delete this last point, the envelope from this point forward leaps up to the value of the previous breakpoint, which should be somewhere around 0 dB. Let's make sure that it is exactly on 0 dB so the rest of the track plays back at that Track Volume.

19. Find the (new) last breakpoint on the One Shots Track. Put your cursor over it. Live displays the value of that breakpoint next to your cursor. If the value is not 0.00 dB, drag it upward or downward as needed until it is 0.00 dB.

Now the Track Volume slider will sit at 0 dB for the remainder of the track (unless you add more automation breakpoints).

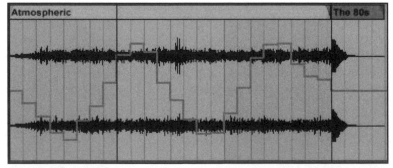

Pic. 8.07: A blue Track Volume breakpoint and its displayed current value.

8.1.5—Editing Automation Envelopes with Draw Mode On

Sometimes you know exactly what you want the automation envelope to look like and it would be quickest to simply draw it in with the mouse. That is what Draw Mode On is for, and it works in Arrangement View just the same way it does in Clip Envelopes: If Snap to Grid is set to On, you will draw segments that are the grid value in length. If Snap to Grid is set to Off, you can draw any shape you like freehand, and this works well for making gradual curves.

When you recorded your Track Panning envelope, you may not have achieved the exact shape you were going for. A nice round, smooth pan back and forth across your speakers would sound great here. Let's draw this in:

20. In the Control Bar, make sure that Draw mode is set to On, which is indicated by the pencil icon button being yellow.

When you place your cursor over the Track Panning envelope now, it becomes a pencil. Be sure to zoom in on the range you intend to draw across, and expand the Track height as much as you need to make an accurate envelope drawing.

21. Draw in a rolling sine wave that oscillates up and down across the center point a few times between bars 1 and 13.

Pic. 8.08: A hand-drawn Track Pan automation envelope with Snap to Grid set to On.

Because Snap to Grid was still set to On, the shape you drew came out like a series of stairs because each segment is one grid value in length. Let's try this again with Snap to Grid set to Off.

22. Turn off Snap to Grid by pressing [cmd-4/ctrl-4] or going Options > Snap to Grid.
23. Redraw the rolling sine wave of Track Pan automation.

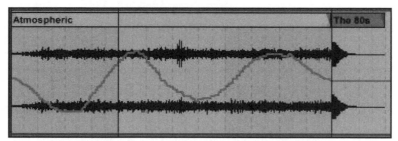

Pic. 8.09: A hand-drawn Track Pan automation envelope with Snap to Grid Off.

This time it is much smoother without the grid quantizing our values.

8.1.6—Editing Ranges of Automation Envelopes

Sometimes you like the shape of the automation gesture that you make, but you wish that the whole gesture had happened a bit earlier, later, higher, or lower. Not a problem. Live offers you a number of ways to work with a series of breakpoints all at once.

24. Press [cmd-4/ctrl-4] to enable Snap to Grid again.
25. On the One Shots Track, click-and-drag a selection across bars 1 through 17.

Note that if you click-and-drag your selection on the top lane, all lanes of Track automation are selected. If you click-and-drag on a lower lane, only that lane is selected.

26. Click-and-drag any breakpoint on the Track Volume envelope to the right so the fade-in happens a few bars later.
27. Click-and-drag any breakpoint on the Track Volume envelope upward slightly so the entire fade is louder.
28. Make a new selection of just a few bars of the Atmospheric Clip's Track Volume lane, say between bars 3 and 9. Click-and-drag the selected part of the envelope up or down to move just a portion of it.
29. Now do one of the following to delete the currently selected breakpoints:

   • Press [cmd-delete/ctrl-delete].
   • [Ctrl-click/right-click] on the selected envelope and choose Delete Envelope from the contextual menu.

The selected breakpoints are deleted and the envelope now directly spans the next two nearest breakpoints.

30. Choose one of these two ways to remove all automation from the Track Volume parameter:

- Click once on the Track Volume box to select it. Press [cmd-delete/ctrl-delete].
- [Ctrl-click/right-click] on the Track Volume box. Choose Delete Automation from the contextual menu.

The red automation indicator disappears, as do all breakpoints on that parameter's envelope.

31. Reset the One Shots Track Volume to 0 dB if it is not there already.
32. Hide the second automation lane by clicking on its Remove Automation Lane button, which looks like a minus sign.

Pic. 8.10: The Remove Automation Lane button.

"But we just deleted all my beautiful Track Volume automation!" I know, I know. But here is a better way to make a gradual fade-in.

8.1.7—Clip Fades

Volume automation is great for making subtle adjustments over time, but there is an easier way to make a Clip gracefully fade in or fade out using the Show Fades command.

33. To show Clip Fades, do one of the following:

- With a Clip on the timeline selected, press [cmd-opt-f/ctrl-alt-f].
- [Ctrl-click/right-click] on a Clip and choose Show Fades from the contextual menu.
- Click on a Track's Device Chooser and select Fades from the pull-down menu.

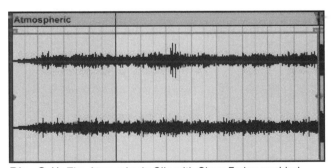

Pic. 8.11: The Atmospheric Clip with Show Fades enabled.

A new set of red controls appears on the Clip, and the Device Chooser for the Track switches to Fades Chooser. Clip Fades consist of two controls on each end of the Clip: a Fade Handle and a Fade Curve Handle.

34. Move your cursor to the upper left corner of the Atmospheric waveform at 1.1.1 over the new red circle there. This is the Fade-in Handle. Click on the circle and drag it to the right to bar 9.
35. Solo the Track and play the Clip from the start.

A long, slow fade-in is created, and the waveform behind the fade controls changes to reflect the Fade setting.

36. Halfway up the fade, at about bar 5, is a second red circle. This is the Fade In Curve Handle. Click-and-drag it and move it up, down, left, and right.

The Fade Curve Handle changes the shape of the fade, subtly or dramatically, and the waveform behind the fade controls changes to reflect the Fade Curve setting.

You can also make crossfades between two directly adjacent Clips using the Fade Handles:

37. Click on the Fade Out Handle in the upper right corner of the Atmospheric Clip just before bar 13 and drag it to the right to bar 14.
38. Play the new crossfade.

Crossfades fade one Clip out while fading the adjacent Clip in. This is useful for easing the transition from one Clip to the next. A fade (or a crossfade) can be only as long as one loop of a Clip. If you need a longer fade, use Track Volume automation or a Clip Envelope.

Since this crossfade wasn't very interesting or useful, let's undo it:

39. Undo the previous crossfade with [cmd-z/ctrl-z].

8.1.8—Automating Parameters Using MIDI Controllers

Now you can record in automation with your mouse, draw in automation with your mouse, and edit automation with your mouse. But this is where it really gets fun! Creating automation with a controller is a lot more musical, and you can modify a bunch of parameters at once. You can, of course, map a controller to any parameter of any device on any Track, and then record automation gestures of those parameters. But remember all that time you spent making those complex effects and Instrument Rack Macros that do all that amazing stuff? Well, now you get to actually *perform* with them and record that performance with automation! I'm going to show you one example, and then turn you loose to do the rest.

The Smoother-Cruncher Audio Effect Rack you made on the Synth 1 Track has only three Macro controls mapped, but each of the Macro controls does a bunch of things at once. Let's use this device as a test subject:

40. Double-click on the Synth 1 Track name to bring up its Track View.
41. Click once on the Smoother-Cruncher Audio Effect Rack's title bar to select it.

If your MIDI controller is natively supported, it should auto-map your controller's knobs when you select the device. If so, you can skip the next step.

42. Enter MIDI Map mode and map three of your MIDI controller's knobs or faders to control the three active Macro dials, and then exit MIDI Map mode.
43. Put your insert point/Arrangement position at bar 25 or so and press Play. Turn your controller's knobs and practice what you can do to the Postwarvar Clips with the Rack's Macro dials.
44. When you have a series of performance gestures you like, enable Arrangement Record and do it again from the same position to record your automation moves. You may want to go ahead and keep recording through bar 82 and put some moves on the s2s_dt_synth_mornvar1_A#m Clip as well.
45. Stop playback to stop recording. Play back your moves.

If you want to add more controller moves or redo one or more parameter's automation, simply go back and record again. Any control that you move will immediately start recording over what was there before, while any control that you do not adjust will remain unchanged.

Try using this same method to automate:

- The Bass 2 Redo Macro dials for both the MIDI Effects Rack Arpeggiator pattern switcher and the Instrument Rack's Elek7ro-II Macros.
- The Sliced Drum Rack Macro controls.
- The Send A and B levels for the various synth tracks.
- The Center Frequency and Bandwidth of the Ping Pong Delay on Return Track B.
- Track volumes and panning as needed.

And so on.

8.1.9—Group Tracks

A Group Track is like a subgroup on a mixer: it is an additional summing point for signals on their way to the Master Track. Group Tracks are a wonderful way to bring together similar elements for processing and volume management.

Let's select all of the rhythm and percussion tracks for grouping:

46. Click on the name of the first track: Beats.
47. Shift-click on the Perc Track to also select the Sliced, Perc Rack, Impulse, and Perc Tracks.
48. [Cmd-click/ctrl-click] on the One Shots Track to also select it, while leaving the Bass and Bass2 Redo Tracks unselected.
49. Do one of the following to group the tracks to a Group Track:

- Press [cmd-g/ctrl-g].
- Go Edit > Group Tracks.
- [Ctrl-click/right-click] on one of the selected Tracks and choose Group Tracks from the contextual menu.

Pic. 8.12: Six Tracks grouped together onto a Group Track.

A new track appears named 1 Group that encompasses the six previously selected Tracks.

50. Rename the new Group Track "DRUMS."

I like to use all capitals for Group Tracks to remind me that it is a Group Track. I also like to use color:

51. [Ctrl-click/right-click] on the new DRUMS Group Track and select a color for the DRUMS group.
52. Repeat this process for the two Bass Tracks to create a BASS Group Track.
53. Repeat this process for the three remaining Synth Tracks to create a SYNTH Group Track.
54. Play your arrangement.

Note how signals now flow: they merge at the Group Track before they are sent to the Master Track. Group Tracks have Volume, Pan, Mute, Solo, and Send controls like any other track, and Group Tracks can contain Audio Effects or Audio Effect Racks.

55. Adjust the Track Volume of one of the Group Tracks to hear the result. Try the Group Track's Pan, Mute, Solo, and Send controls as well.
56. Save your Set by pressing [cmd-s/ctrl-s].

Overriding Automation and the Re-enable Automation Button

Just like in Session View, if you try move a previously automated control, Live will let you, but the automation envelope will turn gray, indicating that you are overriding the parameter's active automation. Additionally, the Re-enable Automation button will turn orange, indicating that you have deviated from the automation as it currently is recorded. This functionality allows you to try out changes to any parameter, even though the parameter may already have been automated. To go back to hearing the automation as it is written on

Pic. 8.13: The Re-enable Automation button.

the track, simply press the Re-enable Automation button. The envelope will return to its normal red color, indicating that it is active again, and the Re-enable Automation button will be disabled back to gray.

MIXING AND MIX AUTOMATION TIPS

I'm guessing that you are now experiencing a combination of raw excitement and head-spinning overload with your newfound ability to automate nearly every parameter in your mixes! It is pretty overwhelming, but if you focus on a section at a time and remain objective, you can sculpt just about anything you can imagine with time and effort.

Here are some helpful tips for making the most of your Arrangement mixes:

- A quick way to adjust an automation Envelope for the length of one Clip is to click on the parameter to be adjusted and then click on the title bar of the Clip on the timeline, which will select the range you want to adjust. Then, click-and-drag the envelope inside of the selection, and all the automation for that parameter will move together as a unit, even if the parameter is not yet automated.

- You can cut, copy, paste, and duplicate envelopes independently of their respective Clips: [ctrl-click/right-click] on a selected range of automation to view the Envelope edit options and their shortcuts. You can even copy an envelope and paste it to another parameter, another Track, or even another parameter on another track. This can be a very creative tool, much like copying MIDI notes to play a different instrument on a different track.
- Don't forget that you can automate Audio Effects on Return Tracks or the Master Track.
- Sometimes it is useful to move the Clip but leave the Envelope where it is. [Ctrl-click/right-click] on the Envelope and choose Lock Envelope from the contextual menu. The Clips on the Track will now move independently of the Envelope.
- Group Tracks provide an easy way to manage a collection of similar Tracks and process them together. Try putting Audio Effects on a Group Track to process the sum of the grouped Tracks together. This can help solidify disparate sounds to make them feel like they "belong" together.
- Since the internal resolution of Live is 48-bit floating point, you cannot actually clip the meters on individual tracks in Live. Track levels can go well above the top of the visible Track meter and not clip, so there is no need to be overly concerned about the level of individual track outputs. Conversely, it is very possible to clip some third-party plug-ins, hardware inputs and outputs, and the Master output when exporting to a final output file, so pay closer attention to those meters.

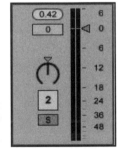

Pic. 8.14: Expanded Tracks and meters in the Mixer.

- Live has a peak level indicator on every track, but it is hidden by default and few users know about it: In Session View, drag the divider at the top of the Mixer upward to reveal the peak level indicator and the numeric Track Volume box. As well, expand Session View tracks horizontally by dragging their Track Name dividers to show numeric decibel levels next to the level meters.

Master Track Plug-Ins

- I try to avoid using a lot of large EQ adjustments like Band-Aids on the Master if at all possible: Fix EQ issues on individual tracks and Group Tracks as needed. If I do use EQ on the Master, it is a highpass filter to remove needless rumble: I do this on almost every song, but usually at the mastering stage. Also, sometimes a Master Track compressor has changed the tone of my mix, and needs subtle EQ correction as a result.
- Try managing the dynamic range of your song with dynamics processors on individual tracks and/or on Group Tracks, before adding them to the Master Track. Single compressors are a challenge to get right, let alone trying to differentiate the effect of two in series. Try mixing the entire song with no compressors/limiters on the Master Track, and then only add them at the very end to subtly tighten the overall sound if you still think it still needs it. Try to keep gain reduction under 3dB on Master Track compression.
- Attack, release, ratio, and knee times on compressors are the key to a song's punch and groove. Spend quality time on these settings.
- Resist the urge (and popular trend) to make your song seem louder by crushing it with limiters or maximizers on the Master Track. If you want to hear what your song will sound like when it is louder, turn the volume up on your speakers. Adding a few decibels of gain reduction with a limiter on a Group Track to smooth out levels is fine. Six or more decibels of gain reduction on

a Master Track limiter is too much. Leave final dynamics for the mastering stage, or mastering engineer.

- If your music is going to go to vinyl, then you really want to avoid Master Track limiters. Vinyl has strict level tolerances for different frequencies. You should seriously consider paying to have a professional master your material if you are going to release it on vinyl.

- Use the finest plug-ins you can afford on the Master Track. Since your whole mix will be subject to their quality limitations, bring out the best you have. They may take more CPU than the rest, but you can always Freeze some Tracks to regain some processing power. If possible, use linear phase plug-ins on the Master Track. Linear phase plug-ins are more expensive and CPU-intensive, but they are significantly more transparent, meaning that they will not smear or otherwise degrade your sound.

- If you are going to have your song mastered by a pro in a mastering studio, export your song without any Master Track dynamics processors. Use the Master Volume slider to take the output level down if your levels go into clipping after bypassing. Set the Master Volume to ensure that your highest peaks are somewhere between –6 and –3 dBFS before exporting.

EXPORTING YOUR MIX TO A FILE

Okay. You've finished your mix, and it sounds great. Now you want to make a stereo file to play elsewhere. It is time for a mixdown. Go File > Export Audio/Video.

This dialog box will allow you to export audio (or video with audio) to a number of specifications. Let's walk through the various controls, and then talk about useful settings for different applications.

The most important thing to remember about this dialog box is that it will export from exactly the state Live was in when you invoked the Export Audio/Video command, so double-check that what is playing is what you want to export. Although we are currently talking about this function in the context of exporting a mixdown, you can use Export in a manner that is similar to the Resampling function. Here are some things to keep in mind about exporting:

- If you are in Arrangement View when you execute the export, and you have neither a selection nor the Arrangement Loop switch enabled, Live will default to exporting the entire timeline from the start of the first Clip to the end of the last Clip. This is great for mixing down your entire Arrangement to a file.

Pic. 8.15: The Export Audio/Video dialog box.

- If you are in Arrangement View with a selection when you execute the export, Live will export the range of your selected bars. Use this to export a specific portion of the timeline.

- If you have the Arrangement Loop switch enabled when you execute the export, Live will export the Arrangement loop's range of bars from the timeline.

- If you have loops playing in Session View when you go to Export, those will be played throughout your entire exported file in addition to Clips playing on the Arrangement timeline (if any). Clicking on Stop All Clips or on the Back to Arrangement button before exporting will ensure that only what is playing in the Arrangement is exported.
- If you are in Session View when you export, Live will ask you how many bars you would like to export of the currently playing Clips. Use this to submix a group of Clips to a new Clip. Be aware that if you have tracks playing in the Arrangement at the same time, they will be audible in the export as well.
- If you have any tracks soloed or deactivated at the time of exporting, they will be audible in the export in that state. Check to make sure that all the tracks you want to export are playing in the way you want them to before exporting.

Now let's have a look at the various controls in the Export Audio/Video dialog box:

Rendered Track—This pull-down controls which track or tracks you are sourcing for the export:

- **Master**—The Master Track's output will be used as the source for exporting.
- **All Tracks**—This handy setting will export each of your tracks individually for the selected length. Using All Tracks is a great way to exchange files for mixing or remixing with someone who uses a DAW other than Live. Individually exported tracks will *not* be subject to any Master Track processing, but Live will export your Return Tracks and the Master Track as a part of the All Tracks export.
- **Individual Tracks**—This setting will export only the selected Track for the previously selected range of bars. Again, individually exported tracks will not be subject to any Master Track processing.

Normalize—If this is selected, Live will Normalize the exported file. Normalization means to turn the gain of the file up as high as it can go without clipping. Normalization does not employ dynamic compression or limiting—it is simply a volume adjustment. The highest peak in the file will be 0.00 dB after normalization. If you observe your mix levels carefully, you will never need to use this function.

Render as Loop—If you select this option, the exported file will contain all included effects, as though the loop had already been playing previously. In fact, Live plays through your selection once before beginning the export so that any time-based effects tails, such as reverb or delay, will already be echoing out at the start of the loop.

File Type—Choose WAV or AIFF here.

Convert to Mono—Select this option if you would like to export a mono file.

Sample Rate/Bit Depth—Choose the desired settings for your destination file (discussed below).

Dither—Live offers five kinds of dither to choose from (discussed below).

Create Analysis File—If you intend to use the exported file in a Live Set, enable this option and it will speed the importing of your file.

Using Dither

Dither is a low-level amount of noise that can be applied when you are exporting to a lower bit depth than the one that you are presently using, and it can help smooth the loss of resolution and even recover additional dynamic range. The trick is to use dither only once in the entire life of your song: multiple layers of dither will degrade the sound quality, so it should be the absolute last process that happens to your file. Here are some guidelines:

- If you are exporting a file that you intend to use again in your current Set, or in another Set, export at the sample rate and bit depth you are currently using, as set in your Preferences. Do not apply dither.
- If you are exporting a mixdown that you intend to play out of Live as part of a DJ set, again, export at the sample rate of the other tracks in your DJ set. Use 24-bit—there is no reason not to. Do not apply dither.
- If you are exporting a mixdown that you intend to make an MP3 from, export at the sample rate and bit depth you are currently using. Do not apply dither. The MP3 encoder—such as iTunes—will do a better job of making the MP3 with the higher resolution source than if you had exported to a 16-bit file with dither first.
- If you are exporting a mixdown that will be sent to a mastering studio for processing, call the studio and ask the people there what audio-file specifications they prefer. More than likely, they will say to export at 24-bit, and the sample rate you are currently working at, and not to apply dither.
- If you intend to do any more processing on the exported file, such as your own mastering, export at the Set's current sample rate and 32-bit floating point, and do not dither.
- If you are ever exporting at a higher bit depth than you are currently using (for some reason), do not add dither.
- In short, the only time you should apply dither is when you are exporting the final mixdown that will not be changed again in any way, and you are lowering the bit depth during the export—for example, from 24 bits that you have been working at in Live, down to 16 bits for burning to an audio CD.

When you do use dither, here are your various dither options:

- **Triangular/Rectangular**—Provided by Ableton, these two options are the safest to use if you think there may be any possibility of making additional changes to the exported file.
- **POW-r 1, 2, and 3**—These three industry-standard dither types offer increasing amounts of dither that sit above the frequency range of human hearing. Use one of these when you are certain that your file will not be altered after exporting. Try exporting a small section of the quietest portion of your song, and try each of these dither types to see which one works best with your song.

SUMMARY

- Nearly every parameter in Live can be automated, and this automation can be edited with breakpoint editing or in Draw Mode.
- If a parameter has a small red square on it, this indicates that the parameter has automation present. Clicking on the parameter will display its automation envelope overlaid on the Track's Arrangement timeline.

- The Device Chooser and Control Chooser allow you to choose which automated parameter you would like to look at. You may add and subtract additional automation lanes by pressing the Add Automation Lane button.
- Ranges of automation Envelopes can be cut, copied, and pasted, as well as duplicated and deleted via a contextual menu.
- In addition to volume automation and modulation, Clips can have Clip Fades for easy fade ins and fade outs. You can also use Clip Fades to crossfade between two adjacent Clips.
- Group Tracks are a handy organizational tool, allowing you to process multiple tracks with a single effect simultaneously.
- You may continue to manually adjust parameters with recorded automation, and doing so will temporarily suspend the automation. The Back to Arrangement button will revert all suspended tracks back to observing their automation values again.
- You can export your song—or a selected part of it—to a file using the Export Audio/Video command. A dialogue box will allow you to select the parameters you want for the exported file.

Using Live... Live!

So far in this book we have primarily been working with Live as a studio DAW for creating and mixing music, which Live is quite handy at. But as the name implies, Live was developed with an orientation toward using the program in a performance setting as well. I hear about new ways to use Live all the time, and the possibilities seem to be ever expanding. I will list some key features here that will hopefully inspire you to invent some new performance techniques yourself.

But first, let's bring this series of tutorial Sets full circle—and to a close—by preparing it to be performed live back in Session View.

EXERCISE 9.1—PREPARING FOR LIVE PERFORMANCE IN SESSION VIEW

I've taken the liberty of doing some additional mix work on the Live Set from chapter 8, which you can see the results of in the provided Exercise 9.1 Set. Or feel free to use your own music that you have been working on up to now. We'll use this Arrangement as an example of a completed song that you might want to perform as part of a Live Set in Session View.

9.1.1—Consolidate Time to New Scene

DO IT!　　Two Ways to Get Started:

- You can continue from right where you left off at the end of Exercise 8.1 and use Save As to save the Set as My Exercise 9.1.als, or
- You can open Exercise 9.1.als from the supplied Sets in Book Content > Book Exercises Project, and then perform a Save As and save your Set as My Exercise 9.1.als.

Let's assume that your mix is done, and that you now desire to play your song in a performance setting. There are many ways to go about this—in fact, the rest of this chapter discusses a few of the more obvious options—but the following technique accomplishes a number of important things:

- Instead of just DJ-ing a mixed down stereo track, you will still have control of all of your individual tracks for "mixing on the fly" in performance.
- All your Arrangement View mix automation will still be present in Session View.
- We will learn a handy new Live 9 feature for making this happen quite easily!

Just as we started this song in Session View for ease and flexibility, and then moved into Arrangement View when the time came to commit to an arrangement, now it is time to put our Clips back into Session View with a handy new Live 9 feature called Consolidate Time to New Scene.

1. If you are using the supplied Exercise 9.1.als Set file, you will notice that I've deleted all the Clips and Scenes from Session View. If you are using your own Set at this point, go ahead and do this yourself by highlighting all the Scenes and pressing [delete]. You should start the next step with only one Scene, and it should be clear of any Clips. This step isn't necessary, but it will help keep things clear and organized.
2. Switch to Arrangement View.
3. On the first bar of any empty track, click-and-drag a selection that spans 1.1.1 to 13.1.1, which is 12 bars in length. This selection goes from your Locator named Intro to the one named Add Bass. The selected bars turn blue.
4. Do one of the following:

- Go Create > Consolidate Time to New Scene
- [Ctrl-click/right-click] on the selection and choose Consolidate Time to New Scene from the contextual menu.

5. Switch back to Session View and look at the new Scene that was created from the opening Clips in your song.

While you only selected bars on one track during this time range, all of the Clips within the time range across all tracks were consolidated to a new Scene in Session View. Remember Consolidate from chapter 4, where we combined the three postwarvar Clips into one new Audio Clip for easier editing? This is the same idea: for each of the three Clips in the selected time range in Arrangement View, Live has made a new continuous 12-bar audio file, and placed it in an Audio Clip in a new Scene. Let's look specifically at what Live did so we can predict the behavior in the future:

- **MT_Beats**—In Arrangement View, this was a two-bar looping Audio Clip. After Consolidate Time to New Scene it is a single 12-bar Audio Clip (with Looping enabled by default).
- **Lightribal**—This was a two-bar looping Audio Clip that began at bar five in the Arrangement View. If you look at the new Clip in Session View, it is a 12-bar Clip and the first four bars are silent.

- **Atmospheric**—This was originally a 16-bar Clip that we shortened to 12 bars, added a sixteenth-note repeating stutter, and used a Clip Fade to fade the volume in. Now, the new Consolidated Session View Clip is exactly 12 bars in length, the audio turns on and off every sixteenth note, and the waveform fades in of its own accord without a Clip Fade or Envelope.

In essence, you can see how Live has taken all your performance edits and "printed" them to a new file. The new files incorporate Clip Gain, Warping, and Transposition, including modulations of these respective Clip Envelopes. However, notice that Consolidate does not "print" the track effects to the new file; you would need to use the Freeze or Resample functions for that, which we'll discuss shortly.

Let's continue with this process, shall we? But let's use a slightly different way to select the time range:

6. Switch to Arrangement View.
7. Click on one of the Clips starting at bar 13, such as Lightribal or Bass 2 Redo 1.

With a single click, you've selected the range between the Add Bass and Buildup Locators, which is exactly what we need. So long as there is a Clip that spans the exact range you want to Consolidate Time to New Scene, use it! It can be a lot quicker and easier than trying to click-drag a range of empty bars.

8. Execute the Consolidate Time to New Scene command again.

The same thing happens as before, with the new addition of our Impulse and Bass Redo MIDI Clips: these have been Consolidated into eight-bar MIDI Clips from the four repetitions of two bar looping MIDI Clips. So this process also works for MIDI.

You will also note that any Arrangement View autotmation carried over into Session View Clip Envelopes, and when you play back your newly Consolidated Clips in Session View, you will hear, for example, any of the Panner Pad Instrument Rack Macro dial automation you may have recorded in Arrangement view. This allows you to hear the Arrangement mix automation you made in the live performance of your Session View Clips.

COOL! Group Tracks in Session View have Launch buttons: you can launch all the Clips on the same Scene in a Group Track—such as the DRUMS Group Track—with a single click. When the Group Track is minimized, this can be very handy. You could, for example, use Group Tracks to contain an entire song's worth of Tracks, and lay out all your songs for a performance horizontally in a series of Group Tracks, and mix and match Scenes between them, expanding the Group Track when you needed to "get inside" of a song's individual parts.

9. Continue this process of highlighting ranges of your arrangement between Locators and Consolidating them to new Scenes in Session View until you have the entire song transferred.

10. You now have your final song in Session View again, and you can make choices on-the-fly about which Clips and Scenes you want to play, and for how long.

11. If you like this new Session View layout, don't forget to save your Set.

IMPROVISING IN SESSION VIEW

The non-linearity of Session View offers an extremely versatile way to interact with your Clips and devices, many of which we have already covered. But here are a few more features and techniques geared specifically toward performing with Live that you will want to know about.

Tempo/Time Signature Scene Names

As you move through a Set, it is likely that you will want to vary your music's tempo and time signature. We learned how to do both of these in Arrangement View in the context of a single song, but what about when you're working in Session View? Live offers a very simple means for addressing this need. To designate a particular tempo and/or time signature for a particular Scene, you simply include this information in the name of the Scene. The syntax for doing this is simple: a number followed by "bpm" for tempo, and/or a time signature with two numbers divided by a forward slash. For example, name a Session View Scene "Breakdown 110 bpm, 6/4." You will notice that the corresponding Scene Launch button will turn orange, and both the global Tempo and Time Signature boxes in the Control Bar will acquire red automation indicators. Launching this Scene will change the tempo to 110 bpm, and the time signature to 6/4. Notice that you can still include other characters in the Scene name, such as "Breakdown" in this example, and Live will still extract the pertinent tempo and time signature information. You need only enter this information for Scenes where you want these values to change, for example, at the start of a new song or song section. Until Live receives a new tempo or time signature value from a Scene name, Live will continue to use the current values.

Pic. 9.01: A Scene name containing tempo and time signature automation instructions.

Matching Clip Levels With Clip Gain

When switching between Clips and Scenes during a live performance, you do not want to be surprised by mismatched levels or tonalities. Ideally, you want to be able to launch any Clip in your Set and have it sound good with the Clips before and after it without any additional adjustments by you, so you can focus on other things, such as what Clips to play next or what effects to apply. Here are some ideas for achieving that:

- **Clip Gain**—The first step is to go through your Session View Set and adjust each individual Clip's Clip Gain to balance their respective levels. There is no need to obsess over making all the Clips as loud as possible. Instead, aim for a consistent somewhat conservative level so if you become inspired to play all your loudest Clips at once, you *still* would not have to worry about clipping the Master output. If you need more overall volume at the gig, turn it up outside of your computer at the mixer or amplifiers, *not* inside Live with a Limiter.
- **Clip Volume Envelopes**—If you have a Clip, for example, that starts at a good level, but it changes unnecessarily before it's over, use a Clip Volume Envelope to smooth it out. Alternately, if you want a Clip to slowly fade in or out, Clip Volume Envelopes can accomplish this, too. Use Unlinked Envelopes to vary the Clip Volume over multiple repetitions of a loop as needed.
- **Track Plug-in Automation with Clip Envelopes**—Remember that Clip Volume Envelopes vary the gain *before* any plug-ins. If you want to vary the Clip's volume *after* a series of plug-ins, insert a Utility Device and use a Clip Envelope to vary the Utility's Volume dial.
- **Resampling Troublesome Clips**—Some Clips need more than a simple volume adjustment to fit in. If need be, remember you can always use Resampling to make a version of them that works in your set. For example, let's say you have a track of drum loops that you are assembling for a show, and one of them is too dynamic and too bright compared to the others:

1. Drag the offending Clip to a new track for making adjustments.
2. Add a Compressor and an EQ Three and adjust to taste, comparing the adjusted results to other Clips on your drum loops track.
3. When you have a result you like, Arm the drum loops track for recording and set the input to Resampling, or from the output of the new adjustment track Post FX, and record the processed Clip back to a slot on the drum loops track.

Device Automation With Clip Envelopes

Remember that you can use Clip Envelopes to automate almost any variable! This is extremely useful when building a Set for performance in Session View, as every Clip can contain all kinds of mix-specific information. Here are a few techniques to get you started. Use a Clip Envelope in a Session View Clip to:

- Enable/disable a particular Audio Effect's Device Activator on the track, such as Chorus, Delay, Overdrive, Amp, etc.
- Change/vary a device's Dry/Wet mix dial, such as a Reverb or Flanger.
- Change/vary a track's Pan or Send levels.
- Change/vary an Audio Effects Rack's Macro dials or Chain Selector. You could create a new Rack Chain for each song in your set and select it with the Chain Selector via a Clip Envelope!

I would generally avoid using Clip Envelopes to vary your Track Activator or Track Volume, as these tend to be controls that are fun to manipulate manually during a show. The same could be said about the Track Pan and Send levels. If you are manipulating a parameter with a controller *and* you have Clip Envelopes changing the same parameter, you may find yourself fighting against your own automation data. I try to do one or the other for any given parameter.

Launch Modes

In every Clip View Launch box, there is a pull-down menu that chooses from four available Launch Modes. Launch Modes govern how a Clip responds to one or more Launch commands, be it from a mouse click, computer keyboard mapping or MIDI device mapping. Additionally, two Modes respond to both a "down" and a "up" state, such as the pressing "down" of a mouse button on a Clip's Launch triangle, and the releasing "up" of mouse button from the Clip's Launch triangle, or the same with a mapped computer key or MIDI note.

Pic. 9.02:
The Launch Mode pull-down selector.

- **Trigger**—Each new Launch command will restart the Clip from the beginning in Trigger Mode.
- **Gate**—In Gate mode, the Clip only plays as long as the Launch button is held. A "down" state launches the Clip, and the "up" state stops the Clip.
- **Toggle**—Similar to Gate, except that a new "down" state is required for start and stop: Click the Launch button once to start the Clip, click it again to stop it.
- **Repeat**—On a "down" state, the Clip will play and repeat the first part of the Clip, the length of which is determined by the Clip Quantization value (see the next section). Once the Launch button is released with an "up" state, the Clip will continue to play normally. So if a Clip's Clip Quantization was set to quarter notes, clicking-and-holding the Launch button will loop the first quarter note until the button is released, at which time the rest of the Clip will play.

The default Launch Mode for new Clips is Trigger, but this can be changed in Preferences > Record Warp Launch.

Clip Quantization

This Clip View Launch box pull-down menu performs exactly the same function as the Global Quantize value, in essence moving a Launch command to the next selected Quantization value to maintain sync when Launching Clips. The only difference is that the setting here is on a per Clip basis, and it overrides the Global Quantize value. The default setting of Global defers individual Clip Quantization to the current Global Quantize value.

Pic. 9.03:
The Clip Quantization pull-down menu in the Clip View Launch box.

Legato Mode

This seemingly simple toggle switch opens up numerous possibilities for live Clip juggling. Instead of starting each new Clip from 1.1.1 when Launched, a newly Launched Clip will pick up playback at the previously playing Clip's position. The switch between the previous and next Clip is still governed by the Global or Clip Quantize value.

One useful application of this function utilizes multiple variations of a single Clip, such as four duplicate two-bar drum loops stacked vertically

Pic. 9.04:
The Clip View Launch box's Legato switch.

on the same track in Clip slots. Set each of the bottom three to activate a different Audio Effect on the track with a Clip Envelope, such as Erosion, Flanger and Beat Repeat. Set all four Clips to Legato, and set Clip Quantize to "none." As the dry version of the Clips plays, Launch any of the other three effected Clips at random. Because of the Legato setting, switching will maintain the continuity of the loop's playback, yet will activate a differently effected version of the Clip. You can add a lot of variation and "glitchiness" to your drums this way. Used in conjunction with Follow Actions, Legato mode allows for rather impressive beat juggling.

Launching Clips From Your Computer Keyboard or MIDI Controller

You will notice that when you enter Key Map or MIDI Map Mode, all Clip and Scene Launch buttons change color to indicate their ability to be mapped to either a computer keyboard or a MIDI control. This is certainly a lot more musical and flexible than clicking with a mouse, and you will find that mapping Clips in this way will dramatically open up your Clip Launching possibilities. Also, when entering either of these Mapping Modes, note the sudden appearance of four new buttons on the Master Track below the Stop All Clips button: Scene Launch, Scene Up, Scene Down and Scene Select. Each of these new functions is available for mapping to a control, which greatly expands Scene Launching possibilities. The Scene Select value is best mapped to an endless encoder (a MIDI knob that can spin endlessly in either direction) so you can select any Scene for Launching with one knob.

Specialized Ableton Performance Controllers

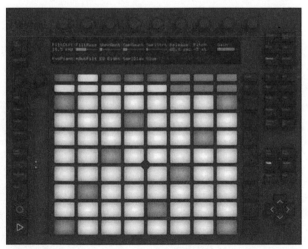

Pic. 9.05: The new Ableton Push hardware controller.

There are a number of hardware controllers available that offer a unique Session View Clip Launching experience, as they are built with Session View improvisation in mind. These include the Akai APC40 and APC20, the Novation Launchpad, and the new Ableton Push. Each of these devices offers visual feedback about which Clip slots have Clips in them, which Clips are playing and which slots are recording. Some devices additionally offer Track Volume, Pan, Sends, Mute, Solo and Arm for each currently depicted track. If these controls are used to their full potential, you need never touch your laptop during a performance. And because a large section of the Clip Grid is at your fingertips, launching and stopping multiple Clips at once is quite simple.

However, Ableton's new Push controller is in a class by itself. In addition to all of the above controls, Push includes a mode for playing Drum Rack pads like a pad controller, a step sequencer mode for making MIDI Drum Rack beats on the fly, and a truly innovative "keyboard" mode that allows you to play the pads as if they were an interwoven series of keyboard keys. You can even load Clips and Effects from Push, which further removes your need to touch your computer during a performance. The pads themselves can display a wide range of colors, and feel amazing, allowing for an expressive playability I have not previously experienced in a Live-specific controller. I have been playing with Push for several weeks now, and have yet to find a limitation worth mentioning. If building tracks and performing them live is your mode of expression, this device is equally at home in the studio or on the stage, and worth checking out.

IMPROVISING IN ARRANGEMENT VIEW

While it may seem counter-intuitive to "improvise" in Arrangement View, it can be done, and perhaps more effectively than you might think. In addition to working creatively with the Arrangement Loop Brace, here are two other functions that can add interest and variety to your Arrangement View playback:

Locator Navigation Mapping

In either Key Map or MIDI Map Mode, note that you can map a control to any Locator, as well as to the Previous Marker, Next Marker, and Set Marker buttons. With a little mapping

and practice, this can yield some beat-juggling-like results. You can lay out an entire performance on the Arrangement View timeline and use Locators to select the next section to play on-the-fly.

Tempo Master/Slave button

You may have noticed the stealthy appearance of a new Clip View Sample box switch for Warped Clips in Arrangement View that says "Slave" when deactivated, and "Master" when activated. This button allows for easy Global Tempo control

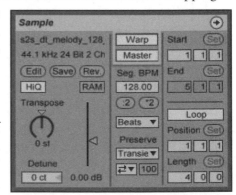

Pic. 9.06: The Tempo Master/Slave button in the Arrangement Clip View Sample box.

options in Arrangement View Clips. When set to the default, Slave, Warped Clips will play back at the current Global Tempo in the Control Bar. When a Clip is set to Master, as soon as the Clip starts to play, the Global Tempo will switch to the Clip's Warped tempo. When you have multiple Clips set to tempo Master, the Clip on the lowest track will take precedence. The benefit here is that all tempo sync'd Audio Effects—such as delays, Beat Repeat, and any effect with an LFO in it that follows the Global Tempo—will create their effect in sync with the new tempo. The alternative of playing an un-Warped Clip on the Arrangement timeline would produce effects that were in sync with the Global Tempo, but out of sync with the playing Clip.

DJ SETS USING LIVE

The ambiguous title of "DJ" has grown to include an ever-wider assortment of skills, styles, and tools over the past several decades. Does a DJ play other people's tracks like a traditional radio DJ, do they play original music that they themselves have created, or some kind of hybrid of both? Do DJs play records, CDs, or files from a laptop? Do DJs play only mastered stereo tracks, one at a time, or are they mixing many individual elements on-the-fly? It would seem that the answer to all of these questions is "all of the above."

Luckily, due to Live's supreme flexibility, a laptop DJ does not have to choose any one way to work. They can mix and match elements as they see fit, creating a custom style that matches their skill level and desires.

Let's start by looking at source quality and learning various techniques to beat map imported song files. Next, we'll explore Live's Crossfader and how to monitor cueing up your next track. And although an entire book could be written on the subject, we'll close by illustrating a few basic styles of using Live to DJ, in increasing orders of complexity.

Wav Files vs. MP3s

For DJing, I strongly urge you to do what you can to start with the highest-quality song files possible, ideally a .wav file ripped from a CD or downloaded from an online vendor. Importing a .wav file to Live results in no translation, and the source material will be full, crisp and dynamic. If you start with a compressed file, such as an MP3, you will be working with compromised quality to begin with, and Live will have to transcode your compressed file into a .wav file anyway, using up additional hard drive space to do so. Once you start mixing two MP3 sources together, adding Audio Effects, or amplifying your mix over a large sound system, you will clearly hear the diminished quality. Sure, .wav files are a lot larger and take up more space, and they do not support ID3 tags for meta data such as artist/album name, but to me, the superior sound quality is worth the extra hassle.

Working with Entire Song Files

As a DJ, it is likely that you have a large music collection that you want to pull from as you perform. While it is entirely possible to grab and use any desired audio file on-the-fly, Live's analysis of a file on import takes time, and you will not be able to play the file in sync right away. As well, Live's Warping engine does a great job of beat mapping new tracks, but it is not flawless, and you may get some surprises. You will get better results by doing a bit of preparatory work ahead of time on a selection of files you intend to play. Once you have gone through the Auto Warping process a few times, you will know what to expect, and it will go quickly.

The goal of Warping long samples is to have an accurate beat map that spans the entire song so the song plays back at a consistent tempo, which allows you to easily play tracks in sync with each other at any point in any song. Depending on the imported material, Auto Warp will function somewhere between perfectly and disastrously! It is up to you to help Live when it fails. Thankfully, you only have to go through it once for each track: once the beat mapping is correct, click the Save button in the Clip View Sample box to save the beat map with the song file.

The more rigid the tempo of the song, the more likely Live will guess the tempo correctly. This covers most electronic, pop, and hip hop music. If you are importing a song that does not have a clear, regular beat, or was not created/recorded to a click, Live will have a much harder time with the beat map. This includes a lot of rock, ambient, folk, and classical music. Let's go through a few typical scenarios:

Live guesses the tempo and downbeat perfectly—You're good to go! If the song starts with a downbeat and has a consistent tempo, Live will usually get it right on the first try. Live will insert a Warp Marker at the start of the song and at the end of the song to maintain a constant tempo.

Live guesses the tempo correctly, but misses the downbeat, consistent tempo—If the tempo is consistent, Live will often put in just a single Warp Marker at the start to govern the tempo, but sometimes will miss the downbeat. When this happens, the solution is simple:

1. [Shift-click] on the first Warp Marker, and drag the waveform left or right until the downbeat lines up with the first Warp Marker.
2. When you have the downbeat lined up, move the Clip Start and End Markers into place so the whole Clip plays the way you expect it to.

Live guesses the tempo correctly, but misses the downbeat, fluctuating tempo—Sometimes, Live has mapped the tempo for the entire song, getting rid of minor tempo fluctuations and locking it to the beat—say, for a rock song—but has misplaced the downbeat, so the beat counting is consistently off by a beat or two. This is also easily fixed:

1. [Ctrl-click/right-click] in the Warp Marker zone directly above the Clip's downbeat and choose "Set 1.1.1 Here" from the contextual menu. This will move the beat grid to start at your selected downbeat. Previous intro bars, if any, will have negative values. You can still move the Start Marker to wherever you want the song to start.

Live gets the tempo wrong, but guesses the downbeat correctly—This gets a little trickier. If the song's tempo is consistent throughout, and you know the tempo, simply enter it into the Seg. BPM box in the Clip View Sample box. If the song's tempo is consistent, but you do not know the tempo, you can figure it out using the following method:

1. Disable the Warp button for the Clip so the song plays back at its original tempo.
2. Play the track. While it plays, click on the "TAP" Tap Tempo button in the Control Bar to the beat of the music on the quarter notes. The Global Tempo changes to reflect the tempo you are tapping. Turn on the metronome if it helps to hear a click.
3. When you see an average tempo emerging, stop tapping. Refine the Global Tempo to your best guess for the average tapped tempo if it is not there already.
4. Re-enable Warp for the Clip in the Clip View Sample box.
5. In the Sample Editor, [ctrl-click/right-click] on the first Warp Marker and choose "Warp From Here (Start at n BPM)" where n is the current Global Tempo. This will tell Live to try tempos around the current Global Tempo you just tapped, and will often result in a correct beat mapping. If not, continue on to the technique in the next section.

Pic. 9.07: The Tap Tempo and Metronome buttons.

Live guesses the tempo and the downbeat incorrectly—This is usually due to tempo fluctuations in the song you are importing—for example, a live recording of a band. When you are importing this type of file, you will need to do a little hand-holding to get the beat map correct. First, try the Tap Tempo technique above. It may be that the Clip's original tempo and the current Global Tempo value when you imported the file were too different, and Live made some bad assumptions. If you set the Global Tempo more closely to the Clip's original tempo and then use "Warp From Here (Start at n BPM)," Live may get it right on the second try. If this doesn't work, the following technique is your only hope:

1. Click on any of the Warp Markers to select it. Press [cmd-a/ctrl-a] to select all Warp Markers. Press [delete] to delete all but the first Warp Marker.
2. [Shift-click] on the first Warp Marker, and drag the waveform left or right until the downbeat lines up with the first Warp Marker.
3. Press play. Manually add new Warp Markers every few bars as needed, and drag them to fit the intended beat grid. Continue through the whole song, adding Warp Markers as you go. Turn on the metronome if it helps, and use Follow [cmd-f/ctrl-f] to keep your view aligned with playback as needed.

Using the Crossfader

The Crossfader is a ubiquitous tool in DJ culture, allowing the DJ to deftly control the fade between two sources for ease of transitions between one track and the next. Turntablist DJs have taken the art of the Crossfader to the extreme, using it for all manner of scratching and beat juggling. I think we have only begun to see all of the permutations unfold in this arena.

In Live, the Crossfader allows you an elegant way to crossfade between your existing tracks. Unlike a DJ mixer, you could assign dozens of tracks to each side of Live's Crossfader. It is not essential to use the Crossfader, but it does add some interesting functionality.

To begin, do one of the following to show the Crossfader Section:

- Click the Show/Hide Crossfader Section button in the lower right corner of the Session View grid (the circle button with the X).
- Go View > Crossfader.

Pic. 9.08: The enabled Crossfader Section and the Show/Hide Crossfader Section button.

With the Crossfader Section showing, you will now see the Crossfader on the Master Track, as well as new A and B Crossfader Assign buttons under each track in the Mixer. The A/B buttons allow each track to have one of three different states:

- **A selected**—The audio on any track with A selected will play with the Crossfader hard left, and will fade out as it is moved to the right past the center position.
- **B selected**—The audio on any track with B selected will play with the Crossfader hard right, and will fade out as it is moved to the left past the center position.
- **Neither A nor B selected**—On tracks that have neither A nor B selected, the Crossfader will have no effect, and audio will play normally on the track regardless of the Crossfader position.

How you assign tracks to the Crossfader is a matter of personal taste and desired functionality. As we go through the various DJ setup styles below, we will look at some creative ways to use the Crossfader.

Cueing up Your Next Track in Your Headphones

Another important part of DJing is being able to listen to, or "cue up" your next track while another one is already playing. You can do this one of two ways, both of which require an audio interface with at least two pairs of outputs:

- If you own a DJ mixer, you can simply output multiple stereo pairs from your tracks in Live, through your audio interface, into the DJ mixer's various inputs. In this scenario, you can use the DJ mixer's cueing system, crossfader and channel volume sliders to do all your mixing. Enable multiple stereo outputs in the Preferences > Audio tab for your audio interface, and then assign various Ext. Outs on your tracks in Live. Leave all of Live's Track Volumes at 0.00 dB, and disable Live's Crossfader.
- If you prefer, you can do all of your cueing and mixing in Live, and then simply output your mix to the speakers directly, or run it through a channel in a DJ mixer that you never touch again once you set a decent gain. The latter often happens when you are playing at a gig with other DJs who do use the DJ mixer, and the P.A. system is set up to come from the outputs of the DJ mixer. The following section will walk you through setting up this type of internal cueing.

Cueing inside of Live is fairly easy to do, provided you have a soundcard that has at least two pairs of outputs: one pair plays the material going out through the speakers to your audience, while the second pair is reserved for cueing the next song on your headphones, which the audience will not hear until you are ready for them to.

To set this up in Live, do the following:

1. In Preferences, on the Audio tab, select the Output Config button and enable outputs 1/2 (stereo) and 3/4 (stereo). This will give you a pair for your main output and a pair for your cue output.
2. In Session View, Show the In/Out Section. On the Master Track in the In/Out Section you see two pull-down menus: Cue Out and Master Out. These settings control which hardware outputs each of these signals is going to. Set Cue Output to 3/4 and Main Output to 1/2.
3. The third step depends on your audio interface and the software that came with it. Most interfaces come with a program or control panel that will allow you to select which output the headphone jack on the audio interface is monitoring. You will need to learn how your interface handles this, and set the headphone jack to only monitor outputs 3/4. This way, when you divert a track to the Cue Out, you will hear it on your headphones, and not through the Master Out speakers. I have seen audio interfaces that only allow you to monitor outputs 1/2 on the headphones. In this case, set your Master Out—and connect your speakers—to outputs 3/4, and set your Cue Out to 1/2.
4. Back to Live. Now that you have different physical outputs for your Master and Cue Outs, a previously inactive button becomes functional in the Master Track next to the Master Volume: It says "Solo." Click it. It now says "Cue." This button changes all of your Track Solo buttons to Cue buttons, and they now all have a headphone icon rather than the usual S.
5. To Cue a track on your headphones, enable its Cue button. The track's audio will be heard on your headphones.

IMPORTANT! Note that enabling the Cue button on a track does not disable the track from *also* outputting to the Master Out! You will have to do that yourself. More than likely, this will solve itself if you are using the Crossfader: If you assign one track to A and one track to B and use the Crossfader to mix between them, you can safely use the Cue on the opposing track you have crossfaded away from since it will not be heard through the Master until you bring the Crossfader back to that side.

Pic. 9.09: A selection of song Clips on multiple tracks in no particular order.

DJ With Live #I: DJing an Improvised Set Using Whole Tracks as Clips

The simplest notion of DJing in Session View involves dragging entire beat-mapped tracks into Session View Clip Slots. You can simply stack up several tracks with Clips of songs you want to play in the Clip Grid. As you prepare to play a Clip, assign the track to one side of the Crossfader, or use the Track Volume fader, and fade into it. Obviously, you can't play two Clips in a row from the same track unless you want jump abruptly between them, but you can always move a Clip to a different track and play it from there. Put an EQ Three on every track so you can adjust for tonal differences as you go, and play multiple tracks at the same time without clashing.

DJ With Live #2: DJ a Planned Set with Whole Tracks as Clips, Plus Effects

The above scenario is fun for a casual setting where you are just choosing tracks as you go. You will spend a lot of your time cueing the next track, and working with EQ and volumes. If you want spend more of your DJ time working with effects, try planning your song order ahead of time so you know exactly what you intend to play and in what order.

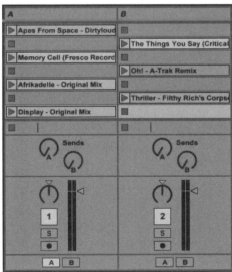

Pic. 9.I0: Checkerboarded Clips on opposing tracks in the Clip Grid.

1. Put your song Clips on alternating tracks, checkerboarding them so that launching a Scene will only launch one Clip on one track. Remove all Stop Buttons for the empty slots.
2. Assign one track to A and the other to B on the Crossfader. Now you can step through your set using the Scene Launch button, and crossfade between the tracks at your leisure without a lot of cueing.
3. Set up some Send effects, or make some interesting Audio Effects Racks on both Clip tracks, and/ or the Master.
4. Map your Scene Launch, Crossfader, Track Volumes, Track Sends and Audio Effects Rack Macros to a MIDI controller for maximum playability, and rock out!

DJ With Live #3: Split Songs into Looping Clip Sections and Stack Them in the Clip Grid

If you want to get more intimately into rearranging songs on-the-fly, or making mashups of two or more popular songs at once, this method may be for you.

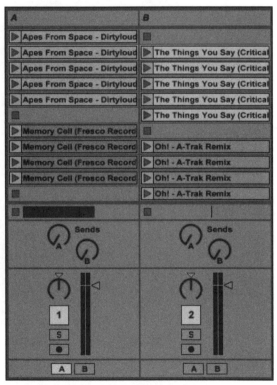

1. Instead of importing your songs directly to the Session View Clip Slots, drop them on the Arrangement View timeline first. Use [cmd-e/ctrl-e] to Split the track into logical sections: intro, kick drop, bass drop, main groove, first breakdown, etc., or intro, verse 1, chorus 1, verse 2, bridge, etc.
2. When you have done all your Splitting, select all the separated Clip sections at once, and use [cmd-x/ctrl-x] to Cut them from the Arrangement. Switch to Session View. Click in an empty Clip slot on a track and press [cmd-v/ctrl-v] to Paste the separated Clip sections vertically down the track into Clip slots.
3. Go through each Clip section and add a loop for the entire Clip, or part of the Clip, but leave the Clip Start at the beginning of each Clip so that it will start normally and eventually play into the loop. If you like, add a follow action to go to the next Clip after a period of time.
4. Now as you play through the song, you will be in charge of advancing from one section to the next. A Live hardware controller makes this process easy and fun, or assign Launch buttons and Scenes to a MIDI controller.
5. Do this for multiple songs, and pair song chunks that work well together on neighboring tracks. Use the crossfader to switch between them at will.
6. Add effects to individual tracks or the Master to add interest.

Pic. 9.11: Chunks of songs stacked in the Clip Grid.

DJ with Live #4: The Free-for-All Multi-Clip Jam

If you prepare well ahead of time, you can make a Session View Set where all the Clips generally work well together, volume and tone-wise, and then you can trigger Clips at will and not ever go completely wrong. Grouping Clips by type on various tracks—or by using Group Tracks—can help make sense of this maelstrom: beats, percussion, bass, pads, leads, vocal samples, etc. As you practice with this Set, you may find that some semblance of an order starts to emerge, so rearranging Clips vertically so you move through your set from top to bottom might keep you building toward some semi-planned climax or resolution. Again, a Live controller makes this type Set a lot more fun to execute.

Elements	Humans	Animals	Perc 1	Perc 2	Bass	Misc	Musical	VST	Loop Audio
underwater									
37 bpm A#8 pol		eagle	darbuka2	percussion_loo		groofie			
drippy rain	marketplace			percussion_loo	158 BILL LA				
shell	22 Market Place, Wa		100 doumbek effects	percussion_loo					
merulaST	walking traffic ambi		BL		077 Innercit	twinkle_fx01			
sibylla Long	pods					weirdsound			
lake water	kids		AK	conga_loop2	Looper0009	hipiano_fx01		3 9-MIDI	
waves		44 Tropical Daw	100 kool and the ga	tsuzumi		cowbells		1 9-MIDI	
thunderStorm				conga_loop2				1 9-MIDI	
sandcrabsHI	Crowd ambience (4)		060dlp01	conga1		spookipiano	Looper0004	1 9-MIDI	
04 30ft Yacht - A	Crowd ambience (2)	insects Dreame	Allan - Zaozara Inna	conga_loop2		TK	Looper0008	3 9-MIDI	
25 Sailing Dingh	Crowd ambience (5)	cricket1 Long	Atoms Family Feat.	conga1	158 BILL LA			13 9-MIDI	
07 30ft Yacht - A	24 Karate Class, Ap	cricket1 Long	111 daft punk fill	089 crooner dub	077 Innercit	089 sainkho dub		13 9-MIDI	
48 Ring-Tailed L			BOB JAMES Take m					13 9-MIDI	
crazy jungle	089 sainkho dubbed		118 Thai Awaits	tabla beat 80bp		Looper0006 10-			
station 1	Kenyon - Om Sri Gar	frogs Thailand	118 Thai Awaits	Tappatai090(trp		43 Tennis		1 9-MIDI	2 10-Audio
		45 Iberian Marsh				36-17 Glass Milk			
EQ-Epi015 Chd	21 Baby, Happy Sou	45 Red-Throated	116 K Hole	124 BagOf Choc	Looper0009	06 High Street, \		2 9-MIDI	3 10-Audio
EQ-Epi001 Chd				SlickDrm10 75		Looper0007 10-	Looper0004		
Looper0001 10-	21 Baby, Happy Sou	47 Willow Warbi	StrtBts 72 Slowburn	conga_loop2	158 BILL LA	Looper0005 10-	Looper0008		Looper0001
Looper0002 10-			ZG HH absolutely tri						

Pic. 9.12: A multiclip jam Set.

DJ with Live #5: The Scene-by-Scene Semi-Linear Attack

This is my personal favorite, as I feel it is the most creative, but it can take a considerable amount of preparation. Let's say you have made a series of original songs that could be presented together, but you don't want to just play the mixdowns: you want to mix each track's individual elements live. Try some version of this:

1. Open the first song's Live Set. Use Save As to save it as "(songname) live.als" or similar, so you are not working directly on your final version of your song.
2. Freeze and Flatten any MIDI Tracks that you don't want to manipulate Live, or for simplicity, Flatten all your MIDI Tracks.
3. Go through, track by track, and export logical looping sections of each track. If you built the song in Session View, this should be pretty straightforward. If you did it in Arrangement, highlight and export in logical chunks. Name the exported files something logical like "(songname)-(instrument)-(partname/number).wav".

4. When you have done this for all your tracks, move on to the next song and repeat.
5. When you have exported parts for all your songs, open a new Live Set and begin to build a Session View Clip Grid that moves you through your various parts of each song, Scene by Scene.
6. As you step through your Set, discover how you can add interest with Effects, and imagine how transitions between songs might work smoothly.
7. Although your songs are laid out in Scenes, this doesn't mean you can't stray from simply launching Scenes in a linear fashion. On the contrary, having all the parts broken out like this will allow you to remix your tracks on-the-fly with a great deal of room for creativity.

Things to consider as you prepare:

- You should take the time to plan what the various tracks in your final live Set will play and submix things accordingly: kick, clap, hats and percussion, bass, pads, leads, vocals, etc. If you are using a Live controller, perhaps you want to limit the number of final elements/tracks to eight so you can have a fader for each track without having to refocus.
- You should also plan what effects you will want to control in your final live Set, and disable this type of effect in each song before you render the individual parts.
- If you decide not to Flatten your MIDI Clips, it is entirely possible to build an Instrument Rack that will play a different Instrument Chain for each song, or even each Scene of each song! You can then create a Chain Selection for each MIDI Clip to make sure it plays the right Instrument Chain. Depending on how creative you want to get with your Instrument Racks, and how powerful your laptop is, you may never have to Flatten a single Clip!

Loops1	Loops2	Electro Revival	Battery	Blue	Bass 1	Bass 2	Piano
			2 5-MIDI	34 6-Blue	43 7-Bass 1	43 7-Bass 1	65 11-Piano
			2 5-MIDI	34 6-Blue	43 7-Bass 1	43 7-Bass 1	10 3-Piano
EQ-Lp627 BlastN2 100			2 5-MIDI		43 7-Bass 1	43 7-Bass 1	
					Fm	Fm	
		3 4-Electro Revival		13 5-Massive	Fm	Fm	20 3-Piano
EQ-Lp631 BlastN5 100	EQ-Lp608 A-Line1 100			13 5-Massive	15 7-Bass 1	15 7-Bass 1	20 3-Piano
EQ-Lp637 Digity2 100	EQ-Lp612 A-Line5 100	3 4-Electro Revival		13 5-Massive	Fm	Fm	20 3-Piano
EQ-Lp634 Creedz 100	RL TBL R 102			13 5-Massive	15 7-Bass 1	15 7-Bass 1	20 3-Piano
EQ-Lp631 BlastN6 100	RL TBL R 102	3 4-Electro Revival		13 5-Massive	15 7-Bass 1	15 7-Bass 1	20 3-Piano
					15 7-Bass 1	15 7-Bass 1	15 6-Predator
2 1-Audio					15 7-Bass 1	15 7-Bass 1	

Pic. 9.13: Songs divided into Tracks and Clips for remixing on-the-fly.

Whew! That should give you some DJing ideas to chew on!

Best Practices

If you intend to spend a lot of time with Live, you will want to immerse yourself deeper and deeper into the tool. Mastery of anything consists of living and breathing your craft. And with Live that means keeping up with updates, file management, knowing what all the Preferences do, visiting the Ableton website and forums, and keeping up with the greater Live community.

What follows here is wisdom distilled from having used the program regularly for many years.

ABLETON LIVE PREFERENCES

The Preferences options seem complex when you first start using them, but before long, you should grow to know them all intimately. I have met users who complain about a particular feature, and when I say, "Well, you know there's a Preference for that, right?" their eyes bulge and they shower me with thanks, as if I unlocked some magic treasure chest for them. But it is all right there—you just have to be willing to look.

I will elaborate here on only the Preferences that are exceptionally useful, are not self-explanatory, or could benefit from more detail:

Look/Feel

- **Follow Behavior**—This is a matter of taste, or "preference," if you like. I find I use the Page setting the most, as it seems less taxing on my system and eyesight.
- **Hide Labels**—A non-trivial switch. Once you get a big session going, reclaiming even a little screen real estate is a cause for joy, and once you know what everything does, Hide Labels will clean things up a bit in the Session View In/Out section.

- **Zoom Display**—This is a Preference that can solve a lot of eyestrain issues and allows you to customize the view for your monitor and viewing distance. Now, if I could just assign this value to my mouse wheel…
- **Skin / Brightness / Colors**—Probably the Most Popular Preference award would have to go to the Skin chooser, which is on this page. It may seem hokey at first, but when you spend long hours in front of the same interface, making it easy on the eyes is no small matter. There have been times when I get stuck on a song and will flip to a random skin and keep working. Try it. Sometimes a fresh visual perspective can seriously reframe your creativity. The new Brightness and Colors values should allow you to achieve just about any hue you desire.
- **Multiple Plug-in Windows**—Often it is useful to compare the levels and settings of two or more plug-ins, so having more than one window open at a time is essential.

Audio

Undoubtedly the most used Preference page on my system. Get to know it well.

The Audio tab in Live's Preferences offers you control over how Live interacts with your audio interface. You may find that you need to continue experimenting with the settings on this page until you get your setup to an optimized state. This is normal, so do what you can to get comfortable with the variables on this page. See the appendices on digital audio and latency for even more detail.

- **Audio Driver Type**—The first step is to choose the audio driver type from the first pull-down menu. If your audio interface has multiple driver types, consult its manual about which driver type you should use. If you are unsure, try one and see if your device shows up in the Input/Output pull-downs in the next step.
- **Audio Input Device and Audio Output Device**—Select your sound card in these pull-down lists.

Your audio interface comes with some number of audio inputs and outputs, typically a combination of each between 2 and 18. Some inputs and outputs may be analog, some digital. The next two steps will allow you to choose which ones you want to work with in Live:

1. Click on the Input Config button. If you chose your device in the Input/Output Device selectors, the selected device's available audio inputs should be listed here. Depending on your device and driver, your inputs may be listed here twice: as individual mono channels and as stereo pairs. The choices you make here will dictate which mono and/or stereo inputs you have available for recording on your Audio Tracks in Live's In/Out section of the Mixer. You can select any/all of the inputs you plan to use with Live, but keep in mind that every input you enable here does utilize some of your system's resources, so it is a good idea to enable only the inputs you actually plan to use. You can always come back and enable more inputs as you need them later.
2. Click on the Output Config button. The same rules apply here as they do for inputs. You may decide that you need only one pair of outputs for sending Live's output to your speakers. Then again, you may be doing some external processing or working in a multispeaker surround environment. Again, enable only the outputs you actually plan to use.

Here are some other important settings to consider on the Audio tab:

- **Sample Rate**—Your audio interface will likely be able to operate at a number of sample rates. Sample rate represents the number of amplitude measurements taken in a given second of recording by your audio interface. Reduced to its simplest terms, the higher the sample-rate setting, the higher the quality of the recordings you make, and the higher the quality of all internal processing done to the files, such as plug-ins, volume, panning, and so on. At the same time, the higher the sample rate, the larger the recorded file size will be, and the more computational power your computer will need to work with your files. If you work with a sample library whose sample rate is largely 44,100 Hz, or if your computer is an older model, try starting with a sample rate of 44,100 Hz. If your computer can handle working with higher sample rates, by all means, do. But if you find that your computer is struggling for resources when you are working on a reasonably complex Set, try lowering the sample rate to 44,100 Hz for future Sets. See a more detailed description of "sample rate" in the appendix on digital audio.
- **Buffer Size**—Your computer has a temporary repository of data that it holds in memory before handing it to, or taking it from, your audio interface. The size of this temporary repository is called the "buffer size." The lower the setting, the less delay (known as "latency") there will be as audio travels in and out of your computer, but the more of your computer's resources it will require. As the buffer size goes up, it becomes less taxing on your computer, but the latency for audio passing through increases. The best way to go about setting this is to start with it low and increase it as necessary. If you encounter clicks and pops while you are working, come back and raise the buffer size until the clicks go away.

Handily, Live provides you with a way to test this setting without ever leaving the Preferences window:

1. Set your buffer size as high as it will go.
2. At the bottom of the Audio Preferences tab is a Test section. Take the CPU Usage Simulator as high as it will go, to 80%.
3. Turn on the Test Tone generator. You can adjust the tone's volume and frequency to your liking, but for this test, only a comfortable volume is required and the defaults may be just fine.
4. Lower the audio buffer size until the Test Tone starts to audibly distort. You must press Apply (or [Enter]) after each adjustment. When the tone starts to distort, raise the buffer size in small increments until it no longer distorts. This is the lowest buffer size that your computer will be able to handle at near maximum CPU load. Remember this setting.

In short, if you are making an audio or MIDI recording, and you need to reduce latency, you can and should. Conversely, if you are just mixing and not recording, you can safely turn your buffer size up as high as it will go to put the least amount of strain on your computer and put all your resources toward making complex mixes with lots of plug-ins and software instruments. You will lose some responsiveness from Live's transport controls as you increase the buffer size—stopping and starting will be a bit more sluggish because it takes longer to fill the larger buffer—but your system will be as stable as possible. Note that this buffer size setting will be different for different audio interfaces and at different sample-rate and bit-depth settings. You may want to start a list of workable settings for each interface you plan to use.

See a more detailed discussion of managing latency in your recording process in the appendix section.

- **Driver Error Compensation**—If you find that the timing of all your recordings is off by a consistent amount, it is possible that your audio drivers are improperly reporting their overall latency to Live. You can use this value to nudge the timing of your recordings in either direction to compensate for this error. There is a good tutorial in Live's Help View lessons that will walk you through how to calculate this value.

MIDI Sync

This is the second most used Preference page, if you work with MIDI Devices. This Preference page is covered in detail in chapter 8.

File Folder

Lots of goodies on this page:

- **Save Current Set as Default**—This one is quite useful and is covered later in this chapter in the Templates section.
- **Create Analysis Files**—This switch is a trade-off between speed and clutter: if it is turned on, Live will create an analysis file (.asd) for any audio file loaded into a Set. This tiny file sits in the same folder as the audio file and has the same name as the audio file, but with the .asd extension. It contains information about the file's tempo and waveform, and this will greatly speed the future loading of the paired audio file into a Set. For longer files, this time savings is noticeable, and when you click on the Save button in the Clip View Sample box, Live will save all your Clip settings to the .asd file. The trade-off, however, is the creation of literally thousands of additional files on your hard drive. I just did a search for .asd files on my laptop and found more than 10,000 of them, totaling 500-plus MB. I guess it comes down to the question of how much hard-drive space your time is worth to you.
- **Sample Editor**—If you own a sample-editing program such as BIAS Peak or Steinberg WaveLab, you can specify its location here. Then, when you click on the Edit button in a Clip's Sample box, it will launch this editor and open that Clip's audio for editing. You can make destructive changes in this external editor, resave the file, and return to Live where the changes will be reflected.
- **Temporary Folder**—The location you set here will determine where new, unsaved Set data will live until you save it. If you open a new Set and make a recording, it will be saved here. You will want to clean out this folder from time to time, and you must do it manually.
- **Maximum Cache Size / Cleanup**—If you attempt to import a file type other than a WAV or an AIFF, such as an MP3 for example, Live will have to turn it into a WAV or an AIFF format before it can use the file. The decoded files live at this location, as do temporary files used during installations of updates and such. You can limit the total size of these cache files, as well as delete them periodically with the Cleanup button.

- **Rescan Plug-ins**—If you add, move, or remove plug-ins from your plug-ins folders outside of Live while Live is running, you can click on this button to have Live rescan the folders and relist them.
- **Use Audio Units/Use VST Plug-Ins System Folders (Mac only)**—AU plug-in files (.component) and VST plug-in files (.vst) are stored in Library/Audio/Plug-Ins/Components or VST respectively, and are shared by all applications that use these plug-in types. Live's use of the plug-ins in these two system folders can be turned on/off with these switches, which can be helpful when trying to isolate a buggy plug-in that is crashing Live.
- **VST Custom Folder (Mac only)**—In addition to the aforementioned system library VST folder, you can specify a second VST folder for plug-ins here. Some uses of this second folder could include having a separate folder of VST plug-ins that you use only with Live, or to have a second folder of newly installed freeware/betaware VSTs that you are still testing for stability. This way, you can always turn off the Preference for using this additional folder when doing mission-critical work or when performing live, for which having stability is essential. When a new plug-in has proven stable, move it from this secondary location into the main VST folder in the system Library. I like to keep an alias (shortcut) to both VST folders on my desktop (or in the Finder sidebar) so that when I get new VST plug-ins, they can easily be placed in one of these two folders.

Library

- **Collect Files on Export**—Whenever you export a Clip, Track or Preset to the Browser by dragging it there, this preference will determine how its associated files will be handled. For example, if you have an Audio Track with a number of Audio Clips on it that you want to export for use in some other Project, you can have Live automatically copy the Clips to the new location, not copy the Clips, or ask you if you'd like Live to copy the Clips. I leave this on "Ask" so that I have the option to decide each time.
- **Live Pack/Library Locations**—Here you can select a destination for these important supporting files. In my Mac Pro I have a hard drive dedicated solely to sample libraries and presets, so I also store my Live Packs and Libraries there as well.

Record Warp Launch

Some of these Preferences have been mentioned in chapter 6, but let's cover a few more of them here.

- **File type**—Here you can change the file type of newly recorded files between .aif and .wav, but there is no appreciable difference between the two, so either setting is fine. The .wav file type seems to be a bit more commonly utilized, so I use that, but I've never had a problem with either.
- **Bit Depth**—One of the more important settings for audio is not found on the Audio tab, but rather on the Record/Warp/Launch tab, and it is called Bit Depth. This setting works together with the Sample Rate setting to determine the file size and resolution (quality) of your recordings and processing. Bit Depth determines the resolution of each amplitude measurement taken by your audio interface when recording. The choices here are 16, 24, or 32. To a greater degree yet than sample rate, I encourage you to work at the highest setting your computer can handle. The file sizes will be bigger than 16-bit recordings, but they will benefit from wider dynamic range, more detail, and a lower noise floor. My advice is to start at 32 bits and take it downward if you find that your computer is struggling. See a more detailed description of Bit Depth in the appendix on digital audio.

- **Exclusive Arm/Solo**—Enabling either Arm or Solo causes Live to arm or solo just one Track at a time. If you select Arm or Solo on a second Track, Live will switch the arm or solo to the new Track rather than arm or solo them both. You can still override this Preference by holding down the [cmd/ctrl] key while clicking on either button to arm or solo multiple Tracks. Handily, the opposite is also true: if this Preference is disabled, Live will arm or solo as many Tracks as you click on, and you can still override this with a [cmd/ctrl]-click to force a single arm or solo at a time.
- **Record Session Automation in**—The two options here toggle between the ability to record Session Automation into all tracks at once, or only into the tracks that have their Arm buttons enabled. I prefer the latter, as it allows more flexibility, and I can specify exactly which tracks I want to record automation to.
- **Loop/Warp Short Samples**—This setting determines how Live will handle the importing of new, short Audio Clips. The Auto setting works for my needs most of the time, but if you work with one kind of file a lot—one-shot drums on the timeline, for example—you can make another choice here that will be more useful for you.
- **Auto Warp Long Samples**—Long samples can take a while to auto-Warp, so if you don't often want long samples to be Warped to tempo, turn this second setting off—importing will be far faster.
- **Default Warp Mode**—Beats makes sense if you use a lot of drum loops, but perhaps you make a lot of ambient music and prefer the sound of tones. Perhaps you have enough CPU to always use Complex or Complex Pro by default. A well-chosen setting here can save a lot of extra clicking in Clip View.
- **Create Fades on Clip Edges**—Enabling this preference enables the Fade button in the Sample box for all new Audio Clips. The Fade button puts a 4 ms fade-in/-out at the start and end of a Clip to mitigate audio files whose waveform does not start in silence, which usually results in an audible click. On some percussion samples with a very fast attack I can hear a slight decrease in punch, so I leave this preference off, and enable the Fade button in the Sample box manually on an "as-needed" basis.
- **Start Recording on Launch**—This setting is discussed briefly in chapter 6. Enabling it will allow you to start multiple Clips recording by launching a Scene. If you have a group jamming to a loop or the metronome, launching a Scene with one or more armed Tracks will begin recording Clips to the empty Clip Slots. This could also be useful for recording multiple takes of a section to multiple Clip Slots triggered with a footpedal.

CPU

- **Multicore/Multiprocessor Support**—Definitely leave this setting enabled if you have multiple processors/cores, which most computers do these days. This allows Live to spread the computational load out among the multiple CPUs.

RESOURCE MANAGEMENT

There are a number of places in Live where you can manage Live's usage of your computer's resources. Understanding how Live uses these resources will allow you to make prudent trade-offs between quality and stability.

64-Bit Compatibility

Until recently, operating systems were 32-bit capable, meaning that the way the OS processed data was limited to a data path of 32-bit resolution. One practical limitation of this is that a 32-bit OS, and all 32-bit programs running within that OS, could only address up to four gigabytes of RAM. With the advent of 64-bit operating systems, such as Mac OSX 10.5 or newer, and Windows Vista or newer, programs can now theoretically address up to 16 *exabytes*—that's 16,000,000,000 gigabytes!—of RAM. In mid-2012, Ableton released a 64-bit version of Live 8.4, and Live 9 also offers a 64-bit version. When you buy Live, you are authorized to use both 32- and 64-bit versions of the program, and you can even install both versions on the same computer.

While the immediate benefit of addressing additional RAM is a significant improvement, you should be aware that not all third-party plug-ins have 64-bit capable versions available, and your 32-bit plug-in versions will not natively work in the 64-bit version of Live. However, there are some work arounds, such as the inexpensive jBridgeM, which will allow you to use your 32-bit plug-ins with 64-bit Live.

If you have more than four gigabytes of RAM, my advice would be to keep track of 64-bit availability of your third-party plug-ins, as well as Ableton's integration of Live's own 64-bit features that you use, and make the move to 64-bit Live when the time is right for you.

CPU Load Meter

The percentile bar gives you feedback about how hard your computer is working to reproduce the current Set's audio and MIDI calculations. Keep in mind that every aspect of the program—from playing back a file to changing volume to an EQ plug-in—is math, and as your Set gets more complex, so does the math to play it back properly. There are many components of your computer working in concert to carry out the tasks that you are requesting of it, and your computer is only as fast as its weakest link. Read appendix D, "The Makings of a DAW," for more detail on this subject. Here is a list of the things that contribute to an overloaded CPU load meter:

Pic. 10.01: The CPU Load Meter in the Control Bar.

- **Non-Live background functions**—Turn off any other unnecessary background applications while Live is running. Every running application consumes CPU that could be devoted to Live instead. I've known some people who even disable their network capabilities to keep the CPU load meter down even further.

- **Sample Rate and Bit Depth settings**—The choices you select in your Preferences about which sample rate and bit depth you are choosing to work with will greatly affect the CPU load meter. Any calculation on an 88,200 Hz sample-rate file will take twice as much math to accomplish as a 44,100 Hz file. The same goes for bit depth, so an 88,200 Hz sample rate 32-bit file takes roughly four times the math of its 44,100 Hz, 16-bit counterpart. So these two settings are a trade-off between audio quality and track quantity.

- **Plug-ins and Instruments**—Every plug-in device is a series of math algorithms. The more complex the plug-in, the more math-intensive it is and the harder it is on your CPU to run it. Live's own plug-ins are optimized to be as low overhead as possible, but they will still add up. Third-party plug-ins and Instruments can range from being very light to being CPU vampires. The easiest way to tell what impact a plug-in device is having on your CPU is to bypass it while Live is playing and see how much CPU load is recovered. If you find a device that is hogging resources, you can disable it, replace it with another lighter plug-in, or "Freeze" the Track to recover some CPU power (see the next section for more on Freezing and Flattening). Aside from getting a faster CPU, having as much RAM as possible installed on your computer will allow you to run more plug-ins and Instruments simultaneously.

- **Hi-Quality/Oversampling mode for some Audio Effects**—Dynamic Tube, Flanger and Saturator have a Hi-Quality mode, and EQ8 and Glue Compressor have an Oversampling option. These modes will add some audio quality at the expense of CPU. By default, these modes are disabled when you add these Devices, but you can save their default settings with Hi-Quality mode turned on if you choose to. To toggle these modes on or off, [ctrl-click/right-click] on the title bar of the device and select Hi-Quality/Oversampling mode from the contextual menu. You will see the Save As Default option there as well. Additionally, note that the Reverb

Pic. 10.02: The Hi-Q High-Quality Rate Conversion button in Audio Clip View.

  plug-in has three modes of its own, each with increasing quality and computational complexity: Eco, Mid, and High.

- **High-Quality Sample Rate Conversion**—In any Audio Clip View there is a Hi-Q button in the Sample box that is enabled by default. This button governs the algorithms used for pitch transposition and real-time sample-rate conversion to the current sample rate. Disabling this button on Clips that are transposed or are being sample-rate converted will regain some CPU at the expense of some audio quality. A better option would be to sample rate convert all your samples to the same sample rate in another program so Live does not have to do it on-the-fly during playback, which is computationally complex, and therefore taxing on your CPU.

- **Complex/Complex Pro Warp modes**—Warping is definitely a CPU-intensive task, and these two Warp Modes multiply that complexity considerably. The default Warp Mode is Beats in Live's Preferences, which is one of the lightest on the CPU. Change this to one of the Complex modes only if you have the CPU overhead to do so. Another option is to Freeze Warped Tracks to recover a bit of CPU (see the next section, "Freeze Track," for more on Freezing and Flattening).

- **Audio Interface I/O**—Every enabled input and output on your audio interface will contribute to the CPU load meter. If you aren't using an input or output, disable it on the Audio Preferences tab to recover some CPU. See chapter 6, "Recording Audio with Live," for more on setting up your audio interface.

Audio playback functions are given the highest priority of all functions in Live. So when Live is reaching its CPU limits, other "secondary" functions (such as screen redraws of the interface) may become sluggish before you hear any audio dropouts. This is a good thing, as an audience won't mind if your screen redraws are sluggish!

Freeze Track

There will be times when you run low on CPU, even when heeding all of the above advice. Your only option at that point is to remove some Devices or to use Freeze Track to recover some CPU. Freezing is a function that turns your computation-heavy tracks, such as Instruments and complex Racks, into comparatively straightforward Audio Tracks by "printing" the device's output to one or more audio files and then disabling the original Devices. While the result is quite similar to recording or "resampling" a Track's output to another track, Freezing has the significant benefit of being reversible. Freezing can be done on any track, and the amount of CPU recovery will depend on the complexity and number of Devices that you are Freezing.

To Freeze a track that is CPU intensive, select the track in question and do one of the following:

- [Ctrl-click/right-click] on the track and choose Freeze Track from the contextual menu.
- Go Edit > Freeze.

When you do this, Live will present a progress bar as the chosen track is rendered to an audio file. This file is saved in the Project Folder > Samples > Processed > Freeze folder. If you Unfreeze a track and make even one change to a device on the track and re-Freeze it, a new audio file is created. When you are done working on a Project, it is a good idea to manually delete unused Frozen files, or use the File Manager (described later in this chapter) to remove the unused files.

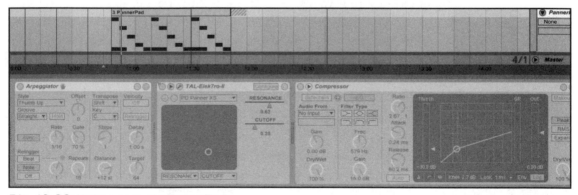

Pic. 10.03: Various parts of a Frozen Track.

When the Freeze Track operation is complete, the Frozen Track will now appear in an icy white color in Session View and Arrangement View, and so will all Devices on the track in Track View. Now that the track is Frozen, all device automation has been printed to audio, and no additional changes can be made to any of the track's Devices without first Unfreezing the track. However, here is a list of operations that still can be performed to a Frozen Track:

- Edit, cut, copy, paste, duplicate, and trim Clips.
- Draw and edit mixer automation and mixer Clip Envelopes.
- Consolidate.
- Record Session View Clip launches into the Arrangement View.
- Create, move, and duplicate Session View Scenes.
- Drag Frozen MIDI Clips into Audio Tracks.

IMPORTANT! Note that edits such as cutting and pasting sections of a Frozen Track will not cause the Frozen Track's temporal effects to be recalculated and re-Frozen, so you may end up with some unexpected reverb or delay tails. To avoid this, Unfreeze the track first, make the edits, and re-Freeze the track.

Frozen Tracks can be Unfrozen to make changes, which can be accomplished by selecting the desired Track(s) and doing one of the following:

- [Ctrl-click/right-click] on the track and choose Unfreeze Track from the contextual menu.
- Go Edit > Unfreeze.

Unfrozen Tracks regain all their original editing properties, as well as re-incurring their original CPU load.

As a Set becomes more CPU intensive than your computer can handle, try Freezing a track that is complex in its number and type of Devices and is a track that you may not need to make a lot of changes to. If you run into further CPU limitations, continue to Freeze more tracks. You may get into a more sluggish work flow of Freezing and Unfreezing Tracks as needed, but this work around will allow you to work on complex Sets far beyond what your computer would otherwise be capable of.

Flattening Tracks

Flattening a track consists of taking a previously Frozen Track and permanently transforming it to an Audio Track. All notes, Instruments, effects, and device automation is printed to one or more Audio Clips, and all Devices previously on the track are deleted. CPU recovery is permanent, but undoing can only be accomplished by stepping backward through the Undo history to a point before Flattening.

To Flatten a Frozen Track, select the Frozen Track and do one of the following:

- [Ctrl-click/right-click] on the track and choose Flatten from the contextual menu.
- Go Edit > Flatten.

While the Flatten command's undoable nature may seem disadvantageous, keep in mind that you can import tracks from previous Sets, so if you save a version of the Set just before Flattening, you can always reimport the un-Flattened Track at that state in the future. (There is more about importing tracks and Clips from other Sets later in this chapter.) Flattened Tracks also reacquire all the usual editing capabilities of a typical Audio Track, such as reversing, transposition, Warping, and so on, so these are more reasons that you might opt to Flatten a track.

Hard-Disk Overload Indicator and RAM Mode

Just as it is possible to overrun your CPU's ability to keep up with computational tasks, it is equally possible to overload your hard drive with data read/write operations. This is unrelated to running out of space on your hard drive, which is also a possible issue, of course. Instead, the Disk Overload Indicator comes on when your hard drive has exceeded its ability to keep up with storage and retrieval requests.

Pic. 10.04: The Disk Overload Indicator in the Control Bar.

A hard drive can read and/or write only so much data at a time. Standard-issue hard drives (especially in laptops) spin at a slower speed of 5,400 rpm, as opposed to the faster, media-optimized drives that spin at 7,200 rpm. In essence, the faster the rotational speed, the more read/write operations the drive can accommodate simultaneously, and the more heat they tend to put out. Newer solid state drives (SSDs) can yield higher throughput yet than 7,200 rpm spinning platter drives. (See more detail about this in appendix D, "The Makings of a DAW.") So the primary solution to disk-overload challenges is to be working with a fast hard drive to begin with.

Some other solutions to disk overload include the following:

- Turn off any other background applications that might try to access the hard drive while Live is running, including virus scanning, auto-saving, network sharing, file downloads/uploads, and so on. For maximum potential, quit all unnecessary applications other than Live.
- Put your audio files and Live Sets on a separate drive from your application drive that runs your operating system and Live. Dividing these tasks between different hard drives means each drives has to work less.
- Reduce the number of audio channels by recording in mono instead of stereo where possible.
- Reduce the number of Audio Tracks that are playing at one time by merging Audio Clips using "Resampling."

- Place some of your shorter Audio Clips into Clip RAM mode, which will store the Audio Clip in RAM rather than reading it repeatedly from the hard drive. Use this option carefully, because every Clip you put into RAM mode will then contribute to your overall CPU load.

Pic. 10.05: The Clip RAM mode button in Clip View.

Device Delay Compensation

Every plug-in or Instrument Device incurs a measureable amount of latency in addition to adding to the overall CPU usage. Literally, the math involved in a plug-in doing its job takes time, and so an audio signal that passes through the plug-in arrives later than if the plug-in were bypassed. Thankfully, all of the calculations to keep your signals in step with each other are handled by Live internally through a process called Device Delay Compensation. While this is a selectable option in the Options menu, it should be left on in most instances. Without it, tracks with a lot of plug-ins will fall noticeably out of sync with the rest of your Set.

FILE MANAGEMENT

Using a computer to produce music, you will quickly discover how crucial file management becomes: buying, storing, and organizing a sample library; naming, organizing, sharing, and backing up Sets; recording multiple takes of each section of each track to new files; rendering mix, submix, and resampled files; Live's Library, Presets, templates, and Live Packs—there are a lot of files to keep track of! Here is a collection of best practices for keeping your files functional. But first, a word about quality source materials.

Digital Audio File Types and Data Compression

If you were building a house that you intended to live in, you would likely not go to the lumber yard and buy the cheapest materials you could find. You would instinctively know that a quality house requires quality materials. The same concept applies to making music: you want to make and work with the best recordings possible. There is a time-honored phrase in the audio-engineering community that sums this idea up nicely: "Crap in, crap out." Meaning, if you start with compromised quality, you will end up with compromised quality.

Due to the advent of the Internet, data-compressed audio files such as the MP3 have become a ubiquitous delivery format. The standard 128 kilobits per second (kbps) MP3 is 11 times smaller in size than an uncompressed 16-bit, 44.1 kHz CD quality WAV file you would find on a CD. Think about that: take away 90% of the data, but still try to maintain the original's quality! The data compression used to make an MP3 definitely compromises the sound quality, but it is also amazing that it works at all!

The key phrase in the above paragraph is that an MP3 is a "delivery format," not a source format. When you are completely done with a mix (including final mixing and mastering at the highest resolution possible), then—and only then—it is time to make a low-resolution MP3 out of something if you must for delivery online. Even though Live supports them as an input type, you want to avoid using loops, samples, or recordings that are in a compressed file type (MP3, AAC, OGG, or FLAC) in your Live Sets if at all possible. Playback and mixing of one or two MP3s for DJ'ing is one thing. Mixing together many sections of many MP3s and trying to make a quality mix or remix is to fight a serious uphill battle. You will never achieve the results you are seeking if you start with compressed file types. Do a comparison between an original WAV file and an MP3 version of the same and be prepared to be amazed.

When you import a compressed file type into Live, the first thing Live does is to convert it to a .wav or an .aif for use in your Set, but do not be fooled into thinking that this somehow restores lost audio quality. This is the equivalent to taking a cassette and making a CD from it: it will simply be a quality recording of a low-quality source. There is no program or plug-in in the world that can restore an MP3 to its original quality. Lossy compression is a one-way ticket.

Making quality music means using uncompressed Pulse Code Modulated (PCM) files, which typically come in two flavors on personal computers: WAVE (.wav) and AIFF (.aif). These are the two formats that Live records in, and they are virtually identical in every way. They will each produce identical levels of quality at your chosen sample rate and bit depth. Look for, and make source materials in, these two formats. They may cost more and take up more hard-drive space, but isn't your music worth it?

You will also encounter a few application-specific file types such as REX files and file types designed for specific samplers; these are also uncompressed and perfectly acceptable to use for their given purpose.

Live Project Folders

The pivotal point for files used in Live is the Project folder. It is the point of file creation, integration and processing, and may also be the destination for file exports such as resampling and rendered mixdown exports. Like your bedroom, a Project folder can be either a relaxing expression of Zen minimalism or a virtual disaster area requiring protective clothing and a backhoe to navigate. How you choose to keep your files (and your bedroom) is up to you, but here are some tools for making sense of everything:

A Project folder consists of the following:

- **The Ableton Project Info folder**—a folder used by Live to store several small files needed to run the Project. Do not use or delete this folder.
- **Live Sets**—The Live Sets that are contained by the Project, often iterations of a single song, set, show or idea, but not necessarily so.
- **Presets folder**—If you save any Live Device Preset to a Current Project folder (there is one of these inside every Live Device Preset list), Live will make a new Presets folder in your Project folder that will contain your saved Presets.

- **The Samples folder**—Audio files created by the Project's Sets. This folder may contain one or more of the following subfolders:

  ○ **Imported**—Files imported to the Live Set from elsewhere, but were copied to the Project folder at some point as the result of a Collect All and Save command.

  ○ **Processed**—Files created by Live as a result of some processing action. Live creates subfolders for each of these processes, such as:

    ▸ **Consolidate**—Any audio files that are consolidated together will show up here as a single new file.
    ▸ **Freeze**—Frozen Tracks will render their results here. Each new Freeze is a new file.
    ▸ **Reverse**—Clips that have been reversed with the Reverse button in Clip View will write a new file here.
    ▸ **Waveforms**—Any samples used in a Simpler, Sampler, or Impulse that were copied here as the result of a Collect All and Save command.

But a Set can reference audio and MIDI files from anywhere outside the Project folder as well. For example, you might choose to use additional audio from the following places:

- The Live Library.
- Your own sample library from purchased data CDs, from DVDs, downloaded from websites, or recorded in the field.
- Your own digital music library, perhaps consisting of MP3s.
- Other Sets you have made.
- Audio files on a server on your local network.

In essence, you might use an audio file from anywhere you can get your hands on it! When you drag a file into a Live Set, one of two things happens:

- If the file is already in an uncompressed file format that Live can use natively (AIFF, WAV, REX, SDII [Mac]), Live will simply use the file as is, and the source file stays where it is.
- If the file is a compressed file type that Live recognizes (MP3, AAC, Ogg Vorbis, Ogg FLAC, or FLAC), the file is quickly decoded into a new WAV or AIFF that is stored in Live's Decoding Cache. The original file stays where it is.

Note that in neither case is the imported file moved or copied into the Project folder, added to the Live Library, or put in your own sample library. This is both good and not so good:

- It is good because you likely want the original file to stay where it is: perhaps it is part of another Project, the Live Library, your own sample library, or your music library, and moving it would harm other uses of the file.
- It is not so good because the files needed for your current Project are not all kept together in one place, and if any of those external files are moved, renamed, or deleted, your current Project will no longer work properly. Also, if you share the Project folder with someone, it will not have all the files needed to play properly on their system.

The only files that are stored by default in a Project folder's Samples folder are the ones created or modified within the process of building you Set. These include the following:

- Audio that's been recorded into your Set from an external input or that's been Resampled between tracks.
- Frozen, Flattened, consolidated, and reversed Clips.

The remaining audio files used in your Set stay where they are—unless you tell Live to do otherwise, such as using the following function: Collect All and Save.

Collect All and Save

Collect All and Save is an invaluable function in the File menu that copies external files currently in use in the Set into the Project's Samples folder. This function makes the Project folder self-contained so that it may be moved and used elsewhere or backed up to an archive without potentially having to track down missing external files later. You should use this function whenever doing the following:

- You are going to share your Project with someone else.
- You are going to use the same Set on another computer that may not have all the same files.
- You are going to archive the Project and want to make sure that the archive is self-contained.

When the function is invoked, a dialog comes up that asks you which file types you want to collect into the Project folder.

You may choose any or all of the four source locations:

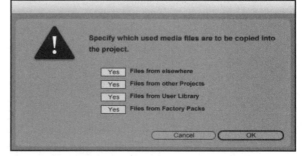

- Files from Library
- Factory Files from Library
- Files from other Projects
- Files from elsewhere

Pic. 10.06: The Collect All and Save dialog box.

If, for example, you know you are going to reopen the Set on another computer and you know that the second computer has identical Factory Library Files, you could deselect that box and opt not to collect copies of those files to the Project folder, as they would be redundant if they were in both locations.

I tend to share Projects with other musicians a lot, and I try to be vigilant about making regular backups of important Projects. I also find that the Audio Clips that are most regularly external to my Projects tend to be small audio files, such as loops, one-shot drum hits, REX files, and short recordings from my own sample library. So on both counts, Collect All and Save has become part of my standard work flow and it has saved me on many occasions.

The only time I find that I intentionally avoid Collect All and Save is when I have a series of Projects that all reference the same large files, such as DJ Set, or a performance Set of rendered high-resolution stems. In these instances, Collect All and Save would only serve to make redundant copies of large files that are already being backed up anyway, and this would waste time and hard-drive space.

File Manager and Missing Files

The more advanced version of Collect All and Save and many other useful functions can be found in the File Manager, which can be invoked in one of several ways:

- Go File > Manage Files.
- Go View > File Manager.
- [Ctrl-click/right-click] on any Project folder, Set, Preset, sample, or Live Library file and choose Manage File from the contextual menu.

The File Manager gives you access to a whole platter of delicious file-management tasks, including the following:

- Discovering and deleting unused consolidated, recorded, or Frozen files that may have accumulated in your Samples folder and are just wasting space.
- A more detailed Collect All and Save type operation.
- A list of Clips and Presets used in your Project.
- Listing missing files and a way to refind and relink them.
- Exporting Clips and Projects to the Library for future use.
- Creating compact Live Packs for sharing Live Projects with others.
- Working with and repairing your Library.

All of these functions eventually come in handy, but your first use may be when you open a Live Set and discover that files are missing. Missing files occur when you move, rename, or delete files in use by your Live Project. Often this happens due to actions done outside of Live, such as when you are reorganizing your sample library's file structure for some well-intentioned reason. Then you reopen a Live Set and Live cannot find the files needed by the current Project. If you still have the files but they have just been moved, do not panic—you can easily relink them with the File Manager's missing files search tool. If you no longer have the missing file, well…

Importing Sets, Tracks, and Clips

This extremely useful set of functions is also intuitively easy to use. Let's say you are working on a Set and you find that you want to import a Clip, a track, or even another entire Set into this Set. Piece of cake:

- In the Live Browser, navigate to find the Set that contains the elements you want to import.

- If you want to import the entire Set, drag the Set icon onto the empty area after your last track. The entire Set is imported to new tracks, including all tracks, Clips, Devices, and automation.
- If you want to import a track, click on the expansion triangle next to the Set icon to see a list of that Set's available Tracks. Drag one of the Track icons onto the empty area after your last track. That track's Clips, Devices, and automation are imported onto a new track.
- If you want to import a single Clip, open the expansion triangle next to the track that contains the Clip you want to import in order to see a list of its available Clips. Drag the desired Clip onto a track or onto the empty area after your last track to put it on a new track.

The Live Library

Think of the Live Library in much the same way you would a traditional library with books: The sounds and files in the Library are there to be accessed by all your Sets. Just as a librarian curates the books in a library with care and detail, handle your Live Library with the same consideration. Do not arbitrarily move, rename, or delete items in the Library unless you are sure of what you are doing.

Having said that, there are some great uses for the Library. They include the following:

The ability to save a new default Set—This very handy function is initiated from the first button on the Preferences/File Folder page, and it will save your current Set as the default New Set. Once you establish a favorite way of working, you can make a template blank Set that has all of your favorite settings predefined:

- Your favorite input/output setup customized for your audio interface.
- Preset Devices, like EQs and Compressors on every track, a favorite Impulse or Drum Rack ready to go on a MIDI Track, or a favorite mastering Audio Effect Rack on your Master Track.
- Preset favorite Track Groups, names, and colors.
- Predefined computer key mappings and MIDI mappings specific to your Devices and way of working.

Saving default sample drop actions—You can customize what Live will do when you drop an audio file on an Audio Track's Track View or on a Drum Rack's empty cell. Either of these actions typically creates a Simpler Device, and if you have favorite settings that you find yourself using regularly within this device, you can save them as defaults by doing the following:

- Create an empty Simpler (or Sampler if you own it).
- Adjust the parameters as you like.
- Drag the edited device to either the On Drum Rack or On Track View folder, which can be found in the Browser at Library > Defaults > Dropping Samples.

Saving New Audio/MIDI Track Defaults—If you find yourself using the same combination of Devices on new tracks, you can modify the default new track so that every new track starts the way you like it:

- Create a new track of the type you wish to modify.
- Add the Devices to the new track you wish to have as the default for new tracks. Adjust the device parameters to your liking.
- [Ctrl-click/right-click] on the track's name and choose "Save as Default Audio/MIDI Track." All future tracks of that type will include your Devices and settings.

Saving new Slice To New MIDI Track Presets—Live ships with several Slice To New MIDI Track Presets that do some pretty amazing things. If you want to create your own Presets for this function, do the following:

- Create an empty Drum Rack.
- Add an empty Simpler or Sampler to the Drum Rack to create a single Chain.
- Add any additional MIDI or Audio Effects to this Chain.
- Adjust parameters in any of the Devices.
- Assign Macro Controls to any of the controls in the Chain's Devices.
- Drag the entire Drum Rack to the Library > Defaults > Slicing folder.

Saving new Convert Harmony/Melody/Drums to New MIDI Track Presets—If you would like to alter the default device for any of these functions, do the following:

- Create a MIDI track containing the instrument you would like to use as your default for a particular conversion type. Note that default presets for converting drums must contain a Drum Rack.
- Add any further MIDI or Audio Effects to the track.
- Adjust parameters in any of the devices.
- If you're using multiple devices, group them to a Rack.
- Drag the entire Rack to the appropriate folder in Defaults/Audio to MIDI in your User Library.

Saving Presets for Live Devices to the Library—When you save a Preset from any Live Device, it is saved to your Library unless you specifically choose to save it to the Current Project folder in a Live Device Preset list. Presets saved to the Library will be available to any future Sets, while Presets saved to the Current Project are only immediately available to that Project, but have the added benefit of being transferrable along with your Set to someone else.

Ableton Live Packs and Factory Live Packs (.alp files)—An Ableton Live Pack is a means for packing and compressing Projects and additional Library content for archiving or distribution as a single file. Live Projects can be made into Live Packs via the File Manager's Manage Project page. A Live Pack has the .alp extension, and has the benefit of being up to 50% smaller than the Project folder that was used to create it. An .alp file can be unpacked simply by double-clicking on it or dropping it onto an open Live Set. While unpacking, Live will ask you where you want to store the unpacked content. If the Live Pack contains files that I might use in future Projects, I will unpack it into a folder I made in the Library called "Live Packs." Ableton will often distribute new Library content (new Instrument Devices, samples, Presets, and so on) in the form of a Live Pack, and these are called Factory Live Packs. Factory Live Packs automatically unpack their contents into your

Library without giving you any other options. All installed Live Packs can be viewed and uninstalled from the Preferences > Library page.

Saving a MIDI Clip or an Audio Clip to the Library—While it is possible to save MIDI or Audio Clips to the Live Library (either through dragging a Clip into a folder in the Library via the Browser or by using the File Manager's Manage Project page), I don't recommend doing so for the following reasons:

- If you work with your sample files in other audio programs, it is not convenient to go hunting for them inside of the Live Library's folder structure.
- The Live Library is already a fairly large collection of files. Placing a large number of additional samples into it would make it unwieldy.
- The Live Library is a constantly evolving database of information that is updated regularly when you install updates or make upgrades to Live, or when opening Live Packs. While it is unlikely that the Live Library would become corrupted and need to be reinstalled, it is a possibility—and for that reason I prefer to maintain a separate sample library in its own folder structure outside of the Live Library.

Backups

One final thought:

I call the item in the picture above my "Totem to the Impermanence of Digital Data." Barely recognizable, it is a box of floppy disks (remember them?) that melted in a fire that occurred at my sister's house. I don't know what was on the disks, but that is unimportant. I put it on my studio desk where I can see it every day. I use it as a reminder that no digital data is permanent. The loss of digital data is not a question of "if," but rather of "when."

I taught audio-production classes at the Art Institute of Seattle for

Pic. 10.07: My Totem to the Impermanence of Digital Data.

more than a decade. Students came and went with their laptops and portable hard drives containing all their recording work. While there, a fellow instructor and friend, Tom Pfaeffle, would regularly tell his students, "Digital files do not exist unless they exist on at least three different devices." He would then go over to the studio's computer, open a file browser to the storage drive where students recorded their sessions, select all the files, and move them to the trash. If students had not backed up their work to their own external drives as regularly instructed to do, they would understandably panic! Students quickly came to refer to data loss as having been "Pfaeffled." Tom's technique was severe, but the important lesson was painfully clear: learn to back up your data or prepare for disappointment.

Your music creations are important to you. You likely spend a great deal of time imagining, composing, arranging, mixing, and rendering them. The fruit of all this effort is nothing more than a series of ones and zeros, which are kept on some storage device. Those storage devices will fail (or be stolen, dropped, misplaced, eaten by the dog, caught in a fire), and when they will fail is completely unpredictable. So, your only recourse is to have some system of redundancy: storing your files in multiple places on multiple devices. This could be a combination of computers, hard drives and DVD-Rs, ideally stored in different geographic locations. The method of making backups can be as simple as dragging-and-dropping or using a program like Apple's Time Machine.

These days, we are blessed with broadband data connections, and there are now a host of companies, such as Carbonite.com, that offer online data backup that happens seamlessly in the background. I do not rely on such a system as my only backup solution, but paired with redundancy at my home studio, it does add an additional layer of peace of mind.

Appendices

Appendix A: Frequency and Amplitude

Sound is vibration. Air particles are the primary medium that acts as a carrier between the vibration source and your inner ear.

Audio is transduction, the art of turning one thing into another. Your inner ear is a transducer that turns these vibrations into electrical impulses in the brain, which you then perceive as sound.

A microphone is a transducer. Like your ear, a microphone turns vibrations into a tiny electrical current, which when amplified with a microphone preamp to a line level, can be recorded, manipulated, and ultimately amplified and sent to a speaker.

A speaker is a transducer. It takes electrical current and moves a magnetic coil that moves a speaker cone that, in turn, makes new vibrations in the air that your ears and brain can again transduce into sound.

An audio interface to a computer is a transducer. It takes "snapshot" measurements of electrical current and turns them into binary numbers that can be manipulated and stored. Ultimately those numbers can be transduced back into a current by your audio interface and sent to an amplifier, a speaker, the air, your ear, your brain, the world.

There are an infinite number of variables in sound and audio that affect what you hear and how you hear it. The two that you will work with the most as a manipulator of audio are frequency and amplitude.

FREQUENCY

"Frequency" is the rate of speed, or how "frequently" something vibrates. Frequency is measured in hertz, which is a simple way of saying "number of times in a second." At a young age, the average person can perceive up to 20,000 vibrations per second, commonly referred to as 20,000 hertz (Hz) or 20 kilohertz (kHz) meaning "thousands of times per second." On the low end of the scale, somewhere around 20 Hz and below, we cease to "hear" the vibrations as sound and rather "feel" it in our bodies.

Between these two extremes, we experience frequency as pitch. Every doubling of frequency is referred to as an octave. We can hear roughly a ten-octave range of musical notes. The central frequency that we base our Western musical architecture on is 440 Hz, which translates to the note A on the musical scale. The frequency of the other A notes below "concert A" are multiple halves of 440: 220 Hz, 110 Hz, 55 Hz, and 27.5 Hz. The octaves above concert A are logically multiple doubles of 440 Hz: 880 Hz, 1,760 Hz, 3,520 Hz, 7,040 Hz, and 14,080 Hz.

In audio, any circuit or processor will change the frequency makeup of a signal to a greater or lesser degree. Quality audio gear is often known for its "transparency," which means the unit's ability to pass an audio signal with an absolute minimum of unintentional frequency change to the signal it is passing. Some devices are said to "color" the sound passing through it, which can be an aesthetically pleasurable improvement in the sound, or a subjective diminishment. All audio devices, from microphones to mic preamps to speakers to audio interfaces, are sought out (or passed by) for their perceived "coloration" of the sound they pass.

To intentionally manipulate the relative balance of frequencies in a recording, you use an equalizer, or EQ for short. An EQ can raise or lower the volume of specific frequency ranges to alter your perception of the material. There are several different EQ interfaces for making these frequency adjustments, such as graphic, parametric, and paragraphic EQs. But any EQ presents the user with a range of frequencies to manipulate and an adjustment for the amount of boost or cut desired. The art of EQ'ing audio is a lifelong endeavor of careful listening and exploration.

AMPLITUDE

The other important dimension of sound and audio is known as "amplitude," and our brains experience amplitude as volume. If frequency is the measurement of the rate at which air particles vibrate, amplitude measures the amount that they vibrate. Tiny vibrations in the air might be barely audible to our ears, while an enormous volume of sound, traveling in great waves of vibration, may actually overwhelm and damage our ears.

The scale of measurement for amplitude is the decibel (dB). Essentially, the decibel is a relative measurement, meaning that it measures amplitude relative to some known, constant value. There are several different decibel reference points in audio, and as a result there are several different scales of amplitude measurement, and this is what creates a lot of the confusion about using decibels.

The second cause of confusion is that the decibel is a logarithmic scale. The dynamic range of human hearing is so vast that if you used a linear scale to measure it, you would be regularly working with values that were gigantic. Can you imagine saying to an engineer in the studio, "Would you bring the guitar down about 2,000,000 units, please?" Instead, the logarithmic nature of the decibel allows you to use much more manageable numbers, usually less than 100 in size. In logarithmic decibels, every 3 dB represents a *doubling* of volume: 100 dB + 100 dB = 103 dB.

A decibel reference that is fairly easy to understand is known as the Threshold of Hearing, which is the quietest sound you can perceive. The Threshold of Hearing is referenced to 0 decibels (dB) sound pressure level (SPL), or 0 dB SPL for short. Sounds louder than that are given a dB SPL value relative to the Threshold of Hearing. For example, the typical volume for a conversation between two people in a quiet environment is around 60 dB SPL, which means that the sound level is "60 decibels louder than the quietest sound you can perceive." A band in a nightclub can be as loud as 110 dB SPL. The top extreme of the dB SPL scale, known as the Threshold of Pain, is the volume at which sound becomes painful, and that is somewhere around 120 dB. So, from 0 to 120 dB SPL, the range of human hearing, there are 40 doublings of volume. That should give you some new appreciation for what our ears are capable of!

In audio, amplitude can be manipulated in a variety of ways, from a simple push of a volume fader to compressors, limiters, expanders, and gates. Any processor will change the frequency and amplitude of the signal passing through it. The question is how much, and do we like it?

Appendix B: Digital Audio

As mentioned previously, in order to work with an audio signal in the digital domain—such as inside Ableton Live—the audio signal must pass through a stage of "analog to digital conversion" (or ADC) at some point. ADC is the point at which an electronic current is digitized, or "sampled," into numeric values. Later, when the digital audio is played back, the sampled numeric values must be converted back into an analog current that can be amplified and passed through a speaker. This is known as "digital to analog conversion" (or DAC). Two important variables that govern the quality, or resolution, at which these conversions takes place are known as sample rate and bit depth.

SAMPLE RATE

When you watch a movie in the theater, you are not watching continuous motion on the screen. Instead, you are watching a series of still images that fool the brain into believing that it is watching continuous motion. These still images are displayed at 24 images—also known as frames—per second. If the rate of images per second drops below about 15 frames per second, the brain starts to be able to perceive individual still images, and is no longer fooled.

Sample rate in digital audio works in a similar fashion. Like a moving visual image in the real world, sound travels in a continuous stream and has an infinite "resolution," as does an analog audio current traveling on a wire. In order to convert this constant stream of current to into numbers that can be stored in and reproduced by a computer, your audio interface must take a series of regular amplitude measurement "pictures," known as samples. When these samples are later played back and turned back into current by your audio interface, there must be enough information, or "pictures," to fool your ear into believing that what it is hearing is a consistent flow of audio. The more samples per second taken, the greater the resolution of your audio "picture," and the more natural the audio will seem. Without enough resolution, your ear begins to hear digital artifacts interfering with the recorded signal, and is no longer "fooled."

A compact disc (CD) uses a sample rate of 44,100 samples per second. Like frequency, sample rate is expressed in hertz, or Hz, so a CD uses a sample rate of 44,100 Hz, or 44.1 kHz. This standard is considered today to be the minimum resolution for successfully "fooling" the average listener on good equipment in an ideal listening environment. Many higher-end studios today make their recordings at sample rates of 88,200 Hz (twice CD quality), 96,000 Hz (twice DVD quality of 48 kHz), or even 192,000 Hz (four times DVD quality).

Since sample rate and frequency are both measured in hertz, you may have inferred that there is some kind of relationship between the two. Without going into a lot of technical jargon, the relationship can be summed up in this way: the highest frequency that can be represented in a digital audio recording is equal to one-half the recording's sample rate. So the highest frequency that can be represented on a CD would be 22,050 Hz. That frequency is above the range of human hearing, so you might wonder, "Why would you ever need to use a higher-resolution sample rate than 44,100 Hz?" That is a question of constant debate within the audio community.

Here is my take on it: All processing in the digital domain—a reverb, compressor, or EQ plug-in, or even a simple volume change—is math. A mix made in a Live Set is essentially one gigantic equation. So the primary benefit of higher sample rates is not only the increased resolution of each recording, but also the increased resolution of every math calculation made on those files from that point on, such as plug-ins, volume, panning, and eventual merging of signals into a final stereo output.

The same can be said for bit depth, discussed in the next section. (See appendix E, "The Makings of a Producer's Studio," for a discussion on audio-interface quality and its effect on sound quality.)

BIT DEPTH

We've determined that sample rate represents the rate at which your audio interface takes amplitude measurements of an incoming analog signal. Bit depth represents the level of detail—or resolution—of each of those measurements.

If I were to ask you to tell me the value of pi in order to calculate the area of a circle, you might say "pi = 3.14." But the value of pi is actually a number of infinite resolution. You simply chose to use a resolution of two decimal points, and called it "close enough." Calculating the area of a circle using 3.14 would get you pretty close to the actual area, but if you used a value of pi that instead went out to 50 decimal places, you would get a much more accurate answer.

In digital audio, the resolution of amplitude measurements, or bit depth, is measured in bits. A bit is a single binary unit, meaning a one or a zero. Therefore, 16-bit amplitude measurement, which is the bit depth of a CD, might look like this: 0101110101100011 (16 ones or zeros). Counting in binary, there are 65,536 possible values between 0000000000000000 and 1111111111111111. By comparison, 24 bits yields 16,777,216 possible values, which is a significant increase in resolution.

So where sample rate correlates to frequency, bit depth correlates to amplitude. The larger the bit depth, the more dynamic range your recordings can have. Dynamic range is defined as "the difference between the loudest and quietest possible sound." So, you could say that the human ear has roughly 120 dB of dynamic range. In digital audio, every bit represents 6 dB of dynamic range. So a 16-bit recording can have 96 dB of dynamic range and a 24-bit recording can have 144 dB. Again, a significant increase.

The digital audio measurement scale is known as "decibels (dB) below full scale (fs)," or dBfs. In digital, the reference point of 0 dB is at the top of the scale, which represents the largest amplitude that can be measured, and all other measurements are a relative negative value below zero. The reason for this is simple: In the above discussion about 16-bit resolution, there is no way to measure a value above 1111111111111111, which is known as "full scale" because all of the bits are "on." So the standard is to make 1111111111111111 equal to 0 dB, and measure all other amplitudes relative to (and below) that. That is why all amplitude (volume) meters in digital audio use negative values.

Appendix C: Latency

In terms of digital audio, "latency" means the time it takes for audio to pass through your computer, and it is determined by your buffer size setting. You will become most aware of latency when you try to make a recording into Live and there is a noticeable delay between what you play and what you hear coming out of your headphones. If the delay you are experiencing is too long, it can make recording a good performance impossible. Minimizing latency is a daily part of working with computers and audio, and there are several ways to go about it.

Seemingly the easiest method for minimizing latency is to lower your buffer size until the delay is so insignificant that it is no longer a problem. This may work just fine for your needs. A good audio interface with well-written software drivers should have a manageably small amount of latency to begin with. And when you are recording at the early stages of a song when the complexity is low (track counts, number of plug-ins in use, and so on), there may be little strain on your computer's resources, so a very small buffer size may be possible. But as your Sets get more complex, low buffer sizes may not be an option. What to do?

The answer lies in what is known as "external monitoring" or "hardware monitoring." Some audio interfaces have an option for this that is built in, but you can achieve much the same thing using an audio mixer. The idea is to monitor the signal you are recording before it goes into your computer. Consider these three different setups for monitoring:

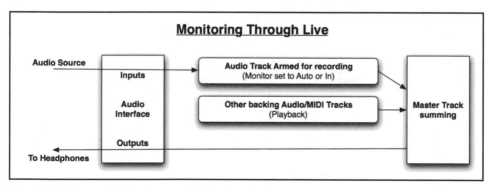

Pic. A.0I: Internal Monitoring: monitoring the signal to be recorded through your computer.

- In this first picture, audio comes out of the audio interface's outputs and connects to headphones and/or speakers for monitoring. The recording track's Monitor is set to Auto or In so that the recorded signal will be heard along with the other Tracks in Live. Since the incoming signal passes through both the input and output buffer of the audio interface before it is heard, latency is incurred. Depending on the size of the Audio Buffer setting in Audio Preferences, this delay may or may not be big enough to present a challenge to the performer.

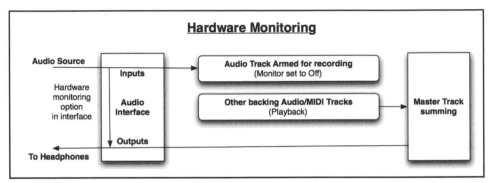

Pic. A.02: Hardware Monitoring: monitoring the signal to be recorded before it goes to the computer using the audio interface's Hardware Monitoring feature.

- In the second picture, the audio interface offers a "hardware monitoring" option that sends a copy of the incoming signal to the headphone jack (or outputs to speakers) so that the performers can monitor their performance, mixed with the backing tracks coming out of Live. Because they are monitoring their own signal before it is digitized by the audio interface, there is no audible latency in their headphones. The input also goes to Live, where it is recorded, and the Monitor setting in Live's In/Out section would be set to Off so as not to hear a second, delayed version of the signal through the computer.

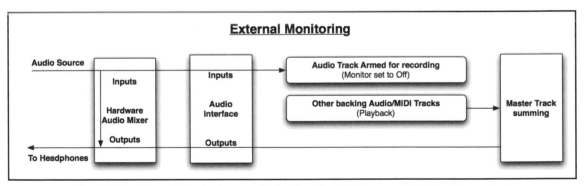

Pic. A.03: External Monitoring: monitoring the signal to be recorded before it goes to the computer.

- In the third picture, a hardware mixer is used to achieve external monitoring of sources alongside of Live's output. This provides essentially the same latency-free solution as hardware monitoring does, through an audio interface that has the added bonus of being able to mix and monitor other sources such as keyboards, drum machines, and so on, and easily incorporate external hardware processing of signals. All these items can be left plugged in, and each can be routed to the audio interface for recording via the mixer's subgroup or auxiliary buses, as desired. In this setup, all monitoring is done at the mixer, and Live's recording channels would again be set to Monitor: Off.

These three methods represent the main techniques for working with—and avoiding—latency. Consult your audio interface's manual for more advice on managing latency.

Appendix D:
The Makings of a DAW

The personal computer is still a fairly recent invention. I remember when I was 12 years old and my father brought home an Apple II+, one of the first personal computers available. It had 64 kilobytes of RAM, a black-and-white 12-inch monitor, a 5.25-inch floppy drive for saving data, and a cassette drive for loading programs. It seemed like a tool of formidable power and mystery to me then, but today, the average cell phone packs more computational power than the Apple II+ had! And while working with digital audio on computers really started to become viable in the mid-1980s, the most prevalent operating systems of the day were built primarily with word processing and spreadsheets in mind. Working with audio (say nothing of video, audio's big brother) on a personal computer has always been something of a niche industry, in which you have to shoehorn the operating system into doing all kinds of things it was never originally intended to do, often at the bleeding edge of its capabilities. This situation has gotten better over the years—quite a bit better—but it still has not yet achieved rock-solid stability. However, along with the improvement of hardware and software, computer audio enthusiasts have chiseled out some best practices for making the bumpy road less bumpy. I share some of these ideas below.

Keep in mind that in addition to Live, your controllers, and all those third-party freeware audio mangling plug-ins, your computer is your instrument. Just the way that John Coltrane knew his horn inside and out, you should get to know how your computer works intimately if you want to excel at your craft. A digital audio workstation (DAW) is a many-headed beast of great complexity. Knowing how to keep it running happily means you will spend more time making music and less time pulling your hair out.

THE COMPUTER

The overall form factors of computers these days come in many sizes, shapes, and prices. You don't need the latest and greatest computer available to make world-class music, but you do need to assess your ever-changing desires and attempt to forecast your future needs. As a regular computer user, keeping up on computer industry trends just makes common sense. Is FireWire being phased out? How fast is USB3? Are solid-state drives up to the task of a running a DAW? Keeping up with trends like these can save you money and headache when it comes time to buy or upgrade to your next computer.

Instead of shelling out top dollar for every latest and greatest computer, I try to buy "just behind the curve." By this I mean that you get the most "bang for the buck" by buying the model that was just replaced by the latest and greatest model. You have to watch for "gotchas" like hardware that is being phased out, or buying something new just before the next generation is to be released, and sometimes the "new and improved" model carries a steep price for only marginal improvements. Watch carefully, assess your needs, and be patient. My rule of thumb has been to "upgrade when a new computer comes out that has four times my current processing power." Think about that.

Laptops provide portability and are quite powerful these days, for sure. If you are a gigging DJ and can afford only one computer, a laptop is the way to go, and they can do a lot. But if you can afford and manage two, having a powerful tower as your home studio workhorse and a laptop for gigging is a killer combo. Towers are less likely to move around, get dropped, or get beer spilled on them in a club. Towers can have motherboards and peripherals that are built for serious speed. Add to that the expandability of additional internal hard drives, higher-quality optical drive burners, more RAM, PCIe cards, faster graphics cards, and multiple monitors. If you spend long hours in your studio like I do, you want a setup that is as reliable and powerful as possible. I make my music at high sample rates at home on my tower, and then render it into parts that my laptop can handle for gigs. The laptop is my "stunt" computer: I will try out questionable new software on it because it is not my "mission critical" studio DAW. If the software works well on the laptop, I may eventually install it on my tower. And I try not to keep anything on a laptop that I would mind losing if I left it in a taxi!

The bottom line: Reducing bottlenecks is the holy grail when it comes to DAWs. Bottlenecks are the weak links in the chain of your system that slow everything else down and prevent you from making more music. You might have the fastest, largest hard drive available, but if you do not have enough RAM, your computer may still seem slow and crash more often. Downtime is also a bottleneck. Therefore, a virus is a bottleneck. If your laptop is your only DAW, losing it means serious downtime, and that is a serious bottleneck! Your job is to find the bottlenecks and remove them as best as you can.

THE CPU

The central processing unit (CPU) is the brain of your computer, and like anything you do on it, audio is just a whole lot of math. From making a 1 dB volume change to employing the fanciest linear-phase EQ or convolution reverb plug-in, it is all just math at the core. So the speed and number of your CPUs doing the heavy lifting on your system will have a great deal to do with Live's responsiveness and upper limits of capability. Thankfully, as of Live 8, the program takes full advantage of multiple processors, spreading the various processing jobs among them. It's like having several computers working together as one, and the improvement is significant. While some parts of your computer can get along just fine with less than the best available, this is one category in which "more is more." Buy the fastest processor you can afford. What is speedy today may be obsolete in a few years.

THE OPERATING SYSTEM

In theory, Live runs equally well on Mac OSX and on Microsoft Windows PCs alike. I am not going to take up a lot of pages and your time rehashing the age-old debate of which operating system is better. I have used both extensively, and both are quite capable. It comes down to what kind of work flow, price point, and interface makes the most sense for you. Without a doubt there is far more software—including audio software—available for a Windows machine, and that is no small thing. If geeking out on an endless sea of esoteric freeware plug-ins is your thing, Windows is the clear winner. However, if day-to-day stability, ease of use, and freedom from viruses and mal-ware are more important to you, the Mac is the clear winner. That is my humble opinion. Your mileage may vary.

HARD DRIVES

When it comes to DAW hardware, hard drives are a central piece of the puzzle. Having speedy and reliable access to your programs and audio data is mission critical. Thankfully, today's hard drives are bigger, less expensive, and more reliable than ever. But what do you need to do it right?

The first and easiest improvement you can make in your DAW is to have multiple drives for doing different tasks. Your operating system (OS) and the programs you run, such as Live, will access the drive they are installed on while you work just to keep the program running. At the same time, recording and playing back of audio requires almost constant access to the hard drive for retrieving the files you are working with. If you can have one drive for your OS and programs and a second drive for your audio, you will notice an improvement in speed and stability. In my computer, I take this concept one step further and have one drive for the OS and programs; a second drive for my Live Library, loops, samples, and soft-synth presets; and a third drive for my Live Projects and their recordings. That way I spread out the data access across three drives so that each can focus on its own task without interference, and in practice it works very well. This is one of the places that a computer tower dramatically excels beyond a laptop. Although I have seen some of the larger laptops boasting two hard drives, the additional hard drive creates additional heat and therefore requires sizeable (noisy) fans to keep them cool. But if a laptop is your only DAW, this might be a worthwhile trade-off.

When purchasing hard drives, you are striking a balance between several factors:

- **Data capacity vs. cost**—The cost per byte of hard-disk drives (HDDs) is on a never-ending trend toward more storage for less cost. We have reached a point at which even the average drive will hold quite a bit of even high-resolution audio (while video, on the other hand, continues to grow in size and gobble up data faster than technological advances can provide it). So unless you are generating huge amounts of data on a regular basis or are working with video, there is not a great argument for buying the absolute largest drives currently available. Instead, I recommend that you buy "behind the curve," where the greatest value lies. If you divide the cost by the total capacity of the drive, you will come to a "dollars per terabyte" value and will readily find the best value. It will usually be around 75% of the largest drive available, in my experience. So if the largest drives available are 3 TB, look at the price per byte of the 2 or 2.5 TB drives.

- **Speed of data access vs. heat generation and noise level**—Here is where the average person's understanding of hard drives starts to fall off. Not all hard drives are created equal. Like cars, some are built to get you from here to there, while others are built for the autobahns of Europe! HDDs typically come in three rotational speeds: 5,400, 7,200, and 10,000 rpm (rotations per minute). A faster rotational speed means that the data on the disk can be served faster, but at the expense of more heat and higher noise coming from the drive. More heat usually means more fans to cool the computer, and thus more noise still. If you intend to record and mix audio with your computer, the amount of noise the computer makes in the room makes a big difference. You want enough speed to deliver potentially dozens of digital audio files at the same time, but you want the computer to be as quiet as possible. You get 5,400 rpm drives if you do not see a rotational speed listed with the computer, and that is typical of an office computer or basic laptop. Drives with 10,000 rpms are made for digital video and servers for which speed is of the essence and noise is not an issue. I have found that 7,200 rpm drives offer a significant performance upgrade over the 5,400 rpm drives, while not being anywhere near as noisy and hot as the 10,000 rpm drives, and so they are the way to go for either a DAW or laptop DAW. A performance 7,200 rpm SATA drive can handle over one hundred 16-bit, 44.1 kHz audio channels simultaneously, and for the home producer/laptop DJ, that should be sufficient. There are indeed other factors such as seek times (smaller is better), burst rates, and cache sizes (bigger is better), but generally speaking these statistics improve or diminish together and a good-quality 7,200 rpm performance drive that works well with your system will have what you need.
- **HDD vs. SSD**—As mentioned above, hard-disk drives use a spinning platter and a reader arm to deliver data to the host computer. Solid-state drives have no moving parts, are less delicate, generate less heat, and make no sound. The only downsides I see are capacity and cost: the price per byte of an SSD is many times that of the more traditional spinning platter HDD. What I have opted to do, for both my desktop and laptop, is to use an SSD for the main OS/application drive, and continue to use HDDs for storing sample libraries, recordings, and Live Sets. So far this has been an excellent solution: my computers boot faster, process faster, and applications respond quickly. As with all things computer related, I'm betting we will move entirely to SSDs eventually, but for the moment it is still too cost prohibitive for most of us.
- **3.5-inch vs. 2.5-inch form factor**—HDDs come in two physical sizes. The smaller of the two, 2.5-inch, is generally for internal laptop drives and smaller external enclosures. Their access speeds are slower than their 3.5-inch cousins, so if you intend to record or play back a large amount of audio with the drive, I would encourage you toward the larger form factor. A small hard-drive enclosure may fit nicely in your pocket or laptop bag and may be fine for backing up your data, but it is not a workhorse in the way the bigger, faster drives are. SSDs, on the other hand, only come in the smaller 2.5-inch size, but you can find mounting brackets that will allow you to use them in desktops that have 3.5-inch bays.

- **Internal vs. external hard drives**—When you need additional space for data, you may be tempted to simply plug in an external hard drive. For additional storage and backups this is a necessity, but in daily practice an internal drive will almost always be faster than an external drive, making it the better choice for your audio Project data. Additionally, how you connect an external hard drive to your system definitely makes a difference. As a rule of thumb, Thunderbolt is faster than USB3, which is faster than eSATA, which is faster than FireWire 800, which is faster than FireWire 400, which is faster than USB2, and speed is commensurate with price. Throughput limitations will directly affect audio track counts in your DAW. An external drive connected to a laptop with FireWire 800 can be plenty fast for direct recording and playback up to its rated throughput, but USB or flash drives, while fine for portable data storage and making backups, are too slow for any serious real-time audio use. Running sample libraries directly from an external drive can be troublesome, because the access speed becomes a bottleneck. Another concern: If you have only one FireWire connection and you use that for your audio interface, then you must daisy-Chain your external drive from your audio interface and they are forced to share an already narrow data channel. I've done it in a pinch, but I try to avoid it as much as possible. In short, favor internal drives when working with your audio, and use external drives to back it up.
- **Reliability, backups, and redundancy**—Data storage of any kind, make or model, will fail. It is not a question of "if," it is a question of "when." And when it comes to hard drives, they either fail imperceptibly or fail completely. All of the big hard-drive makers tout their reliability, but if you check the statistics for this, they are measured in terms of "mean time before failure," which is an average lifespan of the drive before it fails. Some will fail out of the box, some on the tenth day of use, and some on the ten thousandth day of use. There is simply no way to predict when this will happen. And when a hard drive fails, the data on the drive becomes very expensive to recover. So the only antidote to this inevitability is redundancy: keeping multiple copies of all crucial data.

RAM

If the CPU is the brain of your computer, and the hard drives are its long-term memory, then you can think of random-access memory (RAM) as the mind of your computer, or what your computer is thinking about right now. RAM is the high-speed memory that holds the applications and documents that you currently have open. This memory is cleared when you shut the computer down, and it must be reloaded when you next restart the system. Your OS uses some RAM just to operate, as do any programs you have running. But the biggest use of RAM for DAWs are plug-ins and soft-synth instruments: the more RAM you have, the more plug-ins you can use simultaneously. Thankfully, like hard drives, RAM prices continue to plummet as the technology advances, so by all means, load your computer with as much as you can afford. More RAM means more plug-ins and fewer crashes. It's a no-brainer.

DISPLAY MONITOR

While your display monitor does not directly affect sound quality in any way (unless its magnetic field is causing noise on one of your cables), the quality and size of your visual interface will dramatically affect your work flow and your amount of eye and brain fatigue.

Large LCD and LED displays are surprisingly inexpensive these days, and if you plan to spend a lot of time in your studio, do your eyes a favor and get something of large size and high quality. You ideally want to be working at a resolution at which you can see a lot and still be able to read everything easily. Your display should be placed directly between your studio speakers (also referred to as "monitors," which needlessly confuses things) in such a way as to not detract from the sound of your speakers, but still close enough to read comfortably. Live's built-in Zoom Display function in Preferences > Look Feel allows you to scale the interface to work with any screen size and resolution, and this is a tremendous benefit.

While Live's interface does not inherently support multiple displays, having two display monitors is still quite helpful: imagine running Live's interface full-screen on one monitor and all your third-party plug-ins and Instruments on a second. Some plug-ins and Instruments can take up a lot of screen real estate. Imagine them never again obscuring your view of Live's interface, and being able to leave them open all the time on a second monitor! I've done this, and it really is a big improvement. However, I now have a 28-inch LCD display that fits nicely between my studio speakers, and there just isn't room for a second one unless I were to hang it above the first one from the ceiling, which I am seriously considering!

Appendix E: The Makings of a Producer's Studio

A music producer's studio is decidedly not the same as a home-recording studio, although there is a fair amount of overlap. While recording acoustic events—vocals, a bass guitar, the interesting hum of your refrigerator—could be a part of what the home producer does, the main focus often revolves around mixing elements. Those elements could be purchased samples, sounds that were synthesized from instruments or "appropriated" from other recordings, or sound effects recorded in the field. Because of this fundamental shift in focus, and because more and more of the music-making work flow now happens "inside the box," the gear and space needs of the home producer have substantially shifted over the past two decades. This section attempts to identify the most relevant parameters of the space that you choose to work in, and the impact they have on your music-making experience.

THE LISTENING ENVIRONMENT

I know how it is: In addition to all the "normal" things that people own and move from place to place—such as a bed, a dresser, a TV, some kitchen utensils, and clothes—you also lug around an additional set of "stuff" for making music: keyboards, speakers, drum machines, mixers, processors, and maybe a guitar or two. When you rent an apartment, it is as if you have an additional roommate, because you need a second room for all this extra stuff! At the same time, you are an aspiring musician, so perhaps you can't really afford that second room; but you need it and so you get it anyway, and this second "room" is often a hallway, a corner of a living room, or a closet. You get really creative with some furniture you found in the alley, and you manage to stack and cram all of your gear into this secondary little space. When you get it all up and running and finally get some time between your jobs to actually make music, you find yourself wondering, "Why don't my songs sound as good as (insert favorite international artist here)?"

The answer to this question has many facets, as there are many variables that affect sound quality. But the biggest two contributors to the equation (after your ears, of course) are also the biggest influences on your listening environment:

- What are the size, shape, texture, and building materials of the space that you are listening in?
- What kind of speakers/amplification are you using, how are they placed in the room, and where are you sitting in relation to them?

These two factors are your biggest challenges when attempting to make good mixes. If you cannot clearly hear what you are trying to create, how can you know if what you are creating sounds the way you intended it?

YOUR ACOUSTIC SPACE

Let's start with the one that is the hardest to control: the room. The ideal listening environment has the following properties:

1. A mix room should aim to have a flat frequency response across the entire spectrum, ideally throughout the room, but at the very least, at the mix position.

A room is a resonating chamber, just like the inside of an acoustic guitar. Depending on the shape, size, and reflectivity of your listening environment, your room will naturally boost some frequencies and cut others, and these distortions, called "nodes," are your enemy. If your room, for example, naturally boosts sound waves at 100 Hz, then you will likely be unnaturally reducing the 100 Hz frequencies in your mixes with an EQ to make it sound "right" to you in that room. The problem is that when you take that mix to another room that is acoustically flatter, your mix will seem thin because it lacks a proper amount of 100 Hz content. In essence, you will be fighting any tonal irregularities of the room you mix in. So, what room shapes create the worst nodes and should be avoided? Square rooms are the worst, and parallel walls (rectangular rooms) are the second worst. That perfectly describes 90% of all living spaces, doesn't it? It is a challenge, for sure. That is why the finest recording studio control rooms have no parallel walls and are designed by well-paid acousticians. What to do?

- If you are stuck using a rectangular room, situate your speakers along the short wall of any rectangle so that the speakers point into the largest space, which is behind you.
- At the same time, avoid placing your speakers directly against, or within a few feet of, a wall or ceiling. Ideally, there should be more distance between the speaker and the wall (or ceiling) than there is between you and the speaker. Aim to have your mix position at about one-third of the total length of the room.
- Avoid putting a speaker (or your mix position) in a corner of a room.
- Avoid flat, hard surfaces, particularly behind you. An open closet full of clothes is better than a closed closet door, for example. Having a wall of books in a bookcase is better than a flat, bare wall or a window.
- As a general rule, a larger room will be more useful as a mixing environment than a small one.

COOL! You can use the tone generator in Live's Audio Preferences to generate any frequency you like. When you have your room set up, turn on the tone generator and sweep the entire frequency spectrum from low to high. You should ideally hear a smooth representation of all frequencies, without any large spikes in volume at any one point. If you do perceive spikes at certain frequencies, write down the frequencies and be aware of them as you mix. See if you can find a way to treat your room or move some furniture to correct the problem. Low frequencies spikes below 300 Hz will be harder to treat than higher ones.

2. A mix room should have a pleasing, natural decay, neither too short (dead), nor too long (reverberant).

If your room is highly reflective, you will likely be hearing more reflections from your walls than direct signal from the speakers, and that will cause problems. At the same time, absorbing too much of the room's natural reflectivity will leave it sounding dead and lifeless. A common myth is that putting carpet, tapestries, egg cartons, or even acoustic foam on all your flat surfaces will make a room sound better. Those materials will certainly reduce the reflectivity of some frequencies, but by no means all of them, especially the low (bass) ones. While it is possible to build or buy cylindrical bass traps to put into problem corners where bass builds up, you need to be sure that what you are doing does more good than harm. Try clapping your hands in the space: your goal is to get rid of discrete echoes and long reverb tails, but to still hear a short decay.

3. A mix room should have enough sound isolation to keep your sound from annoying others, and to keep out competing sound from outside.

This is fairly self-explanatory, but not easy to achieve. If you have the luxury of building your own space, there are many great books on how to build a room-within-a-room for sound isolation. But at the very least, choose your mix room carefully so that it meets this requirement as well as possible. Stand in the room you are considering mixing in and listen for outside noises. Walk around the building and look for neighbors who share walls in common with your mix room. Sometimes you can find a room in a building surrounded with businesses that clear out at the end of the day, which is ideal if you like to mix at night.

MONITOR PLACEMENT

Aside from the rules of thumb about speaker placement above, here are the other guidelines you should follow:

4. The distance between you and your speakers should equal the distance of your speakers from each other. The two speakers and you should form an equilateral triangle.
5. Your speakers should ideally sit at ear height or just below, and be pointed directly at the mix position.
6. Avoid placing the speakers on any surface that resonates, such as a large wood table or desk. Speaker stands are best.

SPEAKERS

The speakers you use are every bit as important as the room you put them in.

> 7. Your speakers should have as flat a frequency response as possible across as much of the frequency spectrum as possible when outputting a comfortable listening level.

This means that they represent all frequencies equally well, without any unnatural spikes. Speakers that seem to "feature" bass, for example, will cause you to actually lower the bass in your mixes! When selecting speakers, go to the store with one of your favorite, great-sounding CDs that you know very well, and listen to it through the various speakers they have available. You are looking for "natural" and "well balanced" more than "hyped" or "aggressive." A "comfortable listening level" is one you could work in for several hours of editing.

> 8. Your amplifier and speakers should be paired to work well with each other. An "active near-field studio monitor" is a great solution for this, as both the speaker and the amplifier are contained in the monitor and are designed to work optimally with each other.

Near-field monitors are a staple of small and home studios. Find a model that sounds good to you. Some models today even have room-analysis tools built into them to compensate for frequency irregularities.

SUBWOOFERS

I would caution you against using a subwoofer in your studio until you know how to calibrate it properly. Two speakers can be challenging enough without adding a third that only puts out bass! Sure, it is totally sweet when the bass is thumping, but how do you know how much bass is enough?

If making good mixes is your goal, my advice to you is to use two near-field monitors only. Play a CD in a genre similar to yours that you think sounds great through the monitors, and listen carefully to exactly how much bass, mid, and high frequencies you hear. Then go mix your songs, and try to get them to sound like that CD. Keep the CD handy and repeat this process regularly to "recalibrate you ears."

HEADPHONES

Headphones are great for keeping your neighbors and/or family happy. They also give you a second opinion of your stereo imaging and are useful when making acoustic recordings. But they are not ideal for knowing how your mix will translate to another sound system—speakers are far better for that.

AUDIO AND MIDI INTERFACES

The next most important piece of gear after your room, your speakers, and your computer is your audio/MIDI interface. It is entirely possible that you may never feel the need to make a single live recording in the process of making music. Perhaps you are a beginning producer who primarily mixes and remixes previously existing recordings. For those purposes, you may find that the headphone jack that came with your computer is sufficient for your needs. But as soon as you decide you want to start making any kind of recordings with your computer or to play out as a DJ, you will want to look at purchasing and installing an audio interface.

The first, and perhaps most important, role of an external audio interface is to get the delicate processes of analog-to-digital conversion and mic preamplification out and away from the magnetic field circus that is your computer. Spinning hard drives, power supplies, and displays all radiate significant electromagnetic fields than can create noise and distortion on your recordings. An audio interface at the end of a USB or FireWire cable is safely out of harm's way from these disturbances.

After that, the key component of an audio interface is the quality of the clock crystal that governs the timing of the samples of incoming and outgoing audio. The better the clock, the more accurately represented the recordings and playback will be through your interface. Almost any audio interface you buy today will be an improvement on the audio ports that came with your computer, and, generally speaking, you get what you pay for— and you can pay anywhere from $100 to $5,000 for a pair of stereo converters. The more you intend to record, the more you should allot in your budget for your audio interface.

In addition to quality electronic components, you are also looking for quality software drivers—the software that comes with your interface that allows you to access its features— and quality customer service. Your hardware may be amazing, but if the manual is poorly translated from another language and the control panel is buggy, you may be better off with something else.

As far as MIDI support goes, if your other gear is MIDI over USB, you may never need MIDI I/O on actual MIDI jacks. Five years ago I would have said that you needed it. Now, I am not so sure.

There are hundreds of different audio interfaces available to choose from, and they range in features and price. Some have mic preamps, some do not. Some have balanced audio connections, some unbalanced. Some have MIDI I/O in addition to audio, some do not. Some have digital inputs, some do not. Some are USB, some are FireWire. Some have more inputs than outputs, and others the opposite. You should try to imagine all the possible scenarios in which you will use your sound card, and then add a bit more functionality to grow into.

Before you buy, read as many reviews as possible and talk to others who work with audio interfaces regularly to see what they prefer. If you get on a company's support forum website and read posts from people who own the device you are thinking about buying, you will get a great sense about the stability and compatibility of the interface, as well as a preview of what the company's customer support is like. Do an Internet search for your computer and the interface you are considering on the manufacturer's user forum, and see what kind of experiences people have had that have a setup like the one you're thinking of buying.

CONTROLLERS

Choosing a good MIDI controller—or several—is a subjective decision-making process. In addition to doing all the same research outlined above for finding an audio interface, I can't stress enough the importance of additionally trying a MIDI controller before you buy it: features are cool, but essentially you are buying an instrument that you intend to play, so you should enjoy playing it! Go to a store that sells the piece of gear you are considering and try all of its menus, buttons, knobs, and faders. How does it feel? Does it feel musical? Does it inspire you? Does it feel well-built, such that it would withstand years of use? Would the controller be easy to read and use in a dimly lit situation, such as in a club? Would the controller fit in your studio? In a backpack?

MIXERS AND SIGNAL ROUTING: ITB OR OOTB?

If you have several outboard pieces of gear, such as keyboards, synthesizers, samplers, effects pedals or effects Rack modules, equalizers, compressors, and so on, you will likely find yourself wanting a way to incorporate these devices without constantly repatching all of your cables. An audio mixer or a patch bay with enough inputs to handle some or all of your devices may streamline your work flow.

In this day and age, there are two schools of thought about mixing technique, and they are called "In the Box" and "Out of the Box."

"In the box" (or ITB) mixing is a work flow that consists of getting all your source materials digitized into the computer (or "box") and doing all mixing and processing there. The pros and cons of this approach include the following:

- **Pros**—All your mix automation and processing settings are saved in your Set and are instantly recallable and endlessly malleable.
- **Cons**—All-digital processing and summing can sound somewhat harsh, brittle, and less natural than their analog equivalents, although the digital technology gets better every day.

"Out of the box" (or OOTB) mixing work flows often still use a DAW as the recording and editing medium, but mixdown happens on an outboard mixing console, with a liberal amount of outboard analog processing to boot. The pros and cons of this approach can be summed (pun intended) up like so:

- **Pros**—Take all the benefits of editing in the digital domain (cut/paste, automation) and add to that the rich, warm sound of analog processing and channel summing.
- **Cons**—Gear needed for working "out of the box" is many times greater in cost to own and harder to maintain. Saving your mix settings takes considerable time and effort.

Between these two extremes there is a large gray area in which producers regularly combine aspects of both ideals, utilizing some benefits of each. The modern mix environment boasts both plug-ins and select, choice hardware to accomplish specific goals. I encourage you to try both approaches as time and gear will allow.

MICROPHONES AND PREAMPS

Like audio interfaces and vintage outboard gear, microphones and mic preamps are sought after for their particular sound characteristics. If you don't desire to make use of acoustic recordings in your music, you may never own either of these. On the positive side, if you do want to add recordings to your sound, you can likely get away with just a few quality mics and mic preamps, or even one of each, unless you intend to track a live drummer in your sessions, or multiple acoustic musicians simultaneously. In both cases, you definitely get what you pay for.

Microphones come in every imaginable shape, size, and cost. While there are no hard rules about what kind of microphone is used for which particular application, there are definitely trends and fashions, and the pairing of a microphone with a particular application is an art form that is developed only through many hours of experimentation. There are a number of good books on the subject that will get you started.

Mic preamps all do one difficult and delicate job: they boost a mic signal to a line-level signal. You would think that all mic preamps, having such a simple job description, would sound more or less the same, but nothing could be further from the truth. They come in many variants, such as number of mic channels, tube vs. solid state, and class of components. Some also sport built-in EQs, dynamic compression, and even analog-to-digital conversion. Some are known for their "transparency," while others are known for their "coloration" of the incoming signal. Finding a mic and preamp combination that works for you takes a critical ear and some healthy experimentation.

Appendix F: Third Party Devices

Once you have gotten familiar with Live's included effects and Instruments, you will no doubt be hungry for more. Thankfully, the world of third-party effects and instruments is, for all intents and purposes, endless. Over the years, a few plug-ins have floated to the surface that I use every day in my productions. I have described some of my favorites below. In my opinion, they stand out for several reasons:

- Above all, exceptional sound quality. When I hear what they do, I want to use them more.
- An innovative interface that is intuitive, easy, and fun to use. If I have to fight the interface to get the job done, I find I don't reach for it often, no matter how it might sound.
- A friendly, well organized website and good customer service. Important when you need help or an update.

These vendors have allowed me to include freeware or demo installers in the downloadable book content in Book Content > Install. Enjoy them! And if you find any of these plug-ins as captivating as I do, visit the developer's website and purchase your own copy. You will not be disappointed.

CAMEL AUDIO (WWW.CAMELAUDIO.COM)

This company has five great products that do a lot of things simply and well. Two of these are even freeware.

- **CamelPhat**—A multi-effects unit that can do a number of traditional effects very well, but the addition of several unique interface options makes it exceptional. The built-in x-y assignable controller is very Ableton-esque. Like all of Camel Audio's plug-ins, CamelPhat comes with a large, rich bank of Presets, and the Camel signature Randomize button provides endless possibilities by randomizing all the controls. I've found some really "out there" sounds with the Randomizer. The plug-in has an analog-modeled compressor, three resonant filters, two LFOs, and an envelope follower. The filters and distortion are exceptional, and don't sound like any others I've used. Many plug-ins boast an analog-like "fattening" effect, but this one actually does it very well! It's hard to go wrong with CamelPhat.

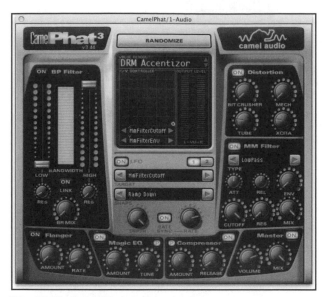

Pic. F.01: CamelPhat multi-fx plug-in.

- **CamelSpace**—Similar to CamelPhat, but this multi-effects plug-in focuses on temporal effects: reverbs, delays, flanger. What sets it apart is its Step Sequencer, which allows you to modulate several of its parameters in a fashion similar to Live's Clip Envelope. This yields some wonderful pulsing variations on whatever you feed into it.CamelSpace is paired with the same *x-y* controller and Randomize button as CamelPhat; I never get tired of this one.
- **CamelCrusher**—This freeware subset of CamelPhat has distortion, compression, and a filter. Like its two big siblings above, the master section has a mix knob so that you can do some parallel processing right in the plug-in, balancing the dry signal with the wet. I am often leery of any plug-in with just one or two knobs for an entire effect, such as compression, because they are typically too limited. But CamelAudio's functions are tuned right to the sweet spot so that you can get great results fast, and from there morph into something completely different with ease. Install this one: you will use it all the time. And it is free!
- **Alchemy**—Without question Camel Audio's flagship product, Alchemy is described as a "sample manipulation synthesizer." Alchemy has quickly become a staple of the EDM community, and the options of this beast are far deeper and wider than CamelSpace and CamelPhat combined. Alchemy is an instrument that allows you to take an audio file and play it like a sampler, but through an array of modulations. In just a short time, I was able to come up with sounds unlike anything I'd ever heard before, and it has since become a regular "go to" synth for me. There are several multi-gigabyte factory patch libraries that you can download with Alchemy, and there are several more for sale.
- **Alchemy Player**—Alchemy Player is the free version of Alchemy, and it even comes with a 1 GB sample library! And although the controls are limited compared with Alchemy's, there is still an impressive amount of functionality here, far more than you would expect from a freeware synth—and it sounds fantastic.

OHM FORCE (WWW.OHMFORCE.COM)

There are companies that make plug-ins that have wacky interfaces, and companies that make excellent-sounding plug-ins, but I have found only one company that does both exceedingly well, and it is Ohm Force. This French company gives you the choice of two different skins for each plug-in: one looks quite traditional and gives you all the functionality in an elegant, compact layout, and the other…well, I'll let this picture speak for itself:

Pic. F.02: OhmBoyz dub delay plug-in.

Yep, that is a plug-in. And an amazing one at that:

- **OhmBoyz**—My first Ohm Force plug-in and still a regular favorite. This plug-in is the ultimate tape-delay emulator and will put a dub vibe on anything you run through it. Up to four simultaneous delays, LFOs, filters, and an amazing distortion/saturation section. Like all of Ohm Force's plug-ins, OhmBoyz can go from subtle to lacerating, sometimes within the same Preset. I haven't found another delay plug-in that can do what this one does, nor have I even been able to re-create its sound with an Audio Effect Rack and a dozen other plug-ins. Highly recommended.
- **Quad Frohmage**—There are boring filter plug-ins, and then there are plug-ins that make you instantly sound like a superstar. Quad Frohmage is the latter. There are four concurrent resonant filters that sound amazing, each with LFOs, delays, and distortion. Different routings allow the filters to feed each other or to happen in parallel. If you make electronic music, get this right now!
- **Frohmage**—This is the freeware version of Quad Frohmage, and as the name implies, it has only one filter, but it is one amazing filter and it is free! Try this one, and if you love it like I do, buy Quad Frohmage.

- **Ohmicide:Melohman**—Again, there are distortion and amp simulators, and then there is Ohmicide:Melohman. If you have heard an overdriven guitar amp feed back on itself, or just about to, you've heard what this plug-in is all about. Most digital distortion plug-ins sound grainy, thin and harsh, but this one sounds warm, fuzzy, and pleasing. And by pleasing, I mean nasty! This is the only distortion plug-in that I know of that feeds back on itself in such a convincing way. From subtle tube warmth to obliterating mayhem, Ohmicide:Melohman does it all. Perhaps its most unique feature is the ability to morph between Presets, which is mind-bending to behold. If you make breaks, dubstep, or drum 'n' bass, this was made for you. Try this on anything, even an entire mix.
- **Hematohm and Mobilohm**—Both of these cover phase-, flanger-, frequency-shift-type effects, but like all of Ohm Force's plug-ins, they have a warm, saturated, analog feel that is so rare in plug-ins. Add a little sparkle or descend into 1970s sci-fi madness. File under exotic and delicious.

TAL (KUNZ.CORRUPT.CH)

TAL stands for Togu Audio Line, and is the brainchild of Patrick Kunz. As far as donationware goes, Kunz is turning out some great stuff. Aside from his creative array of audio plug-ins, what drew me to his work were his soft-synth instruments, the Elek7ro-II in particular. (No, that's not a typo—the name really has a 7 in it!) For a donation of your choosing, this little synth is light on your resources and packs a punch. A basic set of controls provides an impressive range of sounds and is perfect for someone just getting into synthesis.

Pic. F.03: The TAL Elek7ro-II synthesizer.

And kudos to Mr. Kunz for allowing people to make a donation of their choice for his excellent wares! I've had many students rave about how refreshing this approach is.

U-HE (WWW.U-HE.COM)

Each person seems to be born with unique aesthetic preferences when it comes to synthesizers, and mine tend toward smooth, round, glassy, spacious, and dark. And of all the soft synths I have tried, Zebra 2 by U-he hits all of those targets at once.

Pic. F.04: Zebra 2 synthesizer.

Boasting a variety of synthesis engines, modulators, and effects, Zebra 2 is capable of a very wide range of sounds, and there are many free preset banks available from users to show off this diversity. You can even download a slightly modified version called The Dark Zebra, which houses sound banks that Hans Zimmer created for use on the scores for The Dark Knight trilogy. One feature that I think sets Zebra 2 apart is an interface that only shows you the modules you are actually using, which keeps things simple, clear and easy to follow. Having a lot of choices at your fingertips is great, but it can also be overwhelming and mind numbing if you do not yet know what everything does.

U-he produces two other excellent synthesizers: the analog modeling monster Diva, and the graphic patch cable style ACE. Diva is velvety smooth, full of character, and truly worthy of the "analog modeling" title, and serves up the best analog emulations I've yet heard in a plug-in. ACE is enjoyably hands-on, and a great way to learn about synthesis.

To round out the suite, there are three effects products that are very worthy of checking out: the Uhbik bundle, Filterscape, and MFM2.

- Uhbik is actually a collection of nine effects plug-ins ranging from the common to uncommon: reverb, delay, flanger, pitch shift, vocoding, phaser, EQ, filter, frequency shifter, and tremolo. But what is exceptional about these plug-ins is the sound quality! Every preset and knob twist produces a clear, pleasing, inspiring result, without the grainy, smearing, harsh results that many plug-ins produce. If clarity is your goal, this bundle is worth checking out.
- Both Filterscape and MFM2 take common tasks—filtering and delays respectively—and take them to new levels of possibility through the use of highly imaginative user interfaces and modulation matrices. If you have ever dreamt of morphing EQs and filters, or a ping-pong delay on steroids, these plug-ins are for you. Just a quick browse through the effect presets will expand your mind in terms of what is sonically possible. These two effects plug-ins are my new favorite "secret weapons."

D.16 GROUP (WWW.D16.PL)

"Emulation is the sincerest form of flattery." Or was it imitation? Either way, D.16 Group is all about taking classic hardware devices from the past and giving them new life as software, often improving them, or adding sought-after features the originals lacked. Collecting choice old hardware synths can be fun—that is if you find doling out large sums of money for barely working, hard to fix, impossible to upgrade devices "fun!" Sure they sound great (some of the time), but the convenience of software synths is hard to beat. And those classic gear sounds will always be in demand.

Pic. F.05: LuSH-101 synthesizer.

Take D.16 Group's flagship LuSH-101 synth for example: While clearly a respectful nod to the Roland SH-101 from the '80s, the LuSH-101 is vastly more capable, adding MIDI, polyphony (more than one note at a time), and multitimbral playback (more than one sound at a time), just to name a few obvious improvements. And then add to that a modulation matrix, mixer, EQ, and effect sends for all eight sound layers, and suddenly we're making music in the new millennium! The only thing missing from the LuSH-101 is the original's left hand grip with guitar-like pitch bender for keyboard solo rocking onstage.

D.16 Group also offers three classic drum machine emulators, a TB-303 bass line emulator, and a hardy cross–section of great sounding effects. If the classics are your thing, look no further.

FABFILTER (WWW.FABFILTER.COM)

While the underlying code of any software is, at its essence, just math, the variance in the design and implementation of these component parts yields the variety of sound (and quality) differences you hear between plug-in developers. And as the company's name implies, FabFilter has devoted its attention to the quality of its filters, and this entire suite of products clearly reflects this. In the digital world of 1's and 0's, it is quite a feat to create smooth, natural curves, and FabFilter has done just this.

Pic. F.06: Timeless 2 filter delay plug-in.

Like many, I was first introduced to FabFilter's wares via the FabFIlter Micro, which is simply a single highpass or lowpass filter, but it sounds great, and it fits the bill nicely for DJing-type applications. Next I got to know the Pro Q EQ, which has a great interface and sound quality, like the rest of the company's Pro lineup. But my current favorite is the Timeless 2 filter delay.

This one does some simple things elegantly, and some elegant things simply! As with many of FabFilter's plug-ins, you can expand the interface to include a built-in modulation matrix at the bottom to add some motion to the parameters in the top section, and the means for making modulation patches could not be easier. Best of all, the sonic results are rich and sumptuous.

Be sure to check out the full line of FabFilter products—you won't be disappointed.

DMG AUDIO (WWW.DMGAUDIO.COM)

After you are done scouring the web for the latest sample mangler or revolutionary effect plug-in, you may find yourself wondering if you can improve upon the core devices you actually use every day, such as EQ and compression. If EQ and compression are the salt and pepper of audio production, DMG's plug-ins are the butter!

Pic. F.07: EQuality EQ plug-in.

Live 9's EQ 8 seems to have taken a few tips from FabFilter and DMG's EQ interface designs, and that is a good thing, as I think DMG's interface is one of the very best. But above all, DMG's EQ's sound incredible! When truly transparent tone shaping is needed, this is where I turn. Many EQ plug-ins create phase problems that "smear" the sound while changing the tone—I think of it as similar to finger painting with watercolors: the more you play with it, the less distinct it becomes. But with any of DMG's three EQs, the tonal shifts are natural and subtle, without adding harshness, which is what you want when trying to blend a bunch of tracks in a mix.

As well, Live 9's Compressor Device seems to have adopted several of the ingenious graphical elements of DMG's Compassion compressor. Visualizing compression in action has historically been hard to do, that is, until plugins like Compassion. The real-time display of the waveform incurring gain reduction is a revelation for any new user, and I imagine we will see many new compressor plug-ins adopting this approach.

PSP (WWW.PSPAUDIOWARE.COM)

"And the winner for Favorite Compressor goes to…"

Pic. F.08: Vintage Warmer 2 multiband dynamics plug-in.

This is one of my all-time favorite plug-ins. While the controls are a bit unconventional, once you get your head around this one, it will heap a bounty of warm, punchy goodness upon you. Where DMG plug-ins are intentionally transparent, PSP Vintage Warmer 2 is far from it, adding a healthy dose of character while doing your dynamic rage reduction tasks. What adds the character is PSP's implementation of the overload characteristics of various pieces of analog hardware. As a result, you can overdrive this plugin and get the subtle warming of harmonic distortion, or the fuzzy madness of an overdriven circuit. Best of all, you can compress low and high-frequency ranges independently, which is typically known as multiband compression. When I want to "beef" something up a bit, this is the tool I reach for.

PSP also makes many, many other plug-ins. Check the company's site for details.

Appendix G: Sounds to Sample

The mad geniuses over at SoundsToSample.com have been kind enough to donate all the great sounds files that contributed to the tutorial exercises in this book. I asked them in particular

Sounds/To/Sample

Pic. G.01: Sounds to Sample.

because they have a massive selection of high-quality sounds for purchase, as well as an intuitive website for finding what you need.

So much of raw materials for making modern music comes from appropriated sounds, but not all sounds are free for the taking: sampling copyrighted material is illegal, period. You might think you are paying tribute to one of your favorite artists by "quoting" a snippet of one of his or her songs in your own production, but the original artist, record label, and their lawyers will likely not see it that way, especially if you start selling your song containing an uncleared sample. So, back in the early days of hardware samplers, sound designers started to sell their creations as sample libraries, which allows a buyer to use the recordings in their own productions. This practice continues to this day, and the sound selection is unimaginably deep and wide.

The Sounds To Sample content is located at Book Content > Book Exercise Project > Samples > Sounds to Sample and you are welcome to use any of the included sounds in your own songs free of charge or royalty restriction. I highly encourage you to visit SoundsToSample.com site and have a listen to what else this company has to offer.

Appendix H: Warp Academy

Pic. H.01: Warp Academy.

I am as excited as I am proud to announce the arrival of an online Ableton Live Training Academy known as WarpAcademy.com, for which I am the Lead Trainer and Curriculum Director. Headed by founder Drew "Vespers" Betts and myself, our team of Certified Ableton Live Trainers has developed an exhaustive set of training materials for learning Live inside and out. The site consists of both a massive library of videos for learning at your own pace, as well as an ever-expanding rotation of online classes where students interact directly with our trainers on all manner of topics. We are offering the best quality Live education available for a price that is exceptionally affordable. And we are expanding our offerings daily.

I've included some samples of our Live 9 curriculum so you can see the quality for yourself. If you have watched free YouTube tutorials online, you will immediately understand the difference in quality. Our trainers—in addition to knowing an exceptional amount about Live—are able to *explain* what they know in a logical, concise, digestible fashion, and at a pace that you can enjoy.

If you want to go beyond the contents of this book and join in a growing community of Live ninjas, stop by and see what Warp Academy has to offer you.

Appendix I: How to Use the DVD/Downloadable Content

The DVD included with the print version of this book, or the downloadable content for use with the eBook version (both are exactly the same), contains many useful files for your enjoyment. This appendix will walk you through the steps for making the most of them.

DVD CONTENT

1. Begin by inserting the DVD into your computer's DVD-ROM drive. When the DVD icon shows up in your file browser—Finder on Mac, Windows Explorer on PC—double-click it to see its contents. You should see a single folder named "Book Content."
2. Click-and-drag the Book Content folder to your Desktop to make a copy. Many of the included files will need to be modified as you work with them, and the DVD is a read-only storage medium. Having a copy on your Desktop will allow you quick, easy access to the content, as well as provide you with modifiable versions of the files.
3. When the files are done copying to your Desktop, navigate to the new copy of Book Content on your desktop and open it.

Once it has been installed, you should see a folder structure like this:

Pic. I.01: Contents of the Book Content folder (Mac)

The three subfolders contain the following:

- Book Exercises Project—This folder contains all the Ableton Live Sets that correspond to each exercise in each chapter. They are in Project subfolders, divided by chapters. If you want to simply start at the beginning of chapter 1 and follow along with each exercise sequentially, you will likely not need many of these Sets, as each exercise picks up right where the previous exercise left off; you can easily complete the entire book's exercises in this linear manner. But should you desire to double-check your work against mine, or jump ahead a few exercises, these sets are here to allow you that flexibility. As I detail at the beginning of each exercise in the book, my recommendation is to immediately perform a Save As command after opening one of these

Sets, re-saving the set in the same Project folder with a new name of your choosing so that you still have the original Set to re-open should you need or want to. Of course, you still have the DVD with unalterable originals of all these Sets. Should you accidentally modify and save over any of these Sets, you can simply re-copy a Set from the original DVD to your Book Content folder on the Desktop at any time.. I have also included a folder of Live 8-compatible Sets in case you have not yet upgraded to Live 9. Some of the features mentioned and exercise steps specific to Live 9 will not be available, but you can still participate in 90% of the tutorials herein with these Sets.

- Install—The second folder is a sizeable collection of third-party plug-ins that can be used within Live to broaden your sonic palette. These are each described briefly in the previous appendix to help you decide if they would be interesting to you. Some are freeware/donation-ware—meaning you may install and use them without restriction, and the author hopes that, should you decide to keep using the software, you might consider visiting the company's website and making a donation to help with the developer's continuing efforts.

Other plug-ins are demo versions of paid-for products that will cease to function after an introductory time has elapsed. In order to use these plug-ins, open the subfolder (Mac/PC) that pertains to your operating system, then navigate to the installer of the plug-in you want, double-click it, and follow the onscreen instructions. The only plug-ins that don't work this way are the TAL plug-ins, which have no installer application and needs manual installation. The TAL-ReadMe.txt file in the TAL folder will walk you through theprocess of copying the .vst file to the proper system folder. Visit the plug-in vendor's website for more information about purchasing a full version of a plug-in you like, or how to uninstall a plug-in you don't like.

- Warp Academy—This folder contains an assortment of video tutorials from the afore-mentioned WarpAcademy.com for you to enjoy. They expand upon many of Live 9's new features, and offer examples of the quality you will find on our site.

That is a lot of content to work with, and should keep you busy for days and weeks to come. And yet we have only scratched the surface of what is possible and available in the vast world of Ableton Live. I wish you the best of luck in your sonic endeavors.

Index

POWER TOOLS SERIES

POWER TOOLS FOR STUDIO ONE 2, VOLUME 1

by Larry the O

Power Tools for Studio One 2 shows the reader how to get around Studio One and perform recording, editing, mixing, and mastering.

Book/DVD-ROM Pack
978-1-4584-0226-4 ....$39.99

POWER TOOLS FOR STUDIO ONE 2, VOLUME 2

by Larry the O

Studio One maven Larry the O takes users even deeper into advanced applications, such as working with loops and video, mixing, mastering, and sharing your work with the world, exploring each topic in comprehensive detail.

Book/DVD-ROM Pack
978-1-4768-7468-5 ....$39.99

POWER TOOLS FOR LOGIC PRO 9

by Rick Silva

Power Tools for Logic Pro 9 unlocks Logic's immense capabilities to help you achieve amazing results for your audio and music productions with techniques you won't find in beginner-level books or videos.

Book/DVD-ROM Pack
978-1-4234-4345-2 ....$39.99

POWER TOOLS FOR PRO TOOLS 10

by Glenn Lorbecki

See and experience the new features incorporated in this powerful software offering, all the way from the new ways it handles data, memory, and gain functions to some seemingly small updates that make a huge difference in your productivity.

Book/DVD-ROM
978-1-4584-0035-2 ....$39.99

POWER TOOLS FOR REASON 6

by Andrew Eisele

Power Tools for Reason 6 is a comprehensive book that provides a quick-start tutorial that not only gets you up and running quickly, but also delves into advanced sequencing and mixing techniques.

Book/DVD-ROM Pack
978-1-4584-0227-1 ....$39.99

POWER TOOLS FOR CUBASE 7

by Matthew Loel T. Hepworth

Power Tools for Cubase 7 was written with the new user in mind. You'll learn the process all the way from installation and configuration to adding mastering treatments to your mix.

Book/DVD-ROM Pack
978-1-4584-1368-0 ....$39.99

POWER TOOLS FOR ABLETON LIVE 9

by Jake Perrine

Unlike other books about Live that simply explain its features like a second manual, this hands-on-centric book contains a series of exercises that walk you through all the features you need to produce professional-sounding music with Ableton Live 9.

Book/DVD-ROM Pack
978-1-4584-0038-3 ....$39.99

HAL•LEONARD®

www.halleonardbooks.com

Prices, content, and availability subject to change without notice.

0813